education, interaction,
and social change

education, interaction,
and social change

HAROLD L. HODGKINSON
Dean, Bard College

prentice-hall, inc., englewood cliffs, new jersey

LIBRARY OF CONGRESS CATALOG CARD NUMBER: 67-12932

Printed in the United States of America

current printing (last digit):

10   9   8   7   6   5   4   3   2   1

C

prentice-hall international, inc., london
prentice-hall of australia, pty. ltd., sydney
prentice-hall of canada, ltd., toronto
prentice-hall of india (private) ltd., new delhi
prentice-hall of japan, inc., tokyo

for Barbara

acknowledgments

Many people have been involved in the writing of this book. My intellectual debt to Robert Merton, Willard Waller, David Riesman, and Marshall McLuhan is clear. Charles Kakatsakis of the Bard College Drama Department was very helpful with the role chapter; Richard Clarke of the Biology Department equally so on functionalism. Students in my sociology seminars have been unusually helpful in raising questions and posing alternatives. Mrs. Cecilia Hilbrandt typed the manuscript in several drafts and compiled the index. The final responsibility for what is said here rests with the author.

contents

introduction   xiii

1: actors and roles,
audiences and stages   1

cues and strategies, 4; "phonies"—poor and unauthorized perform-ances, 10; role and game theory applied to education, 12; the crea-tion of role consensus in education, 13; intellectual "styles" and social roles in education, 15; awareness context, interaction, and educa-tional roles, 17; identity management, 19; cues, 22

2: bureaucratic structure and personality 25

the concept of bureaucracy—Max Weber, 26; criticisms of Weber's position, 28; the "Hawthorne Effect", 29; resistance to change, 31; efficiency and red tape, 31; in defense of bureaucracy, 33; bureacracy and education, 35; education and power, 36; the problem of change in educational bureaucracies, 38; organizational styles in educational bureaucracies, 40; the "Hawthorne Effect" and education, 44

3: the problem of functionalism 48

manifest and latent functions, 50; equilibrium and conservatism, 52; reciprocity and autonomy—the parts and the "whole", 54; functionalism and values, 56; functionalism and education, 60; educational functions—manifest and latent, 62; curricular functions, 66; the "two cultures" in education—the curriculum and the fun culture, 68; inadvertent learning, 74; reciprocity and autonomy as functions in education, 76; conclusions, 77; EXTRA BIBLIOGRAPHY ON FUNCTIONALISM, 78

4: social stratification— systems of closure 80

the concept of social class—history, 85; social stratification and social class, 87; problems in measuring social class, 88; the assumption of discrete, closed classes, 88; criticisms of the Warner approach, 91; the assumption of social class as a continuum, 92; individual class consciousness, 94; the concept of status consistency, 95; occupational and social class, 97; class and caste, 99; education and social stratifi-

cation, 104; *higher education—"the higher the better"*, 104; *educa-tion and economic status*, 107; *education, social class, and values*, 109; *conclusions*, 111

5: social mobility and "success"— who stole the protestant ethic?   113

the mythology of social mobility in America, 114; *vertical and hori-zontal mobility*, 117; *the measurement of social mobility*, 117; *chang-ing patterns of occupational mobility*, 120; *nonoccupational mobility*, 123; *the decline of the Protestant Ethic*, 126; *family structure and the need for achievement*, 127; *social mobility and education*, 130; *education and the Protestant Ethic*, 134

6: the quest for community   139

urbanization and cities, 141; *the slum and delinquency*, 144; *suburbs*, 147; *the exurb*, 148; *Levittown*, 149; *Park Forest*, 150; *Crestwood Heights*, 151; *megalopolis*, 153; *education and the quest for com-munity*, 155

7: creativity as a social phenomenon   161

creativity and education, 173; *the paradox of socialization in Amer-ica*, 175; *planning for creativity*, 178

8: the impact
of the american college
on student values   182

history, 184; *academic changes in students*, 186; *changes in the student as a person*, 187; ADDENDUM: NEEDED RESEARCH, 196; SELECTED BIBLIOGRAPHY, 197

9: some "revolutions"
of our time—
drastic social changes   200

theoretical perspectives, 201; *i. cybernation*, 204; *ii. leisure*, 208; *iii. the family*, 211; *iv. the evolution of a world perspective*, 215; *conclusions*, 217

index   221

introduction

Our youth now loves luxury. They have bad manners and contempt for authority. They show disrespect for their elders and love idle chatter instead of exercise. Children are now tyrants—not the servants of the household. They no longer rise when elders enter the room. They contradict their parents, chatter before company, gobble up their food, and tyrannize their teachers.

Does this statement have a familiar ring? Haven't you heard it many times? It presents, many would say, the major problem of our time. However, the statement was actually made by Socrates, about 450 years before the birth of Christ.

Such statements have been made continually throughout human history. They present the attitude of adults that youth have not "turned out" as expected, that young people do not behave as they should.

What makes parents and other adults feel that youth *should* "turn out" in a certain way? Why do American children "turn out" somewhat differently from French children? There is no reason to assume that the differences are hereditary, since the child conceived of French parents and born in America will go to school and learn English as his native tongue. There must be some sort of process or machinery whereby American society "turns out" Americans, and French society "turns out" Frenchmen.

At this point we might want to raise several questions about this process if we want to study it more carefully: first, how can we locate it, and second, how does it work? The first question is the easier, because we can say that any person or thing which has direct or indirect contact with the developing child is a part of this process. Thus, home, school, perhaps the church, most certainly the television set, the magazine, the radio, the baseball field, the hot rod would be part of the list of socialization agencies in our country. The reader can add many other items to this list which, for American society, happens to be very long. In some other countries, the list is much shorter (and much more completely controlled by the adults).

When we come to the second question—how does society cause individuals to "turn out" in certain ways—we come to much of the contents of this book, which tries to explain and describe the ways in which people are influenced by the social systems around them. It seems that in every society, some sort of glue, or "social cement," is needed to produce the cohesion and consensus needed for people to be able to live with each other. As the young are socialized by the agencies mentioned above, the cement begins to set. By being exposed to similar experiences, by developing similar perceptions of what they and the world are like, *culture* is created, and youth are inducted smoothly into the adult ways.

However, it is here that we must return to our opening quotation from Socrates. Clearly something is wrong: the young have not been inducted into the culture as the adults had expected they would, either in Socrates' time or in our own. It would appear that all the time the culture was "making" adults out of children, the children were modifying the notion of what an adult should be. Thus, the participants are not only acted upon by social forces; they can, through participation, modify the social forces at the same time. This complicates the picture terribly, since instead of saying that A causes B, we must also admit that at the same time B is changing A! One of the central themes of this book, therefore, is that social systems are people in a condition of continuous and reciprocal interaction. Unlike the biologist, we, unfortunately, cannot take a slice out of our specimen, freeze it or stain it, and then put it under our microscope for examination. Individuals and groups of people will not be people if we do that. This means that our modes of analysis must be dynamic, not static, active rather than passive, flexible rather than rigid, continuous rather than segmented.

In this book, therefore, education will be used not only in the conventional sense of that which happens in classrooms, but also in this broader sense of continuous interaction of individuals and cultural norms. The hot rod and the comic book must be viewed as potentially educative in nature. Another major theme of this book is that many of these informal educational devices are frequently socializing young people into patterns which are in contradiction with the patterns espoused by the formal educational system of schools and colleges. Thus, we must see schools as being in competition with other educative forces in our culture.

This competition is of the greatest importance, both economically and socially. About half of the U.S. population is now under 25 years of age, so that to capture the "youth market" for selling purposes is vitally important for business. Millions of dollars are spent in "educating" youth toward buying a particular product. While the schools are urging that the cultural norms of America involve looking to the future, thrift, and control of one's impulses, precisely the opposite "message" is being transmitted through impulse buying, the installment plan, and constant references to the immediate gratification of one's wishes. In this competition, it must be said that the home and the church, traditional allies for formal educational institutions, have to some extent defaulted in their responsibility for educating the young. Whether or not the schools can "go it alone" remains to be seen. Books dealing with education have tended to view the formal institution of schools and teachers *in vacuo*. It should be clear that we can no longer afford to do this. Schools and colleges must be seen in their interactive context with other social institutions. Current developments make it clear that schools and colleges are rapidly losing the passive, reflective role they have played in our culture, and could well be one of the transforming elements in our society for at least the next several decades.

By looking at formal education as it interacts with other elements in our culture, two other major themes of this book emerge. The first is that the similarities between educational social systems and other institutions, when compared with other formal organizations such as business, are more striking than the differences. The second is that in viewing the various sectors of formal education, the same is true: the kindergarten and the graduate school have some striking similarities in terms of organization, problems to be faced, goals to be achieved, etc., and these similarities are perhaps more important than the differences. We have no single educational system in America; rather, we have a kaleidoscope of rapidly changing confrontations between local, state, federal, private, public, student-centered, faculty-centered, administration-centered, board of control-centered, accreditation-centered, and many other factions. With the divisiveness inherent in this kind of confrontation, it is very important to see these commonalities clearly, if formal education is to assume an innovative or transformational role in our culture.

The title of the book suggests another major theme: the social sciences can be used, both in terms of theoretical concepts and research findings, to illuminate our understanding of the role and function of education in our culture. (In fact, the commonalities just mentioned can only be seen via a theoretical analysis which allows for the existence of such commonalities). The book does not represent all areas of social science research which would be relevant to education; indeed, such a book could hardly be produced, given the current explosion of knowledge. Instead, the book exists as a demonstration of the possibilities of relating social science to education through some carefully selected examples of themes or topics. Even though the chapter topics are carefully pruned, the discussion covers most matters dealt with in courses in social foundations of education, educational sociology, the American school, and the like. Outside of the themes we have mentioned, there is no central principle of organization leading from chapter to chapter. Each one is basically a discussion complete in itself. However, the reader should be aware of three sections of the book, representing three different approaches to the use of social science in education.

In the first section, three theoretical concepts are made the topics of three chapters: role theory, the concept of bureaucracy, and functionalism. These concepts are analyzed and the results applied to education. In the second section, the topics shift from theory to applied research, mainly on the three problems of social stratification, social mobility, and community organization. In the final section, three somewhat more speculative topics are discussed through the integration of theoretical and (somewhat limited) research evidence: the development of creativity, the impact of education on student values, and a final chapter on selected "social revolutions."

Although there is no central principle of organization leading from chapter to chapter, there is a central theme, or task, which the book undertakes; that is to interpret and expedite, through as many conceptual formulations as possible, the *analysis of change*. Thus, the concepts of interaction are consistently present in each chapter. From bureaucracy to cybernetics, we need to begin to see people and institutions not as static entities but as systems in flux. Teachers at all levels need the perspective of viewing changing students in a changing society. The concepts of sociology are particularly suited to this endeavor.

A word should be added here in regard to the footnotes in the text. They represent not only the usual acknowledgment of others' ideas but also a selected bibliography on the topic. It is hoped, therefore, that the reader who wishes to read further in a topic will consult the footnotes.

It is hoped that the material in this book will be of interest both to the student of the social sciences and to the educator who may find new insights about American education as a social system. As is always the case when two things are related, the trained sociologist may be unhappy about the treatment of some of his pet terms and with having to deal with mundane things, while the teacher or administrator may grumble at having to learn new and occasionally long words. But if the reader can see the fun and excitement of disciplined speculation and the evaluation of evidence, if he can sense the thrill of looking at a familiar situation with new depth of perception by seeing many perspectives simultaneously, then this book will have served its purpose.

the problem of perspective in the social sciences

All of us have, at one time or another, felt the desire to change human behavior, either our own or that of those around us. In fact, a great deal of our time and effort is spent in developing strategies whereby others will respond as we wish them to. In order to find the most effective way of altering behavior, we tend, however casually or unthinkingly, to look for its *causes*.

Immediately we are plunged into the dilemmas and contradictions which plague the social scientist. Our very description of the behavior will limit or partially define what the causes of it might be. Physical reality is hard enough to describe with any objectivity, but social reality is infinitely more difficult. Part of this difficulty comes from the fact that we live *inferentially* and *symbolically*. That is, what we expect a person to do will have an effect on what he actually does. If you, as a stranger, are invited into my house as a guest, I cannot determine "scientifically" that you will not steal my money, but I infer that you will not and proceed accordingly, thereby causing you to behave as a "proper" guest, while you cause me to behave as a "proper" host.

Because it is difficult for me to ask you directly what sort of person you are, I have to infer symbolically, on the basis of what clothes you wear, the way you talk, the way you walk, the way your hair is cut, etc. At the same time, you are making inferences about me in the same way. Neither of us has any evidence, as the physical scientist would use the term, to support our inferences. Yet somehow the game goes on, and we learn from each other. Change the situation from host and guest to teacher and student; the process remains the same, as we shall see.

Obviously, we cannot hope to find a simple, one-dimensional model for social interaction, what Veblen has called "A highly sterilized, germ-proof system of knowledge, kept in a cool dry place." Human beings are simply not that way. They not only respond to experience; they *actively and selectively seek it out*. In this sense, they *create* experience for themselves and others; they are not rats in cages with only one bar to press.

At the same time, modern statistical techniques have enabled us to predict certain behaviors of large groups of people rather accurately. Yet, even here, Presidential candidates have been unwilling to publish poll results which showed that they were ahead, because people tend to vote for the underdog. The impact of the prediction itself had to be taken into account in making the prediction. Here is another problem in causation for the social scientist. The chemist can shout his predictions to the skies; it will not change the rates of combination of the chemicals he is working with, but with people the prediction can actually be a *cause* of behavior. Simply asking a person what he thinks about communism or why he wants to go to college may be an educational influence. Thus, the social scientist's desire for "objectivity," as the physicist might use the term, the wish to withdraw from participation in the social universe and study it "pure" is a vain and forlorn hope. All the world's a stage, the people merely players, including the teacher and the social scientist.

In the same vein, the chemist can start and stop his reactions. When he stores his chemicals on shelves in brown bottles, he can be fairly sure when he goes home for the night that they will not do much while he is gone. People cannot be stored; they are not only names but lives in progress. Behind the basic continuity of habit, each individual is a compendium of shifting hopes, fears, desires, hates, joys, ad infinitum. The chemist can duplicate his reactions with ease, while the duplication of a complex human reaction under controlled conditions is virtually impossible. People's lives are not going to stop while we investigate. The statement from Socrates suggests that young people will grow up, whether we are ready for them or not. Usually we are not, as we have not watched closely what is happening to them. If, for example, we do a careful study of causes of delinquency which takes five years, by the time we announce our findings a whole new set of factors may have come into being which we could not have taken into account, as they did not exist when we began the study. Some social research is therefore obsolete before it is published, particularly in a time of rapid social change such as our own, or that of Socrates.

Additional problems with objectivity occur as we decide to take careful aim on our target. Do we use a telescope or a microscope? Do we consider a man as simply an infinitesimal part of a vast social universe, or do we call the *individual* a universe and look within him for our questions and answers? The first, or macrocosmic view, can give us good information about large numbers of people, but not much about each individual. For example, the Nielson rating system of television programs has a large say in what programs are shown, yet it is simply a measure of how many TV sets, within a "representative" sample, are *turned on*. This tells nothing about whether people liked the program, how many were watching, or whether or not anyone was watching at all, leading to the ludicrous but possible extreme of a program getting very high ratings, continuing season after season, with no one watching, as people enjoy tuning in the program and then going off to do something else! This type of perspective is thus limited because of its tendency to lose individuals. A good group prediction is not necessarily a good predictor for John Smith.

Interestingly enough, the chemist has the same nasty question of probability, prediction and sampling. All the atoms of a substance do not behave in precisely the same way—some atoms are more active than others. There apparently are great individual differences betwen atoms and molecules *of the same substance*. The layman's view of science, that its precision is based on completely identical "building blocks" for each substance, is false. Some day, the chemist may be as concerned with individual differences among atoms of the same substance as the social scientist is with individual differences among people, and at that level of analysis, the chemist's predictions may not be much better.

On the other hand, if we make John Smith himself the object of our study, we may compile a great deal of information on him and his behavior which will allow us to predict his actions and reactions, but if John Smith happens to be a very atypical specimen, we cannot generalize or transfer our information about him to other people. Should John happen to get struck by lightning, our pile of information about him would be of little use if we were to generalize our findings to other people.

Here, then, we have the two extreme perspectives with their virtues and limitations. Group data can be of great help in making group predictions but are of little use in refining our perceptions of individuals. Individual data, on the other hand, are often not transferable to group situations. It is worth pointing out here that the teacher must make the same choice of perspective that the sociologist must make. Many teachers adopt the macrocosmic view and consider each student only within the frame of reference of *all* seventh graders, ignoring any individual behavior which deviates from this rather stereotyped norm. If this teacher expects all seventh graders to misbehave and break the rules, they will usually be happy to reinforce his view. (Again, teacher's expectations determine student behavior, and vice versa.) Other teachers, taking the microscopic view, feel that each individual is a sacred entity, and that trying to classify him at all, as middle class, seventh grade, urban, Southern, or whatever, is a violation of his individuality. Naturally, the relatively few teachers at these two extremes run into precisely the same problems which confront the social scientist who takes either extreme view.

Although it does not represent a solution to all of the difficulties presented earlier, the most sensible point of view for us to adopt here can be called *interaction*. The interactionist realizes that the individual and his society are constantly in a reciprocal relationship with each other. Rejecting the two extreme views we have presented, he looks for *meaningful* general contexts within which to place the behavior of individuals with whom he must deal. Like the skilled clinical psychologist, he *begins with the person and works out*. As his knowledge of individuals and groups increases, he will become aware of small clues which he would have ignored earlier. He is eclectic in his view of man, and selects the definition of each problem that will be most helpful in solving it, instead of attempting to transform everything into *only* Freudian, Marxist, Christian, or other terms. He sees people and groups as constantly changing within a limited framework of constancy, and sees himself in that light too. (How many teachers, like Socrates, condemn the younger generation without realizing that they themselves, and their society, have changed as much as the young?)

He will tend to resist the "basic" arguments—man is *basically* an economic being, man is *basically* a religious being, man is *basically* a family being—as models which tend to obscure the reality of individuals operating within many different systems *at the same time*. This point deserves a bit of explanation. When one picks up an introductory sociology text, one usually is told that people express themselves through *roles:* when one is at work, one plays the worker role; when one is at home, one plays the mother, father, husband, wife, or other roles. One's children play the student role at school, the son or daughter role at home. This picture of people switching roles as they would clothes (one at a time) is somewhat misleading. The child at home is still in some sense concerned with his student role—if a person is to be integrated, these various roles must be fairly compatible so that the person can live with all of them. Every teacher knows that children bring their families to school with them every day, in the sense of their responding to school situations within the home context, to some extent. The switching of roles is not therefore complete; the parts we play *overlap* to a considerable extent. Of greater value than the view of complete switching of roles is the view that roles are situational; that at any given moment one role may be dominant but the others are still present, and are still influencing the person's behavior, albeit in a minor way.

This view is consistent with the interactionist position—just as individuals are interacting socially in a reciprocal way, so the various components of each individual's personality (however we wish to describe them) are in a state of interaction. These dynamic conceptions of activities within and across persons are more complex than the static models, and are much harder to visualize, as they must take into account *change* and *time*.

As Korzybski and others have pointed out, man uses his ability to create symbolic structures (particularly language) to *bind time*—to create an artificial world of permanence in a world which is really full of constant change. The term "apple," for example, blinds us to the fact that the apple is in flux, that it begins as a green bud (or perhaps a flower), then a small green knob, then a larger colored object, then a ripe red fruit, then a mushy brown pile on the ground, to be driven into the earth by the rains and snows. When does it start and stop being an apple? We tend to think of people in the same framework as that we use for things. Our term "Bill Smith" blinds us to the organic and evolutionary nature of the person, just as our notion of "apple" does for the astounding processes that are involved during the interval in which a thing we call an apple becomes, and somewhere, sometime, ceases to be.

Keats, of course, was making the same point about works of art that we are making about language: they achieve a time-binding permanence of perspective which does not exist in the world as we experience it. The young lovers painted on the side of the beautiful Greek urn Keats was describing have a permanence that real lovers can never have:

> Bold Lover, never, never canst thou kiss,
> Though winning near the goal—yet, do not grieve;
> She cannot fade, though thou hast not thy bliss,
> Forever wilt thou love, and she be fair!

The interactionist can also avoid the pitfalls of the heredity *versus* environment argument, eliminating the dichotomy by viewing man as the interplay between heredity and environment, and by realizing that the interrelationship between the two factors is as important as the factors themselves. Other conventional dichotomies such as the mind-body problem, free will *versus* determinism, are met in the same way, by conceding that both extremes are part of human behavior, and that the interaction of the dichotomous elements should be our primary focus. The person who adopts this position (which borders on a philosophy) will be selective in the concepts he uses to describe and analyze human behavior, and will always be willing to shift his perspective on the basis of the evidence *as it comes in*. This person is, in a real sense, educable, and his judgments, perceptions, values, and predictions should improve as he accumulates experience. This book is dedicated to the development of this kind of analytical thinking in the reader, whatever his profession may be. The assumption is that we will be better teachers, social scientists, wives, mothers, fathers, husbands, friends, and citizens as a consequence.

education, interaction,

and social change

1: actors and roles, audiences and stages

All the World's a Stage, and all the men and women merely players. They have their exits and their entrances, and one man in his time plays many parts. . . .

As You Like It, II, 7

The attentive pupil who wishes to be attentive, his eyes riveted on the teacher, his ears open wide, so exhausts himself in playing the attentive role that he ends up by no longer hearing anything.

Sartre, Being and Nothingness

(Philosophical Library, 1950), p. 60

It is probably no mere historical accident that the word person, in its first meaning, is a mask. . . . It is rather a recognition of the fact that everyone is always and everywhere, more or less consciously, playing a role. . . . It is in these roles that we know each other, it is in these roles that we know ourselves. . . . In the end, our conception of the role becomes second nature and an integral part of our *personality. We come into the world as individuals, achieve character, and become persons.*

R. E. Park, RACE AND CULTURE
(Free Press of Glencoe, Inc., 1950), pp. 249–50

We may practically say that he has as many different social selves as there are distinct groups of persons about whose opinion he cares. He generally shows a different side of himself to each of these different groups. Many a youth who is demure enough before his parents and teachers, swaggers and swears like a pirate among his "tough" young friends.

THE PHILOSOPHY OF WILLIAM JAMES
(Modern Library), pp. 128–29

The actor's entire spiritual and physical nature should be involved in what is happening to the character he has imagined . . . (otherwise) he initiates the external manifestations of his feelings, or he attempts to "squeeze out" some emotions for his part. . . . But when he thus violates his psychic organism with its immutable natural laws, he can never achieve any desired artistic results. He can only give a crude counterfeit presentment of an emotion, for emotions do not appear on demand. . . . One cannot play or represent feelings, and one cannot call forth feelings point blank.

C. Stanislavski, STANISLAVSKI'S LEGACY
(Theatre Arts Books, 1958), pp. 174–75

The variety of sources given above represents the range of interest in the conception of a person as a collection of roles or masks. Shakespeare's superb insight told us long ago that people are all actors, both on and off the stage, while Stanislavski tells us that one cannot become, on the stage, a character totally unrelated to his off-stage person. The job of the actor is therefore to respond *with his own being* to the role; not to forget himself and become Hamlet, but to transmute Hamlet through his own personality. Thus, even on the stage, or in the audience, we can never change our own identities and become someone else.

The quotation from James points out another interesting thing about the roles we play: that they often vary a great deal, even to the point of being contradictory. Thus, one individual may be the Gentle Husband, the Stern Father, the Shrewd Banker, the Awesome Uncle, the Genial Rotarian, the Devoted Methodist, and the Dedicated Republican. (The versatility of the performances we give *off* stage would put many professional actors to shame!) Like the actor on the stage, we present only those aspects of ourselves which are relevant to the role and to the people around us. In this sense, the groups of people with whom we learn to relate are remarkably like the audience in a theater, because it is through their cues that we, like actors, learn to play a role "correctly." As newborn infants, it is the responses of our parents to our behavior that guide and mold our consequent behavior. As we get older and go to school, we learn how to play the schoolboy roles by observing the actions of the other children, and by responding to signals they give us about our own behavior. Each new group into which we move will require our learning a new set of cues, and conversely, each new group changes to some degree because we have joined it. The individual and the group are constantly modifying each other.

As we develop as persons, we develop a sophistication and sensitivity to what is the "proper" role behavior for various groups we must meet. With this sort of "radar" we can, in a new group, quickly assimilate our own behavior into the group norms. We are in a sense able to predict the consequences of various behavior alternatives on others without actually performing them, and can select the best role and performance—"put our best face forward." This process, seen as a "dramatic rehearsal," as a "generalized other," or more recently as "awareness context," is the basic core of human interaction, and is as complex as the relationship of actor and audience on a stage. In fact, contemporary drama seems to be self-consciously exploiting this relationship, both in the theater of the absurd genre and in plays like the *Assassination of Marat*, in which the actors are putting on a play-within-a-play, and the "real" audience is expected to play the part of the audience of French *bourgeoisie* viewing the interior play.

Consider for a moment how elaborate the process is when we leave one group and join another. In a sense, we "turn off" one part of ourselves and "turn on" another in a very complex way. Again, the stage provides us with a vivid example:

> We have seen a loving couple immediately after their marriage ceremony slip off their wedding clothes to put on their stage costumes. . . . We have seen a father, broken with grief, entertain an audience and then run into the wings to weep over the news that a member of his family is dying. We have seen an audience whistle down a singer who missed his high note: he was singing on the day he buried his wife.[1]

Most human beings seem to be able to manage this continual modification of themselves without too much difficulty. The fact that it is often done without conscious effort or intent is also interesting. Most aspects of personality can be altered as we shift reference groups; not only manners and other superficial behavior patterns, but attitudes, values, and

[1] C. Stanislavski, *Stanislavski's Legacy* (New York: Theatre Arts Books, 1958), p. 24.

moods as well. Thus, the role of the educational administrator in some faculty committee meetings may be not only dignified and stern, but *pessimistic* as well (particularly if money is to be spent). However, the same person may be joyful, optimistic, and relatively uninhibited with his own children. It is important to remember that roles often require certain emotional and attitudinal states as well as behavior per se, so that the cues we learn from the new group are not only related to what we *do* but also to how we *think* and *feel*. Thus, the actor on the stage can be made to feel certain emotions because of cues provided him by the lines and by the audience. Another way to say this is that the audience puts the mask on the actor. In the same vein, what we are as persons is due largely to our interacting with the various "audiences" (groups) for whom we have "performed."

Thus, one definition of personality would be all the role performances engaged in by a particular individual at any given time or throughout his life. In that personality is determined in large part by the reference groups with which the individual comes into contact, the concept of personality, which is often seen as the territory of the psychologist, can be also the province of the sociologist. But because of the time dimension, our notion of personality must be a *developmental* one, as the individual moves through a small sea of shifting reference groups. It also must be a *relativistic* conception, in that we cannot assess personality merely by one observation, and must interpret what we observe as relative to the reference group (audience) for whom an individual is "performing" *at that particular moment.* (The office grouch at 3:30 may be the life of the party at 8:30. *Both* "shows" are part of his personality.)

The definition of personality allows us to develop an approach to the difficult problem of personality *adjustment* as well. The well-adjusted or "mentally healthy" person is, for us, the individual who possesses a basic consistency in his performance as he goes from role to role. Of course, he will have to shift certain aspects of his behavior, but if these shifts are minimal and not too painful, not involving the basic values of the individual, then we can speak of him as being well adjusted.

Please note that we are not saying here that the well-adjusted individual is necessarily the *conforming* individual, as it is perfectly possible (and often desirable) that the well-adjusted person *reject* the behavior, attitudes, and values of certain reference groups, and often that he alter the group's expectations to bring them into line with his own. Thus, individuals like Albert Schweitzer, Gandhi, Galileo, and Socrates can be called well-adjusted individuals because of their role consistency, not because they gave up their norms to conform with those of the people around them. (They didn't.)

Perhaps the clearest example of this conception of adjustment and role consistency is in the political arena. As the politician climbs the ladder of political power and influence, he must work out from local to state to national groups. In so doing, he must appeal to an ever-increasing variety of people and special interest groups. Thus, John Jones, the candidate, must modify his behavior just enough so that the farmer, miner, housewife, Midwesterner, Easterner, unemployed, bureaucrat, suburbanite, etc., will all think he is *their* man. In order to please one group, he must not modify his behavior so much as to offend another constituency—there must be a common John Jones in whom all constituencies can believe. The easiest way to provide this identification is to adopt some of the superficial behavior and mannerisms of the reference group he is "performing" for at a given moment.

Thus, we may find our man Jones eating corn in overalls in Iowa, wearing a cowboy hat at a barbecue in Texas, and lunching at a Cambridge University club in tweeds. As is true on the stage, some people can adopt these superficial mannerisms in a believable fashion and "carry off the show," while others, often men of equal ability, cannot. (The field of American politics is littered with examples of men of great potential who were simply not able to accomplish an identification with the masses through these minor compromises in role behavior.) But most important of all, there must be an *essential* or basic John Jones, who shines through all the behavioral adaptations as he moves from role to role. His basic commitments and values must remain constant, or there will be nothing in which to believe. Thus, at any given moment, John Jones must be involved with a give-and-take of behavior in "performing" for a given reference group which does not override or alter his basic personality. To the extent that he can remain a consistent person as he shifts from role to role, he fits not only the criterion for a good politician, but also our definition of a well-adjusted person: conscious of the needs and demands of others, but not overwhelmed by them; able to modify his performances without losing his sense of self.

cues and strategies

The problem of cuing the performer exists both on and off the stage. A cue is simply a "trigger" or sign which will produce the required behavior in the actor. This is usually done in the theater by the prompter (who incidentally never has to say more than a word or two), but offstage it is accomplished in many different ways by many people. The prompter in the theater must, if an actor is really confused, select one or two words which will "trigger" the entire line or scene for the actor. In a similar vein, the conductor of a symphony orchestra must, when a soloist skips a phrase or makes a serious error, indicate to the rest of the orchestra precisely where they should begin playing in order to compensate for the soloist's error. In both of these examples, the cue is never direct and complete; it is *inferential, compact,* and *symbolic.* The ideal cue, therefore, generally possesses this quality of "infinite riches in a little room" which we usually associate with *symbols.* Like a good metaphor in poetry, a good cue will tell us many things at once.

One way of looking at human behavior, which has gotten a great deal of attention recently, is to perceive the interaction of persons as a sort of battleground, in which each of the participants is trying to maximize his chances of coming through the encounter well and minimize his chances of emerging with a "loss." Thus, the *strategy* employed by the participants becomes of great importance. If human interaction is seen as a sort of war without guns, all the principles of games (strategies) become relevant, as does the theory of games, with its central notion that each player tries, in each "move" (as in chess) to maximize his chances of "winning" and minimize his chances of losing (the two things are *not* the same). Thus, game theory, widely used to interpret economic behavior, can be used to interpret *any* social system.[2]

If we were to proceed to look at social interaction with this model, it would become clear that our cues, as described here, become the basic elements or "pieces" with which we play the game. Thus, the acquired British accent, the air of haughty disdain, the manner of dress, the display of knowledge of cultural objects, the social skills of smoking, hold-

---

[2] The book which originated the vogue in game theoretical analyses is John von Neumann and Oskar Morgenstern, *Theory of Games and Economic Behavior* (Princeton, N.J.: Princeton University Press, 1947). This lead was followed by works like *Strategy and Market Structure,* by Martin Shubik (New York: John Wiley & Sons, Inc., 1959). Others have taken the theory out of the realms of games and the stock market, setting it up as a major theory of almost all human behavior. (Life is a game; one wins or loses through the strategies one employs and carries out.) See John Cohen, *Chance, Skill and Luck: The Psychology of Guessing and Gambling* (Baltimore: Penguin Books, Inc., 1960); G. L. S. Shackle, *Decision, Order, and Time in Human Affairs* (New York: Cambridge University Press, 1961). J. C. C. McKinsey, *Introduction to the Theory of Games* (New York: McGraw-Hill Book Company, 1952). It should be pointed out that the theory in its original form was almost primarily a mathematical one. The books listed here become much less mathematical as one gets down the list. Probably the most fascinating use of the concept in a totally nonmathematical setting is Erving Goffman, *The Presentation of Self in Everyday Life* (Garden City, N.Y.: Doubleday & Company, Inc., 1959). See also by the same author, *Stigma: Notes on the Management of Spoiled Identity* (Englewood Cliffs, N.J.: Prentice-Hall, Inc., 1964). As well as being a stimulus in the wealth of small group research of the last twenty years, the theory has been used in studies like Edward Walker and Roger Heyns, *An Anatomy for Conformity* (Englewood Cliffs, N.J.: Prentice-Hall, Inc.).

ing spoons and balancing cups, etc., all become weapons in a social war. (In fact, Swift himself suggests that language is becoming so unimportant, men of the future may eliminate it altogether by simply carrying huge bags of things around on their backs. When they meet, instead of conversing, they can simply exchange things. When one drives a station wagon, one wonders what all the space is for!) The things we possess become as important as our conversation, and the actions we exhibit. In fact, as we become more mobile and our human contacts more superficial, it may be that the symbolic importance of *things* in socal inter-action has increased enormously. Our cars, telephones, office furniture, lighting fixtures, bathrooms, vacations, and homes can tell the visitor a great deal about what sort of people we are. The things that we own, therefore, exist as cues to others concerning our social status, and become an important "weapon" in social interaction. A quick glance at almost any magazine or television advertisement will verify the fact that the chief appeal is not in the specific virtues of the product but in the effect that owning the product will have on others. Thus, one major strategy in the contest is the strategy of ownership.

In some cultures at certain times, the skillful use of rhetoric, logic, and argumentation was an important weapon in the social war. For British society at the time of Swift, Dryden, and Pope, the coffee and chocolate houses were scenes of intellectual battle, and one's use of words and logic was the skill by which one won or lost. If one wished to marry a lady, one might write a sonnet, clearly and logically stating the case. It must be said that in many sectors of our own culture, the weapons of social war have little, if anything, to do with the intellect. This anti-intellectual component of American life has been brilliantly perceived and documented by the historian Richard Hofstadter.[3] In fact, the social war in America seems to be carried on through the use of three battlegrounds: sociability, comfort, and fun. Any casual study of media advertising will reveal the enormous evidence that these three areas are of primary importance. It is perhaps the cocktail party which best typifies this type of social setting. The smooth but superficial personal relationships, the rapidly shifting patterns of communication, the explicit expression of how much fun people are having, the unwillingness to commit oneself by pursuing any issue in depth or getting emotionally involved with the argument—these all add up to a social event highly characteristic of our highly mobile, fluid society. (We will return to this example later.)

Although game theory is comparatively new, the conception of hu-

---

[3] Hofstadter, *Anti-Intellectualism in American Life* (New York: Alfred A. Knopf, Inc., 1963). The concluding section on education in America should be required reading.

man interaction as a battleground is certainly not. In fact, it could be considered as a major theme in literature, from Pope's "Rape of the Lock" to T. S. Eliot's "Love Song of J. Alfred Prufrock"; from Kingsley Amis's *Lucky Jim* to Eric Sanson's *A Contest of Ladies*. "The Rape of the Lock" is particularly and humorously clear in pointing up the weaponry used in the "battle of the sexes" in a very sophisticated era. Although the style of the mock epic points up the absurdity of it all, nevertheless we are able to recognize many, many cues that are relevant to our own time. The whole art of "one-upmanship," which is new in name only, is simply the proper selection of cues and strategies in order to overcome your partner in almost any social enterprise (who is seen, almost universally, as the opponent).

Probably some of the best advice to those who wish to follow the game theory model comes from Machiavelli:

> Whence it is to be noted, that in taking a state the conqueror must arrange to commit all his cruelties at once, so as not to have to recur to them every day, and so as to be able, by not making fresh changes, to reassure people and win them over by benefitting them. Whoever acts otherwise, either through timidity or bad counsel, is always obliged to stand with knife in hand, and can never depend on his subjects, because they, owing to continually fresh injuries, are unable to depend upon him.[4]

Pascal's famous wager concerning whether or not God exists is another example of the use of the game theoretical model in an earlier time. The problem is established in terms of the lack of clear-cut evidence as to whether or not God exists; the solution (seen in terms of the earthly life and the life hereafter) is that in order to maximize your chances of "winning," you should behave *as if* God existed. (Whether or not He really does exist becomes in a sense subservient to the possibilities for gain of the individual—a crucial point.)

However, it should be pointed out that the "mini-max" model for social interaction leaves much to be desired. In the first place, according to the model, benevolent, cooperative, or charitable activities are impossible, unless the actor does them for purely selfish reasons (and of course, if he does, they could hardly be called benevolent). It does not seem reasonable to assume that *all* human activity (the death of martyrs, for instance) can be explained away in terms of selfish desires to enhance the self at the expense of other selves. To assume that Joan of Arc was operating out of self-interest alone seems to miss much of the point.

Also, few of us look at all of our contacts with other human beings

[4] N. Machiavelli, *The Prince* (New York: New American Library of World Literature, Inc.), p. 69.

in strategic terms of exploiting the self. (What marriage could long endure if one or both participants were constantly employing the "minimax" strategy? On the other hand, this may be a new explanation for our high divorce rate!) The theory is probably close to universal in explaining our behavior in meeting people for the *first* time; however, as our knowledge of them increases, we can "let down our guard," at least in certain areas of relationship. Thus, for old friends who have enjoyed each other's company for many years, the theory is of very little use, either in explaining or predicting their behavior.

The theory also seems to assume that in all areas of our lives we try to exploit people with equal intensity. There are few people who would make a strategic campaign out of ordering a hamburger at a restaurant, compared with the reactions of these same people in an interview with their bosses in which they explain why they should be given a raise. We all, then, will use a strategic approach in certain areas of our lives, and not in others. The theory also seems to neglect individual differences in the sensitivity to, and ego-involvement in, various cues and strategies. Certainly, any analysis of a cocktail party will reveal that certain individuals have a particular expertise in dealing with large numbers of individuals on a transitory basis, making precisely the right "ploy" with one person, then moving on to the next, picking the right strategy and scoring another "victory." In terms of military tactics, some people desire to seize the offensive, make the first strike and win the day, while others prefer the counterattack, waiting for the opponent to make a false move before "putting him away." However, it is just as easy to find others who are obviously and determinedly *not* playing the game. They will tend to stay by themselves and not be drawn into a "duel" with the other participants. (In fact, in some social situations, the "ploy" of disdaining the rules of the game, and the game itself, becomes an index of high status. Thus, the person who makes it clear from his actions that he considers the others not worth playing the game with may carry the day.) Our first type achieves victory by vanquishing the enemy, while the person we describe here "wins" by saying that the enemy is not worth vanquishing.

It also becomes abundantly clear to anyone watching such an affair as a cocktail party that people vary in the *involvement* they have in the game. For some, the game is life and death; for others, it hardly matters at all.

Even with these limitations, the game theoretical model has become extremely popular with sociologists and social psychologists, and many research studies are now being done using the model. (The fact that the game theory paradigm has been accepted so quickly may tell us something significant about social scientists as a group.)

"phonies"—poor and unauthorized performances

Another major relationship between the world of the stage and the world off stage is the amazing ability most human beings have of detecting a false performance. The actor who is simply mouthing his lines and waving his hands is quickly detected. In the non-theater world, we are more likely to say something like "He's putting up a false front" (an interesting expression). How do we know it is a *false* performance? A major distinction can be made here between the *poor* performance and the *unauthorized* performance which may still be of excellent quality. The first can be seen nicely in the quotation from Sartre with which this chapter began—the student who is trying to play the role of student so hard that he ceases to hear anything and learns nothing; hence he cannot fulfill the student role. The hockey player who is constantly thinking of what he is doing and what the coach thinks of him, who is *thinking of himself playing hockey*, is a lost cause. Thus, one major cause of poor performances is often obsessive self-awareness and self-consciousness over the role we are playing. (How many people have been on quiz shows on radio and television and not been able to answer ridiculously easy questions that would have been easily answered in the comfort of their own home? Their concern with their own selves has effectively blocked their ability to concentrate.)

It is, therefore, almost impossible for an individual to play a role well and think about himself playing the role at the same time; we must to some extent "lose ourselves" in the role. Stanislavski has pointed up the theatrical problem nicely:

> Find out all the reasons which justify the action of your character and then act without reflecting about just where your "own" actions end and "his" begin. The one and the other will merge of their own accord if you have followed the procedure I have indicated to you. . . .
>
> In life a man who weeps is concerned about restraining his tears—but the actor journeyman does just the opposite. Having read the remark of the author (he weeps), he tries with all his might to squeeze out tears and since nothing comes of it, he is forced to grasp at the straw of the stereotyped theatrical cry. The same is true of laughter. Who does not know the unpleasant, counterfeit laughter of an actor? [5]

As it is on the stage, so it is elsewhere. The stage is indeed a mirror held up to nature—human nature.

[5] Consecutively, the first from "The Hard Job of Being an Actor," in *Stanislavski's Legacy, op. cit.*, p. 12. The second from *Acting—A Handbook of the Stanislavski Method* (New York: Lear Publications, 1947), pp. 118–19.

The second type of "phony" performance, the unauthorized performance, is also interesting. Here the performance of the role may be of high quality, but somehow it does not match the consensus of the reference group—it is a wrong or inappropriate performance. This is perhaps most easily seen in terms of people who *act* as if they had a higher power, office, or status than we know they really have. While we usually feel some compassion for the first type of "phony" (the *bad* performance), we usually respond to the *unauthorized* performance with deep bitterness and sincere ill will. The reason for this is simple. In order for a social system to work, participants have to believe that the rules of the game will be adhered to by all players. But when the boss's secretary begins to talk *as if she were* the boss (acting the boss role), then the rest (especially the other secretaries) must realize that this is taking unfair advantage of the system, and that if it continues, they can no longer have faith and trust in the system. Thus, the unauthorized performance puts the position of each individual, and of the system of orderly relationships among the employees, into jeopardy.

Another interesting thing about unauthorized performances is that the closer the performer is to the person and position he is imitating, *the madder we get*. Thus, when the third assistant office boy "plays the boss" with a pillow under his coat and smoking a pencil instead of a cigar, we (including some bosses) will be inclined to laugh. But if a vice-president begins to hand down edicts *as if he were the president*, we will be angry, even if his performance of the president's role is an admirable one. Note that a major distortion of the system by the performer in an unauthorized performance does not often bother us much, as the third assistant office boy could not, in that position, *be* the president—our own positions are, therefore, not threatened. However, a minor distortion of the system on the part of a person who, because of his position, could be "the boss," results in extreme anxiety. A rough theatrical parallel to this might be the art of "upstaging," in which an actor who is not supposed to be in the center of the stage manages to maneuver the other actors around until he is in the central position, so that the actor who carries the major lines cannot be seen—an unauthorized performance if there ever was one!

"Getting ahead," whether it be on the stage, in the classroom, or in the office, generally requires a testing of skills *through time*. The unauthorized performance is undertaken by the person who wishes to "short-circuit" or leap this time barrier. Social status is, in a game theoretical sense, an investment problem. The players must invest time and activity in order to "make a gain" in the market. If a person can make a gain *without* investing a certain number of months or years of his life, then the central principle of the market (status equals time plus work) is violated. This violation is made abundantly clear in the musical "How To Succeed in Business Without Really Trying." As in education, achievement without obvious effort is becoming a clear-cut goal. To admit that one has worked hard on anything is becoming a social sin.

It should be clear from this discussion that any performance, in order to be effective, must agree with the *consensus* which surrounds it. There are, of course, unauthorized performances that *do* work, but when they do, it is because a new consensus is created around the new performance. There are Horatio Alger cases, but not many, due mainly to the relative decline in importance of individual mobility and the increase in importance of group mobility in our society. Thus, the group consensus on what the acceptable performance of a role is will undoubtedly become more important in the future, and the coercive factors brought to bear on the individual to conform to this performance (particularly in occupational roles) will increase in strength. We will probably hear more and more often things like: "If anyone in our group goofs (deviates), the whole group will be held back, so nobody rock the boat." As Whyte cogently pointed out quite a while ago, if one's position in the group of people of similar status and activity level is crucial, then social performances will often become as important as "job" performances. (In fact, many salesmen are held back from promotion because they sell *too much;* the reasoning being that if they are that aggressive, they do not belong in a management job.) Thus, the unauthorized performance may be even more dangerous in the future, because it may destroy an entire *group* of people, not just the deviating individual.

role and game theory
applied to education

In this brief discussion, an attempt has been made to present an analogy between the roles of the actor on the stage and in social and game theory, in relation to some kinds of human interaction.

The relationships between this discussion and strictly educational situations is so obvious as hardly to require comment. What teacher, in elementary school or graduate school, has not walked into a classroom on the first day of the new term with the conscious intent of presenting himself in a certain way? In similar fashion, what student (elementary or graduate school level) has not put on a concerted effort to impress a certain teacher? What person in any level of administration has not manipulated an assortment of cues and strategies in order to get the "proper" responses from the person or group sitting on the other side of his desk? Whether conscious awareness was present or not, have not the strategic and tactical aspects of "mini-max" been brought into operation? What member of a football team has not been irritated at the "third-string" quarterback who *acts as if* he were in charge of the team? Similarly, the faculty member who acts as if he were the chairman of his department?

Education takes place, at least in contemporary societies, in highly organized social institutions. An organized institution is defined (at least in part) as a clearly codified set of functions and sanctions, performed by a variety of people whose position in the hierarchy is determined and regulated by the functions they perform. Thus, the judgments of the performance of academic *and* social roles is bound to be a major component of all educational systems; and a major problem of all educational institutions is to decide which performances are the important ones, *who shall judge* the quality of performance, and by what criteria.

the creation of role consensus in education

One difficulty with role consensus in all educational institutions is in the rapid and continuous shifting of clientele. Every year, semester, or whatever, a new student group comes in at the bottom, while the most mature group of students leaves at the top. Even neglecting faculty attrition, the school principal or college dean of students must see that every year a new consensus or climate is created. (One of the most frustrating aspects of this job is that the group of students with the greatest maturity, wisdom, and influence with their peers is always just preparing to leave the institution. Here is a major difference between education and business as a social system: most businesses are established on the basis of the "steady customer" who adds stability and continuity to sales. There are no "steady customers" in education.)

Just as the administrator must face this problem on an institutional level, so the teacher must face it at the classroom level. He must not only learn who and what is behind the blur of new faces on opening day, he also must structure for them a set of roles he wishes them to play, and give them clues as to what he means by a "good performance." For reasons not yet clear, this work is usually done inferentially and often symbolically, seldom if ever directly and openly. (Why human beings cannot simply *tell* others what role performances are desired is a fasc:-nating problem.)

Likewise, the students, as they gain in experience with teachers, are changing their criteria for a "good" performance by a teacher or a fellow student, or an administrator. They are the most continuously variable segment of the educational institution, and in a way the most vital, as all other segments exist only to serve (teach, feed, house, medicate) students. Although they may not know the term, students become much more aware of, and skillful in the use of, reciprocal role relationships. Just as an audience can come to realize its power over an actor, so students become increasingly aware of their impact on, and control over, the teacher, while at the same time the teacher is also controlling them. One definition of a good educational institution *qua* institution is that in it, the amount of time and energy devoted to this mutual accommodation of role definitions is minimal. On the stage, the actor must convince the audience as quickly as possible what role he is playing, how he intends to play it, and what he expects of the audience. So in a classroom or an entire school there must be a speedy agreement on what each is to do, and what is expected of the others. Please note that this does not mean that there can be no latitude or flexibility of role consensus in these institutions—indeed, they may well be more flexible and tolerant in the variety and range of roles allowed. One can easily find a rigid, monolithic, single-minded classroom, school, or college in which this mutual consensus has not been reached at all.

No one would argue that role definition and consensus is an end in itself for educational institutions. It is, however, a vital *means* without which teaching and learning (desired ends) cannot be accomplished effectively. Certainly, this consensus cannot be accomplished in an educational institution in which factions are isolated from each other. Edicts issued *in vacuo* by administration or faculty (or students) will not do the job. Because this consensus comes about indirectly and often symbolically, the constituent groups must be gotten to confront each other.

The reason for this confrontation simply cannot be explained by the game theory or "mini-max" models—the object must not be that of a faction "winning" or losing. The object is rather to explore and discover the limits or parameters of roles within which each and all must work. Because teachers and administrators are more permanent than students, and because of their maturity relative to students, they tend to build up a working role consensus without involving the students at all. Exactly how students should be involved in this consensus is indeed a difficult matter, particularly in light of the obvious necessity for formal power and authority to be in the hands of faculty, administration, and ultimately boards of control. Perhaps we should return to our notion of role consistency, and say that in a good educational institution no one should have to take on a role which is totally at variance with his real self. This is emphatically not to say that students need not be made to learn.

Indeed, they often must. But there are many ways of making students (and teachers and administrators) learn, some humiliating and personally destructive, some rewarding and productive.

intellectual "styles" and social roles in education

One of the enormous difficulties in education at all levels is to judge teaching and learning in terms of the student as a person. If we are interested only in the acquisition of factual knowledge, that, of course, is fairly easy to judge. It is also clear that in a very short time, this factual information will be forgotten. One commentator on education is known to have said that the teacher affects eternity; he can never tell where his influence stops. This may well be true, but he also cannot tell where it *starts* either. Anyone who has worked with small groups of students is aware of the difficulty in assessing whether or not he is having any genuine impact on them. The major reason for this difficulty is in the impossibility of divorcing intellectual roles from social ones—the depersonalized intellect does not exist in any meaningful sense. The most enthusiastic student in class, the one we use to justify our claim to skill as a teacher, may simply be playing a "phony" role very well.

Contemporary education seems to be developing as if we did believe that the person and the intellect were two entirely separable things. Teaching machines, television monitors, and all of our vast educational technology seem geared to a disembodied intellect, not to a person. As one example, the author was observing a demonstration of closed-circuit a few years ago in which an excellent TV teacher was giving a demonstration of sculpture techniques to over 3,000 grade-school students in about 20 schools. One little girl in the classroom the author was observing was obviously enthralled with the project as she followed along on her own piece of sculpture. As the program neared completion, she could stand it no longer, grabbed her sculpture, went directly to the television monitor, and said "How's this, Miss Jones?" Miss Jones (on tape) continued blithely on, while the little girl returned to her seat in tears. She thought she had been dealing with a person, and took on a role she usually played with persons. The consequences of this incident on the little girl are interesting to consider. What sort of social-intellectual role *should* she have played?

At the college level also, consistent and spreading protests and unrest of students seems largely a demand for their right to play personal roles within the college or university context. A Berkeley student said to the author recently, "The only way you can be treated as a person here is to mutilate your IBM cards." Because the issues mentioned in student demonstrations vary so widely, it would seem that almost any issue can be used for protest, as long as it allows the students to act as if they were persons, and to be seen by the faculty and administration as such.

All this is not to say that when teacher and student confront each other as persons, "good" education automatically results. It also should not be concluded that a certain type of person (friendly, gregarious, a "pal") will necessarily be the best teacher, nor should it be argued that a lecturer can never be known to his students as a person, or vice versa. The educational environment must, however, make the playing of personal roles possible for teacher and student within that context.

In fact, at earlier levels of our educational system, the reverse problem seems to exist; namely, in elementary schools, children are often not allowed to play any roles *except* social ones. Although there are now serious efforts to correct this, it appeared for a time that the curriculum in the formative elementary-school years would be almost totally the acquisition of skill in playing social roles. Now, some of this is unquestionably needed in a culture as interested in sociability as our own, in which social skills have a pervasive importance to one's future life. But the personal role without intellectual components is as dangerous as its opposite. It is the simultaneous involvement of both factors which should be produced by the educational context. Students must be allowed to be persons while learning.

Another interesting aspect of this topic concerns the various performances or "styles" we characterize in America as being "intellectual." Clearly, the word is not always used to heap praise on the recipient; in fact, in the fifties it became synonymous with "egghead." Bromfield's definition of this term in 1952 suggests one common view of the intellectual style in America:

> Egghead: A person of spurious intellectual pretensions, often a professor or a protegé of a professor. Fundamentally superficial. Over-emotional and feminine in reactions to any problem. Supercilious and surfeited with conceit and contempt for the experience of more sound and able men. Essentially confused in thought and immersed in mixture of sentimentality and violent evangelism. A doctrinaire supporter of Middle-European socialism. . . . Subject to the old-fashioned philosophical morality of Nietzsche which frequently leads him into jail or disgrace. A self-conscious prig, so given to examining all sides of a question that he becomes thoroughly addled while remaining always in the same spot. An anemic bleeding heart.

In 1954, President Eisenhower defined an intellectual as "A man who takes more words than are necessary to tell more than he knows." [6] Thus the social role of the intellectual, at least in this stereotyped view, is

[6] Both Bromfield and Eisenhower quotes from Hofstadter, *op. cit.*, pp. 9–10.

antithetical to the role of masculinity in our pragmatic, "can-do" culture. This attitude has softened a bit in the sixties, but mainly toward "intellectuals" in science and technology. The poet and artist are still viewed by many to be playing un-American and unmasculine roles.

Unfortunately, schools and colleges often seem to support the narrow and stereotyped definitions of the intellectual role present in much of our culture. Many studies have shown that in high schools, the playing of athletic and "sociability" roles is far more important and receives far more status from other students than does the playing of the student role. At the college level, other studies have indicated that, at many institutions, the college situation is remarkably the same.[7] One of the most pervasive components of these stereotypes is their connection with sex role—to be masculine is to be an athlete and have no visible emotions, except perhaps for anger. A young man interested in the arts as well as athletics is considered in many quarters to be something less than a male. As David Riesman has pointed out, we badly need to enlarge the parameters of acceptable sex roles in our culture and cut down on sex-linked stereotypes of subject matter, so that the girl interested in physics and the boy interested in painting can maintain their integrity as persons.[8] If tolerance for the way in which people play the learner role can be increased by a small bit, it will represent a big step forward.

awareness context, interaction, and educational roles

Whenever we evaluate the worth of a role performance, we are judging how good a job an individual did with what he had to work with. We also wish to avoid being taken in by a false, unauthorized, or "phony" performance. One of the major decisions we must make is the amount of awareness the person possesses of himself and us, and we of him. Thus, our interaction exists in a context of awareness (or lack of it), which is the total combination of what each participant in a situation knows about the identity of the other and his own identity in the eyes of the other.[9] The situation gets very complex, even with only two people in the situation. For example, take a seriously

[7] At the high-school level, see C. Wayne Gordon, *The Adolescent Society* (New York: Free Press of Glencoe, Inc., 1961). At the college level, see George Stern, "Characteristics of the Intellectual Climate in College Environments," *Harvard Educational Review,* 33 (1963), 5–41.

[8] See David Riesman, "Some Dilemmas of Women's Education," *Educational Record,* 46 (Fall, 1965), 424–34.

[9] B. Glazer and A. Strauss, "Awareness Contexts and Social Interaction," *American Sociological Review,* 29 (1964) 670. Although the title is abysmal, see also their provocative article "Temporal Aspects of Dying as Unscheduled Status Passage," *American Journal of Sociology,* 71 (1965), 48–59.

Actually, see C. Wayne Gordon, The Social System of the H.S. and James Coleman, The Adolescent Society.

ill person whose doctor tells him he is improving when actually the doctor knows he is about to die. One might assume that the patient was taken in by his doctor. On the other hand, the patient may have guessed the truth but simply "played along" with the doctor's approach. If the latter is the case, then the doctor was fooled. A third variant, however, resembles the two we have stated, plus the doctor's awareness that the patient knows that he is really dying. Clearly, any good analysis of this situation will depend on the awareness context—what each knows about himself and the other. Both people are trying to manage or control the interaction, based on what they know of the awareness context. Thus, different situations will produce different types of awareness context—open (both totally aware of the context), closed (one person does not know his true condition or identity, or the other's view of him), suspicious (variation on closed: one person suspects the true context), and pretense (variation on open: both persons fully aware but pretend not to be).[10]

Some institutions seem designed to develop closed awareness contexts; for example, in a hospital, everything possible is done to make sure that the patient's access to information is limited. Conferences about him are not held within his earshot, all records are kept from him, he is not trained to look for the signs of impending death, he has no allies in the hospital staff, etc. To a considerable extent, educational institutions also seem designed to produce closed awareness contexts on the part of the patients (students). In most schools, intelligence test scores are not given to the student, so that he can never evaluate his performance against his "real" ability; he never knows his true condition. Likewise, in most schools and colleges there is a confidential file on each student, not available to either the student or his parents. Although grades are usually given, the exact criteria for the grades are usually not made completely known to the student.

In fact, one way to define a profession is that it produces a closed awareness context in the client. The advantages of this are clear for the professional: the closed context makes the client very dependent on him and greatly enhances the professional's status. (Most lawyers know what the judge's verdict will be on their clients in advance, but this information is carefully kept from clients, in most cases.) Many school and college administrators also produce closed awareness contexts by not informing students and faculty of important decisions, or of the reasons for them.

The great difficulty with the closed context is that when it is closed for one participant, it becomes closed for all. The doctor who keeps the

[10] *Idem.*

truth from the patient is also keeping from himself the patient's real level of awareness. The faculty member who tells the poor student that everything is going fine, the administrator who fails to inform the staff when money is running out—these also ultimately prove ineffective strategies, as communication and interaction get closed off both ways. It is the open model that, for almost all situations, remains the best working procedure. In medicine, for example, there are many operations which cannot be performed without accurate and continuous information from the patient on what he is perceiving. In law, a lawyer cannot really present a case effectively unless he and the client have an open awareness. Similarly, in education, to admit interdependence and open awareness will ultimately allow each to play his own role better.

identity management

One of the most stimulating and productive writers in the field of social interaction is Erving Goffman. He has been particularly interested in the ways in which authoritarian, coercive institutions ("total institutions"), such as a mental hospital or army base, manage or reconstruct the identities of the inmates.[11] It is interesting to see how efficiently the limits to personal identity within the institution can be set out:

> This clean break with the past must be achieved in a relatively short period. For two months, therefore, the swab is not allowed to leave the base or to engage in social intercourse with non-cadets. This complete isolation helps to produce a unified group of swabs, rather than a heterogeneous collection of persons of high and low status. Uniforms are issued the first day, and discussions of wealth and family background are taboo. Although the pay of the cadet is very low, he is not permitted to receive money from home. The role of the cadet must supersede other roles the individual has been accustomed to play. There are few clues left which will reveal social status to the outside world.[12]

This procedure, designed to divest the recruit from all cues to roles which had meant his identity in the past, can be found in penal institutions, some religious orders, and mental hospitals. After a time, most inmates will tend to take over the identity model the institution gives to them, and will model their behavior on lines of the "ideal" inmate—they accept the role the institution has given them to play.

[11] Three books are especially important: *Stigma; Notes on the Management of Spoiled Identity* (Englewood Cliffs, N.J.: Prentice-Hall, Inc., 1963); *Asylums* (Garden City, N.Y.: Doubleday & Company, Inc., 1961); and *The Presentation of Self in Everyday Life* (Garden City, N.Y.: Doubleday & Company, Inc., 1959).
[12] *Asylums, op. cit.*, p. 15.

No one would suggest that, today, the school functions as a "total institution," in Goffman's sense. But it unquestionably has, virtually throughout the history of formal educational institutions called schools, functioned close to this level, both for students and for teachers. The initiation rites for new student recruits have had the same goal as those mentioned: the creation and management of a uniform, subservient identity for the student. Although particularly strong in Puritan America (particularly in the influence of men like Cotton Mather), it could still be seen in 1870:

> You have come here to learn and I'll see that you do. I will not only do my share but I will make you do yours. You are here under my care. . . . I rule here—I am master here—as you will soon discover. . . . But mark you: The first rule of discipline shall be SILENCE. Not a desk-top shall be raised, not a book touched, no shuffling of feet, no whispering, no sloppy movements, no rustling. I do not use the rod, I believe it to be the instrument of barbarous minds and weak wills, but I will shake the daylights out of any boy who transgresses after one warning. . . . I shall not start you with a jerk, but tighten the reins bit by bit until I have you firmly in hand at the most spirited pace you can go.[13]

Before we condemn too quickly, it might be well to read the response of one of the boys in attendance at this opening class:

> Louis was amazed, thunderstruck, dumbfounded, overjoyed! . . . A pathway had been shown him, a wholly novel plan revealed that he grasped as a banner in his hand. . . . Louis felt that the hour of freedom was at hand. He saw, with inward glowing, that true freedom could come only through discipline of power, and he translated the master's word of discipline into its true intent: SELF DISCIPLINE OF SELF POWER.[14]

It must be admitted that in this context, bearing in mind the master's pedagogical objectives, the management of the student's identity may have been highly effective.

It should also be pointed out that teachers, as well as students, were often involved in a closed system. For example, even in 1936 a teacher's contract in a small North Carolina town could contain the following:

> I promise to abstain from all dancing, immodest dressing, and any other conduct unbecoming a teacher and a lady.
>
> I promise not to go out with any young man except in so far as it may be necessary to stimulate Sunday School work.
>
> I promise not to fall in love, to become engaged or secretly married.
>
> I promise to remain in the dormitory or on the school grounds when not actively engaged in school or church work elsewhere.[15]

[13] From M. Smiley and J. Diekhoff, *Prologue to Teaching* (New York: Oxford University Press, 1959), p. 51.
[14] *Ibid.*, pp. 51–52.
[15] *Ibid.*, p. 32.

Identity management of the teacher could be complete because the institution was total for her. The members of this small town functioned very much like guards in a prison, watching her every move and rewarding any deviation with swift punishment. She came to accept a subordinate role, and existed as a sort of museum of virtue, exhibiting to the children the "correct" behaviors which the townfolk wanted the young to be exposed to, but which they themselves did not necessarily practice. Being perhaps the only virtuous lady in the town, she was of pedagogical value as a symbol. What she taught them in the classroom made little difference; what did matter was that the children were exposed to one who had taken the monastic vows. In this case, the community functioned as a closed institution for the teacher, just as in the earlier example, the teacher's classroom served as a closed institution for the students. Before leaving this last example, it must be mentioned that although much has been said about the role of the automobile in emancipating the teen-ager (the proposal of marriage, previously made in the parlor, with parents listening privately, is now made in the back seat of a parked car), it is far overshadowed by the enormous freedom it has given to the American teacher. No total institution can function if the inmate can be free of it for a large part of time; therefore, the teacher's release came when it was possible to teach in one place and live in another. The teacher was free to be a person after school.

Identity management also occurs at the collegiate level, although it is seldom that the college can act as a total institution. The fraternity system is perhaps the best example of identity management. First, there are the rites of pledging and initiation, calculated to make the pledge take a subordinate role to the regular members, with punishments and sanctions meted out to deviants. Generally, there are visible symbols of his low status, either a special article of clothing, such as a "beanie," or the requirement of wearing normal clothing in bizarre ways, such as jackets put on backwards. One of the major ways fraternities manage identity is in their purveying their collective image or role to the prospective pledge. If theirs is the "athletes' frat," they will tend to attract others of the same predisposition; similarly, others with the "studious grinds," the "social wheels," etc. This limits the need for much coercion in the initiation stage, as only those with interests and roles parallel to those of the "frat" are selected to become members. Fraternities can often function restrictively as total institutions, for they can dominate the complete lives of the members, except for going to classes. The activities, selection of friends, view of the college or university as a whole, and view of the good life can be managed or "packaged" for the individual by the institution.

cues

As on the stage, we are constantly sending out signals to those around us, telling them how we wish them to behave. In the case of the total institutions mentioned in the last section, the cues to desirable role performances are certainly not subtle and not at all ambiguous, since direct and overt punishment can take the form of whipping, mutilation, total isolation, starvation, etc.

Outside the realm of total institutions, however, the proper giving and reading of cues is more complex. Because both people are involved (the sender and receiver) in communicating, the awareness context again becomes important. As a specific example, consider the problem of the student who talks too much in class. One typical teacher cue is to ignore him, calling on others continually, without paying any attention to his waving hand. This cue is easily misread by the student, who may think it a deliberate attempt to persecute him, who may think that the teacher is simply not "seeing" his hand (and therefore tries to "cue" the teacher by waving it even more energetically), or who may decide that his previous comments in class were for some reason not satisfactory to the teacher and simply withdraws from the situation. Note how easily the student's response to the teacher's cue can be misread by the teacher, due largely to his lack of knowledge of the student's awareness context. For example, if the student tries to talk more, the teacher may conclude that he is being perverse and is bent on destroying the discussion, while the arm-weary student may simply be trying to find some style or role which the teacher will approve.

One of the major distinctions we must make here is between the intentional and the inadvertent cue. We must also come to see, as in the last example, that the response to the cue may be the sending of another cue back to the first person, saying, in effect, "How's this?" In most interaction, cues take place on a two-way basis. One example from the author's experience involved a class dealing with (of all things) classical conditioning. It was observed by several members of the class that the instructor exhibited the characteristic of pulling on his ear perhaps twice during the lecture hour, particularly when he was making what he thought was a vital point. (This was a completely inadvertent cue; the instructor was totally unaware that he was doing it.) The topic of the course being conditioning, several of the students organized a procedure whereby every time the instructor pulled his ear, the entire class would smile, nod their heads as if they had just been shown the final truth about everything, and begin to write furiously in their notebooks. After about a month of this, as might be expected, the instructor had changed from one or two ear-pulls per class to between thirty and forty per hour, still totally unaware of what was going on. He was totally unaware of the cues he had been sending out, and was completely misreading the cues that were coming in from the students.

As we can see, the cue is a delicate and subtle form of symbolic communication; like all symbols, full of ambiguities and easily misread. (Some have even suggested that the reason for the high degree of cuing behavior in human beings comes from their innate love of manipulating symbols. The artistic aspect of human courtship rituals, for example, centers around the subtlety of the sending and receiving of infinitely small and very symbolic cues.) With all its difficulties, however, the cue remains the major access route we have to the awareness contexts we have to try to fathom. Although sensitivity to the meaning of cues can unquestionably be developed (we are all better at it than we were when born), it also seems clear that some people are much better at "cue reading" than others. In general, these are the people who are more concerned with how life seems to others, who make an effort to see the situation through the other's eyes. These are also the people whose view of themselves is reasonably consonant with the views others have of them. (This is not to say that they must be *like* other people, only that they must want to understand them.)

Education at all levels is constantly faced with the problem of correcting misunderstood and unintentional cues. Particularly dangerous is the inadvertent cue, because the sender is not even aware that a signal has been sent. In a group situation of more than two participants, the problem becomes even more complex. For example, if the teacher rewards the performance of one student too openly in class with obvious cues, the rest of the class may resent it, the inadvertent consequence of the teacher's cue being that the "honored" student loses status with his peers while he gains status with the teacher. All teachers have a particular problem in communicating things to students without being aware of what has been communicated, partially due to their long periods of exposure to the students. They can plan what to do before a class starts, but, once it has begun, even the best teacher is to some extent swept along, unable completely to control the system of cues and responses. There is no time and little opportunity to check back to see what the students were actually responding to at any given moment.

Cues are not only sent out by individuals. *Institutions* also have ways of transmitting cues, as we saw in the section on closed institutions. In looking at cues as signals in this sense, we must become aware of the whole perceptual field of the student in the educational environment.

Even without the people, buildings and grounds can tell an observant person a great deal about a school. Are the grounds and athletic fields well kept up and the classrooms cracked and unpainted? Has the money been put into the administration offices, while the teachers' offices and lounges look like small closets? How big is the library, and how heavily used by the faculty? Schools and colleges may just now be coming to an important awareness of the importance of nonclassroom cues in the educational lives of students. Dormitories are being planned that will communicate to the students what the educational values of the college are, with small private discussion areas, resident tutors, a core book supply for the dormitory (who has ever seen a bookshelf downstairs in a college dormitory?), food service areas intentionally designed to increase serious student discussion at meals, etc. In similar fashion, new elementary and high schools are attempting to "cue" students into the desired role by architecture designed to allow it to happen: flexible classrooms, learning centers, conference and seminar rooms, etc.

Although this author has no panacea in mind, the need for better return information (or "feedback") on the cues we send out seems essential in education. Role play is one technique by which one can be made to take on the role of the other, as can happen in case analysis. However, it is still not clear that this sort of training will transfer back to the real situation. Much of one's willingness to admit the importance of other people depends on the sort of personality structure one has, and personality is notoriously difficult to alter. Perhaps the simple *awareness* of some of these facts of the nature of human interaction may be as helpful as anything. Certainly the lack of awareness of role playing interaction can seriously damage educational goals:

> Day after day, hour after hour, we misunderstand each other. . . . We make of the other person simply an extension of self, either through the attribution of our own thoughts and attitudes to the other person or by too facile a decision about his nature, after which we go on responding to him as though he were the character we have invented.[16]

[16] Hiram Haydn, "Humanism in 1984," *American Scholar,* **35** (1965–66), 25–26. This is an excellent article, summarizing many facets of the interactionist position and creating a valid philosophical point of view concerning human interaction.

2: bureaucratic structure
and personality

In our time, perhaps more than in any other, the word bureaucracy assumes essentially evil connotations. When we think of a bureaucrat, we think of a faceless, machinelike creature sitting in an office, doing routine, meaningless things. One often hears that bureaucracies restrict the freedom of the individual, that people who work in a bureaucracy become "depersonalized."

Notice the assumptions in these statements. Bureaucracies, it would appear, have the power to *transform* the personalities of those who are involved with them.[1] There are few secondary schools or colleges which would claim that they can do this much, and their *only* business is that

[1] In fact, one study suggests that what is happening in American industry is roughly parallel to changes in the American family, which is shifting from an "entrepreneur" approach to child rearing to a "bureaucratic" approach. However, the use of bureaucratic is somewhat misleading, as the authors really mean to make a distinction between individual-centered and group-centered patterns of child rearing. This research is considered in more detail elsewhere in this book. Daniel R. Miller and Guy E. Swanson, *The Changing American Parent* (New York: John Wiley & Sons, Inc., 1958).

of trying to invoke some change in the minds and hearts of those whom they serve. If the thoughts expressed here are correct (and this is debatable), then one thing is sure: a bureaucracy is a social organization that can exert powerful educational influences. The theme of the depersonalized individual caught in the web of the faceless, nameless organization runs from Kafka's *The Trial* and *The Castle* to Menotti's opera *The Consul,* from David Riesman's *The Lonely Crowd* to W. F. Whyte's *The Organization Man* and C. Wright Mills' *White Collar,* from Arthur Miller's *Death of a Salesman* to the novels of Marquand.

One might well ask here, are these patterns of human organization evil *by definition,* or is it the ways in which they have been used? Could they be used more intelligently and effectively, in term of the human beings involved? In order to answer these important questions, it will be necessary to take a closer look at some of the material dealing with bureaucratic organization, both theory and fact.

the concept of bureaucracy—Max Weber [2]

It is unfortunate that in so many areas of sociology we are dependent to a large extent on theories which were devised to explain *European* patterns of social action. Thus, Weber, who is undoubtedly the founder of the systematic study of bureaucracy, based his observations chiefly on the Prussian models of military and governmental bureaucracies. The differences between these organizations and those prevalent in the United States will be pointed out later.

[2] The most concise statement of Weber's views on bureaucracy can be found in *From Max Weber: Essays in Sociology,* edited by Gerth and Mills (New York: Oxford University Press, 1958), pp. 196–244. An excellent account of Weber as a human being can be found in the same volume, pp. 3–31. Although the book is not new, the best over-all treatment of bureaucracy is still *Reader in Bureaucracy,* edited by R. K. Merton *et al.* (New York: Free Press of Glencoe, Inc., 1952). See also Peter Blau, *Bureaucracy in Modern Society* (New York: Random House, Inc., 1956), and the two excellent chapters on bureaucracy in J. Bensman and B. Rosenberg, *Mass, Class, and Bureaucracy* (Englewood Cliffs, N.J.: Prentice-Hall, Inc., 1963). Outside of the sources mentioned in the text, the reader might look at Charles Hyneman, *Bureaucracy in a Democracy* (New York: Harper & Row, Publishers, 1950); and two older books, James Beck, *Our Wonderland of Bureaucracy* (New York: The Macmillan Company, 1932), and one of the classics in the field, James Burnham, *The Managerial Revolution* (New York: The John Day Company, Inc., 1941). The most interesting recent book on the topic is R. Presthus, *The Organizational Society* (New York: Alfred A. Knopf, Inc., 1962), particularly in the use of psychoanalytic theory in describing the patterns of accommodations that people working in bureaucracies must make. For an interesting view of how the Russians have interpreted Weber's views in their own industrial complex, see David Granick, *Management of the Industrial Firm in the USSR* (New York: Columbia University Press, 1954), pp. 262–71.

For Weber, there were in all social structures certain central tendencies or attributes about which one could generalize. Thus, if one could find a series of defining characteristics for a pattern of social organization, one could set these characteristics up as an *ideal type*—a comprehensive description of how this category of social interaction differs from others. Because he was to a large extent limited to those institutions he knew first-hand, his ideal type bureaucracy represents and reflects his own culture in a particular era.

For Weber, bureaucracy is fundamentally a *rational* system of organizing a collectivity. It is, therefore, a hierarchy of *positions* or titles, each related in a functional way to those above and below. These positions are to a large degree independent from the person who occupies the position. Thus, the position or title of Master Sergeant means that *any* occupant of that position can do certain things and not others, regardless of who the individual is. What he can do is (according to Weber) functionally and rationally related to the prescribed activities of those positions (not people) above and below him.

A central concept of Weber's work is that of the *office*. An office can be looked at as a certain quantity of floor and wall space, with desks, phones, etc. It can also be defined as the position or title occupied by a person—he carries the *office* of vice-president. Or it can be used to describe the *functions* carried out by the office through the person—it is the duty of the *office* of the treasurer (not the treasurer) to issue budget reports monthly. An *offic*ial is, therefore, a person who works in a given *space* called an office, who carries the title or *position* of the office, and who carries out the *functions* of the office.

If we were to look for this ideal type in nature, the closest we could come would probably be the beehive. Here can be found the complete division of activity by function (workers do certain things, drones do other things), the notion of an increasing, rationally organized hierarchy with the queen at the top, a clear set of rules of who associates with whom and in what ways, and a clear subordination of the individual to the collectivity. (Not all worker bees are *exactly* alike, but these differences are of no use to the collectivity, and are therefore ignored.) The advantages of such a system are obvious. There is a very high rate of efficiency in using the energies of all the participants, since there is little confusion and no duplication of function. Because each bee does not need a view of the whole enterprise, only his place in it, he can be almost instantly replaced if necessary. The fact that bees (and more particularly termites, which are similarly organized and are one of the oldest living creatures) have survived for such a long time is a tribute not to the individual bee but to the system of organized productivity that they have evolved.

Weber maintains the same holds true for bureaucratic structures in the human sphere—that they are virtually unchangeable, that they can continue to function in the same way even in a time of drastic social change, that even if new leaders come in on top with new ideas, the bureaucracy, because of its *internally* derived direction, will continue to chug along on its former path. One is reminded of the famous tale of "The Sorcerer's Apprentice," especially in the musical score by Dukas. The apprentice tries to use his master's magic, which backfires as the broom that is to haul water for the apprentice *continues* to do so, regardless of what he does to stop it, until the poor apprentice is nearly drowned by what was to be simply a labor-saving device. The analogy to bureaucracy is clear: the magic broom cares nothing for the apprentice; it is simply doing its job. It has no view of the whole enterprise, and if the apprentice drowns in the process, it is a matter of no concern to the broom.

In order to explain this view of Weber's, which we in America find somewhat distasteful, two things about Weber should be definitely in mind. First, he believed firmly that if sociology were to become a social science, it would have to become sharply divorced from the world of human *values*. A second major thesis of his was the so-called "de-mystification of the world," by which he meant that the world is steadily becoming more rational, less magical. If one holds these two views, it is obvious that Weber's concentration on bureaucracy as a mechanistic system, his total lack of interest in the individual *person* in the bureaucracy, is perfectly consistent. He was, as are we, only a creature of his time.

criticisms of Weber's position

To see how far we have come, one need only quote the amusing central rule of bureaucratic administration for decision making—"Who will be mad? How mad? Who will be glad? How glad?" In our time, a bureaucracy is seen by many as an interacting group of human *personalities*, and the job of the administrator is that of sensitizing himself to the needs, hopes, and values of the individuals with whom he works. The case method of instruction, widely used in schools of business administration (and in schools of law and education), deals heavily with problems of *"How to handle Mr. X in situation Y."* Extensive sections of the case materials are devoted to personal descriptions of Mr. X—how he has responded in the past, and how he can be manipulated in this situation. We have, in our time, tended to reverse Weber and emphasize the individual in the bureaucracy, subordinating the formal organizational structure to a secondary position. In this, we are reflecting the values and assumptions of our own time, just as Weber did for his. However, we have good evidence for believing that a rational pattern of organization is of little use, unless the people involved can work together harmoniously.

the "Hawthorne Effect" [3]

Certainly one of the classic studies in social science is that carried out by Roethlisberger and Dickson at the Western Electric plant at Hawthorne, Massachusetts. Carried out in conjunction with the Harvard Graduate School of Business Administration, it represents the first major study of virtually all aspects of an industrial plant, from carefully worked-out interviewing techniques to the experimental manipulation of variables, such as length of rest pauses, room temperature, illumination, etc.

In the illumination phase of the study, one of the hypotheses was that increased illumination would lead to increased production. In order to verify this, illumination was gradually increased in one assembly section while, simultaneously, the workers involved were interviewed extensively concerning their reactions to the change, how they felt about their jobs, the company, etc. As anticipated, production rates went up. Then (and this was one of the strokes of genius in the study), it was decided to make sure that the experiment was being controlled by *lowering* the illumination back to its former level. It was expected that production would decrease. Lo and behold, production rates increased again! At one stage of the experiment, workers were assembling small induction coils on wooden spools in virtual semidarkness at high rates of speed.

It was clear to the research team that illumination by itself was not responsible for the increase in production, that there were *human* factors that transcended the purely physiological factors of illumination. Further evidence for this position came from another part of the experiment in

[3] F. L. Roethlisberger and W. L. Dickson, *Management and the Worker* (Cambridge: Harvard University Press, 1939). See also Roethlisberger's *Training for Human Relations* (Boston: Harvard Business School, 1954), and his *Management and Morale* (Cambridge: Harvard University Press, 1941). In the same tradition is Elton Mayo, *The Human Problems of an Industrial Civilization* (Boston: Harvard Business School, 1946).

which the workers were told that the illumination would be increased. They then saw an electrician change the light bulbs, presumably to a higher candlepower. Actually the bulbs he substituted were of the same strength. The workers commented favorably on the "increased" light. Then they were told that the lighting would be decreased. Again the electrician changed the bulbs to other ones of the same strength. The workers now responded that the "lower" lighting was not as pleasant to work under. The crucial factor here is that at no time in this experiment did the workers' production change. (Here we have a fine example of the "placebo effect"—people responded to a stimulus as they were *expected* to respond. In similar fashion, a sugar pill can be very effective in curing headaches, if the person taking it is told that it is a new drug discovery for that purpose.)

The so-called "Hawthorne Effect" is now interpreted to mean that increase in efficiency which comes from effective concern for the emotional and personal needs of the individual workers. "Morale" has become a household word largely because of the Hawthorne experiments, and "control" has changed from the barbarities of the early industrial revolutions in England and America to a new view:

> This will be the exercise of "control" by understanding and not by ritualistic, verbal practices which address themselves to human nature in general, but not to *particular* human beings in *particular* places with *particular* feelings and sentiments for which they need concrete social expression.[4]

This rather brief excursion into the Hawthorne experiments should make it clear that, for our time, Weber's view of bureaucratic structure as a depersonalized set of relationships between *offices*, not people, is not overly helpful. However, it should be pointed out that his chief models were the military and political systems of Germany and Prussia from approximately 1880 to 1910. One thing about these bureaucracies is that they do not *produce* anything; they have no product to be sold, and the notion of *output* is not very appropriate. Thus, the bureaucracies Weber knew well probably *were* more or less as described in his ideal type: an impersonal series of relationships between offices.

It is the central concept of output which allows us to approach a bureaucracy with more specific questions than Weber could raise. The experimental method as we have come to know it in the social sciences is not applicable to a situation in which there is no product, as the

---

[4] Roethlisberger, *Management and Morale, op. cit.*, p. 194. (It should perhaps be pointed out that the "Hawthorne Effect" will not increase production *forever;* a slowdown will occur.)

manipulation of variables is of no use unless the consequences of manipulation can be confirmed or disproved in terms of output (as was the case in the Hawthorne experiments).

resistance to change

There is also a considerable body of evidence for calling into question Weber's insistence on a "beehive" model for bureaucracies—rigid, unchangeable because change was not *necessary*. For example, the rise of the Nazi regime certainly caused enormous changes in the bureaucratic structures of the nations involved.[5]

In our time, it would seem that the more adaptable a bureaucracy is, the better its chances for survival. This is why so many large corporations are setting up satellite centers for operations—each one a functioning entity with a great deal of autonomy. In the event of a change in plan (and the speed of innovation in technology today makes the ability to change mandatory), only those satellites involved will have to make the change. This brand new notion of a flexible, adaptive bureaucracy can be seen in such disparate organizations as the Raytheon Corporation and the University of California, which has been referred to by its president as a "multiversity." In the days of the empire builders in America—Ford, Rockefeller, Carnegie, and Hill—the bureaucracy was strongly centralized around one man. The bureaucracy did not adapt; the rest of society had to adapt to *it*. (Ford once said of his famous Model T, "They can have it in any color they want, so long as it's black.") Today, there is a noticeable trend toward a decentralization of operations to increase flexibility. The monolithic dinosaurs of huge corporations, in which all energy was directed *internally*, have been replaced by a speedy, light, flexible organization, which has its attention on the outside world as well as on what is going on inside.

efficiency and red tape

One common charge leveled against bureaucratic organizations is that they are notoriously inefficient. However, these charges are not usually made in relation to the production of goods but to the insistence on a great variety of paperwork, most of which seems quite irrational, before a necessary service can be provided. It is in the getting of a marriage license, a driver's license, returning a defective

[5] Frederick S. Burin, "Bureaucracy and National Socialism: A Reconsideration of Weberian Theory," in Merton, *op. cit.*, pp. 33–47.

piece of merchandise for a refund, applying for a passport, that one is likely to hear enraged citizens talking about red tape. It is therefore not in the production of goods, but the production of services, that the problem comes up.[6]

The person who expresses the cry of red tape is usually someone *outside* the bureaucracy, who is made to do a great deal of paperwork that *he* considers unnecessary to the accomplishment of his goal. Remember that bureaucracy is derived from the French *bureau*, a small piece of furniture in which papers are stored, and that Weber pointed out the necessity for large quantities of paper to operate as a collective memory for the bureaucracy. ("The files" are usually revered by those inside the organization, and the privilege of using confidential files is almost universally a mark of status.)

To the poor outsider, then, the enormous pile of paper he must fill out in quadruplicate seems irrelevant and useless, while to the informed, objective observer, it serves the central purpose of keeping many aspects of the bureaucracy informed of what is going on and storing this information for later use. Red tape is mainly in the eye of the beholder, who does not understand the functional importance of the forms for the bureaucracy. Because of this lack of understanding, the complainer may also feel powerlessness in the face of a system to which he must yield if he is to have his wishes granted, as well as frustration and anger, and a feeling of alienation, of being cut off from this thing which has such control over him.

Everyone has had the experience of walking into an office full of people who, one feels instantly, are on the "in," and who seem to make life as difficult as possible for the "outsider" who needs something only they can grant. Feelings of hostility and alienation almost universally occur, as has been very accurately described in the plays and novels mentioned in the beginning of this chapter.

It is important to notice, however, that the *same* characteristics which produce alienation in the outsider can produce very positive and effective experiences for the insider. Going back to the Hawthorne experiments, it was clear to the researchers that a great deal of loyalty and identification was produced in the workers, which not only increased production but added a dimension to the lives of the workers. They were made to feel not that they were nameless cogs in a huge machine, but that they were human beings whose feelings were of real importance to the officials in the firm. The identification they had with the Hawthorne plant was one of the most positive and important things in their lives.

[6] See Alvin Gouldner, "Red Tape as a Social Problem," in Merton, *op. cit.*, pp. 410–18. See also Peter Blau, *op. cit.*, pp. 102–5.

in defense of bureaucracy

To begin with, there is no question that in the early days of the industrial revolutions, workers were exploited miserably in the sweatshops of the nineteenth and early twentieth centuries. Moving descriptions of these conditions can be found in Upton Sinclair's novel of conditions in the Chicago meat packing industry, *The Jungle,* and in Émile Zola's *Germinal,* which describes similar conditions in the European coal mining industry. However, it is just as clear that we have passed through this stage, and that the manual worker, through extensive unionization in virtually every industry, is comparatively very well paid for his efforts and has a great deal to say concerning the conditions of his employment.

To blame bureaucratic organization for the previous exploitation of workers is as ridiculous as to give it credit for the enlightened approach which is now in effect. Patterns of social organization are after all created, maintained, and altered by human beings who must take the responsibility for them. Bureaucratic structure is per se little more than a "rational" system of organizing a number of people so that certain work can be done as effectively and efficiently as possible. (In this sense, one of the most rational ideas about producing goods is the concept of interchangeable parts and the assembly line. This idea, usually attributed to Henry Ford, can be traced back at least to Paul Revere, who made guns in this way. Yet to call him a bureaucrat is not to lessen his stature as a human being.)

Part of the difficulty is that bureaucracy is virtually the *only* concept we have to describe all large-scale collective organizations that produce goods and services. Yet the Pentagon and the Armour Meat Packing Company are dissimilar enough so that describing them both as bureaucracies indicates the need for some sharpening of terminology. The tendency, mentioned earlier, toward decentralization and the creation of satellites, and the elimination of huge, monolithic, inflexible organizations, also indicates the need for a clarification of terms.

It is certainly possible, in *any* bureaucracy, to build in a meaningful system of personal relationships so that the people who work there can feel fulfilled as persons. This can be accomplished in many ways, such as giving each worker a sense of the *whole* enterprise so that he can appreciate the significance of what he does, by establishing (or allowing others to establish) a system of *informal* organization that will allow workers at various levels of the firm to get to know one another *as equals,* as in the case of bowling and softball activities, by making it clear to the individual workers that their views and feelings are important as participating members of the firm, etc.

In a very perceptive essay that still has much validity, Merton has posed the crucial dilemma for the bureaucratic administrator:

> Thus, with respect to the relations between officials and clientele, one structural source is the pressure for formal and impersonal treatment when individual, personalized consideration is desired by the client. . . . Conflict *within* the bureaucratic structure arises from the converse situation, namely, when personalized relationships are substituted for the structurally required impersonal relationships.[7]

If, in a bureaucracy which has as its primary purpose the meeting of the demands of "the public," the amount of personal attention is given to each client that would make *him* happy, the efficiency of the whole would suffer. There is a built-in conflict between that which would be best for the client and that which is best for the organization. Treading this tightrope is one of the major responsibilities of an administrator of a "service" bureaucracy. In a manufacturing situation like the Hawthorne plant, the same conflict must be resolved for those *within* the organization—total lack of discipline will inevitably result in the collapse of the production process; while total *presence* of discipline with no consideration of the personal needs of the individual workers will seriously reduce production also.[8]

The good administrator, therefore, in either type of bureaucratic structure, will be the person who can select the correct "style" for each situation. The little statement, "Who will be mad? How mad? Who will be glad? How glad?" does have the ring of truth to it. The administrator must be able to predict the consequences of various courses of action *in both personal and organizational terms*. In order to do this, he must be able to do what John Dewey referred to in another context as the "Dramatic Rehearsal"—to evaluate, in advance, the various effects of each possible course of action. As more and more administrators are trained to develop this decision-making "ear" (much as the musician develops his), and as the trend toward the organization of more meaningful bureaucratic units continues, it should be clear that the criticisms mentioned earlier were really leveled at inept administration rather than the notion

[7] R. K. Merton, "Bureaucratic Structure and Personality," in Merton, *op. cit.*, p. 370.

[8] Of course, most manufacturers also have an organization for handling the inevitable problems of the purchasers of their products, so that both forms of bureaucratic organization can be found in virtually all producing companies. The coordination of these two systems represents a major problem for the people in management, since those who are in the "service" component are usually not well informed of the specifics of manufacture used in the assembly procedure.

of bureaucracy itself. Bureaucracy is affectively neutral—it can be used well or poorly, depending on the motivations of those who establish bureaucracies.

bureaucracy and education

Much of what has been said about bureaucracy thus far is very relevant to many perplexing educational questions. A school, or system of schools, represents a combination of the two bureaucratic functions already described—that is, it *both* manufactures something through a process which is very analagous to the assembly line (students move through the school; each "worker" adds some component to the "finished product," the graduate) and must deal with the "outside" public in a variety of ways. The administrator must walk the same tightrope: knowing how to work with the "inside" people to meet their needs and keep efficiency high, and how to deal with the "outsiders" without creating debilitating strains and tensions within the organization.

The primary difficulty in talking of education as an industry [9] involves our lack of definition of what a good "product" should be. It was clear in the discussion of the Hawthorne experiments that the major factor which allowed experimentation to take place was the output factor; quality and quantity of production was a clean, numerical, and unequivocal measure, and variables such as lighting, temperature, humidity, etc., could be manipulated, *holding the other factors constant,* to see the impact of the single factor on output. Educational research has always bogged down on this question, and for this reason, research on education today is little heeded by teachers and administrators, while the results of the Roethlisberger, Dickson, and Mayo experiments of the late thirties were eagerly read by business leaders, who implemented many of their recommendations.

There are some marked similarities between the new organizational patterns of educational institutions and those of business, politics, the ministry, etc. In general, these newer patterns call for the fulfillment of

[9] See Ernest Van Den Haag's fascinating work, *Education as an Industry* (New York: Augustus Kelly, 1956). To see how much the study of educational administration has borrowed from industrial research, see *Behavioral Science and Educational Administration,* NSSE Yearbook No. 63, Part II (Chicago: University of Chicago Press, 1964). The concepts used in this volume, such as work flow, formal and informal organization, open and closed systems, and the bibliography suggest that the fields of social psychology, sociology, anthropology, and psychology (which are, after all, important behavorial sciences) have been shamefully neglected by those who study and write about educational administration.

many more objectives through more complex patterns of organization, greater dealings with a wider variety of "publics"—from local to state to federal, revision of the power alliances within the institution, and major changes in administrative roles, particularly from those of the patriarchal and totalitarian leader to those of the mediator and arbitrator between conflicting factions. This new view of organization has been put nicely by one of its major proponents:

> A university anywhere can aim no higher than to be as British as possible for the sake of the undergraduates, as German as possible for the sake of the graduates and research personnel, as American as possible for the sake of the public at large—and as confused as possible for the sake of preservation of the whole uneasy balance.[10]

These central tendencies (toward the development of the "whole student," toward scholarship as the focal point, and toward "public relations") can be found in virtually every educational institution at .whatever level. The need for multiple focus—looking in and out simultaneously at all the constituent groups—is becoming common to all of education.

education and power

As Weber saw bureaucracy, it was single-minded and monolithic, concerned chiefly with its internal activity. Power (which was defined into various positions in the hierarchy rather than being the possession of individual human beings) was above all rationally and mathematically divided into smaller subcomponents within the bureaucracy. In America, however, there is no single educational bureaucracy, as we have seen. One way to begin to describe these bureaucracies is by looking at the parameters of their influence; that is, how far does their influence extend? There are, for example, *local* bureaucracies like the school system of a city or town. (Increasingly, through the phenomenal growth of the junior and community college movement, the typical local system will include educational levels from kindergarten through college.) The parameters of influence here are largely those of the community itself, although there will be liaison arrangements with larger units. From the local unit, we move into increasingly *cosmopolitan* bureaucracies in which the sphere of influence and decision making is much larger: for example, state departments of education, regional accrediting associations, and the U.S. Office of Education.[11]

Although we use the term every day, power is a notoriously difficult

[10] From Clark Kerr, *The Uses of the University* (Cambridge: Harvard University Press, 1963), p. 18.

[11] The local-cosmopolitan distinction, first used by Merton in a typology of "influentials," seems also applicable to institutions.

thing to define in specific terms. For example, C. Wright Mills wrote an entire book on the subject of power without defining it. Part of the difficulty is that power is so many different things. It is inherent in some positions; e.g., the Presidency of the United States. But it is also inherent in particular people as well; no two Presidents have used the power in the office in the same way. If power in an office is never used by the incumbent, one can ask whether or not the power still exists. What is the act by which we infer power? Is it the ability to *control* the lives of others? Is it the ability and right to make *decisions?* Is it the ability to block or *veto* the actions of others? Is it the same thing as money? Is power in politics the same kind of power as that of military or business enterprises? Much more subtle are the questions we must ask about power occurring outside Weber's formal structure. For example, *influence* (which could be defined as informal or nonpositional power) may be of major importance, even though we cannot see it by looking at an organization chart. It is a commonplace that many of the most influential people in any organization have little formal power; in fact, their lack of formal position may make it easier to acquire influence, since they are less threatening to their fellow workers who see the influential as "one of us."

Although these definitional problems are indeed complex, there are some common factors. Power comes from individuals and groups that have the organizational capacity to manifest and "communicate" it to others. The language of power will differ in different areas of human endeavor, but as with language, there must be some consensus among the participants as to the meaning of power in a given context. Again, power is interactive, involving the sender of the message as well as the receiver. Like electrical power, there must be a mechanism for the sending of power after it has been generated.

Because social power (like electrical power) is based on transmission networks, it would seem that in an era like our own, characterized by greatly increased speed in communication and transportation, power would also be moving out into larger and larger systems of transmission. In the early days of the Republic, travel and communication were so slow that the election of a President took months of time and a special device (the electoral college) to accomplish. Today, election results can be known with as little as 5 per cent of the vote in. Likewise, when the local town was the center, power (heat and light) were provided by the homeowner, and social power was centered in the town. Today, electrical power is produced and distributed by enormously complex interlocking power systems, some of them nationwide in scope. It would be reasonable to assume that social power has also been developing toward larger and larger patterns of organization.

This same development can be seen in the growth of educational bureaucracies. The local school board no longer exists *in vacuo;* there is an active national organization of school boards, as is true for P.T.A.'s, for school administrators, for college faculty, presidents, and deans, students, and boards of trustees. The only educational constituency not nationally organized is the parents of college students. Everyone else has a nation-wide organizational structure.

One important consequence of this development is that power is more and more a *shared* matter between many constituent groups. The college president at the turn of the century was a virtual dictator; today, he is more often a mediator. Just as the "Giant" like Carnegie, who could move an organization singlehandedly, is gone from the business scene, so the "Giants" of the educational world like Eliot, Lowell, and Hutchins, men who transformed complex educational institutions almost by themselves, no longer seem to exist. For every educational giant today, there is a giant-killer. Power in the hands of one man can be used for change. In the hands of many constituent groups, it tends to be used to maintain the *status quo,* as the power of each group tends to be canceled out. (We will deal more extensively with this problem in the chapter on social change.) For this reason, we must say that Weber was right about the difficulty of changing bureaucracies, but not because of their internal cohesion; in fact, just the opposite. It is the *fractioning* of power in the hands of the constituent groups that creates the stalemate.

One productive consequence of this change in organization of educa-tion may be that members of one group may treat the other groups with more respect. If teachers can strike, administrators and school boards can no longer look upon them as powerless. Even at the college level, the first strike of college teachers is now history, and there unquestionably will be more. Similarly, students in high school and college are much more adept at organization today, and thus are able to speak as an efficient collectivity and act on a large scale. As we push social experiences further and further down the age scale, it may well be that high-school students will begin the national coordination movement. But it is not clear at this time whether we have made much of an organizational gain through each group's seeing the others as formidable opponents.

the problem of change
in educational bureaucracies

There are two notions, both pre-sented by Merton in his discussions of bureaucracies, that are enlighten-ing when applied to the problem of change in education. First is his concept of "trained incapacity," which he attributes to both Veblen and

Dewey.[12] Simply, this refers to the tendency to continue to make a given response which has been successful in the past, after the conditions that made the response successful have been altered. An example of this would be chickens who have been taught to come running for food at the sound of a bell. When it comes time for their execution, the same bell creates the same response, with drastically different results. Thus, the more we have done things in a given way in the past, the less likely will we be to see that our response is no longer appropriate or successful.

Because of the specialization and division of labor that characterizes virtually all bureaucracies, workers tend to do repetitive things. This very repetition of a response tends to blind them to other responses that might be more appropriate to changing conditions. When, in response to an inquiry about a given practice, a teacher, secretary, or administrator replies, "But we've *always* done it this way!" one may be in the presence of Merton's trained incapacity. By focusing on what we are *used* to seeing (or doing), we may neglect to see other factors which are also there and might provide us with a better response.

Another factor, mentioned by Merton and others, is closely related. This is the tendency for us to attach personal and emotional values to routine operations we perform, the tendency for us to allow institutional *means* to become personal *ends*. As specialization and trained incapacity increase, we tend to lose a view of the *whole* enterprise and its goals. When we have lost sight of the goals of the education system, the perpetuation of our own habituatetd patterns of behavior becomes an end in itself. Thus, the person who has the major responsibility for the purchasing of pencils for an entire school system will tend to resist anyone who states that there are presently other writing devices markedly superior on all points to the old wooden pencil. The buying of pencils, which is after all only a means to the end of allowing the students to practice their writing, has become an end in itself, something to be fought for and preserved.

Both of these concepts (trained incapacity, and means becoming ends) are important in that they operate to reduce change in all educational systems at *all* levels, from the U.S. Office of Education to the smallest public school or private college. For a teacher to shift to a new method of presentation means both extra work and the threat of the new and untried. His ego-involvement with *present* practices will probably be far greater than their actual worth warrants. In the world of business, the free enterprise system makes it mandatory for new techniques to be adopted, since any firm's competitors who use new, more efficient meth-

---

[12] Merton, "Bureaucratic Structure and Personality," *op. cit.,* pp. 369–70.

ods will have an important advantage over one which does not. In education, however, it is difficult to *prove* the superior effectiveness of new techniques, due largely to the vagueness of the educational "product" mentioned earlier. Educational systems, no matter how bad, seldom go "out of business," although it might be a good idea if they could.

The adoption by teachers of new educational techniques, such as the language laboratory, team teaching, teaching machines, ungraded systems, and the hundreds of new devices from overhead projectors to television, is much more an act of faith than a giving up of one method for something which has been *proven* to be better. Like all acts of faith, it heightens the resistance to further change on the part of the individuals involved. The expensiveness of these new approaches makes it even less likely that they will be voluntarily and cheerfully discarded when *something better* comes along. The language laboratory, as just one example, was hailed as the savior of language teaching when first introduced, and many educational systems became very heavily committed to this approach, both in terms of money for equipment and in the training of teachers in its use. At the present time, there is considerable feeling in the profession that the early claims for this equipment were somewhat magnified, and that new developments in the next few years will make the language laboratory obsolete. When this happens, the educational institutions heavily committed to it will be in a very difficult position, and, interestingly enough, the very willingness to change in the institutions which first went "all the way" with the language laboratory concept may result in their taking a very defensive, reactionary position if new approaches make the language lab notion obsolete. A similar reaction can be seen in the field of educational TV, since many prominent educational leaders have taken the position that the medium is *not* the answer to the problems of mass education. There is no real answer to this dilemma of educational change. It is certain, however, that the "new math" and the "new science" will be replaced by even newer concepts, and we must somehow build into their use a *willingness to give them up in the future.*

organizational styles
in educational bureaucracies

Within the world of education we can see the entire range of views on the question of "good" administrative policies. At one pole are those who basically agree with Weber that a bureaucracy is a formally organized hierarchy of positions, that administration is a rational chess game, that "running a tight ship" is the criterion of a good administrator. A small but identifiable minority seem to feel about teachers in the way Frederick Taylor describes a factory worker:

> Now one of the very first requirements for a man who is fit to handle pig iron as a regular occupation is that he shall be so stupid and phlegmatic that he more nearly resembles in his mental make-up the ox than any other type.[13]

Administrators of this type rely heavily on the *social control of ignorance;* that is, the worker (teacher) must be only a cog in a machine, he must be kept as ignorant as possible of the processes of the firm, and he must not begin to influence decisions, because this is a threat to the administration. Thus, the worker and administrator are in a *competitive* position in terms of power, and the administrator must "keep the worker down."

At the other administrative pole can be found those who believe that administration is fully compatible with democratic processes, that authority is to be delegated, not selfishly guarded, that everyone in the organization should have a view of what the organization is trying to do, that the needs, views, and wishes of each worker are to be respected and listened to, that it is through vigorous social interaction that the best solutions will arise.

Our natural assumption would be that teachers would love to teach in the school of the latter type and dread the former. However, the "democratic" administrator is threatening, too, for certain types of people, since he requires them to take the responsibility for their own actions, which many people are anxious to avoid. In order to escape from this freedom, they may be much more secure and productive in an authoritarian administrative situation in which their every move is dictated from above.[14]

The educational administrator moving into a new job is faced with the problem that, whatever his administrative style, some of the teachers will not like it and will find him threatening. One solution to this problem is that of complementary staffing—selecting people for educational positions partially on the basis of their being able to get along with others.[15] However, this is often interpreted as meaning that we should get

---

[13] *Behavioral Science and Educational Administration, op. cit.,* p. 36.

[14] On this vital point, see Erich Fromm, *Escape from Freedom* (New York: Holt, Rinehart & Winston, Inc., 1941). A good description of personality types and their interaction in bureaucracies can be found in Presthus, *op. cit.,* pp. 93–134, using Harry Stack Sullivan's interpersonal approach to psychiatry as the basis for the typology.

[15] Roald Campbell, "Implications for the Practice of Administration," in *Behavioral Science and Educational Administration, op. cit.,* pp. 279–302.

people *as alike as possible* in order to minimize personal friction. The notion of interchangeable parts is fine for the assembly line, but the idea of interchangeable *people* is not. The job of the administrator is to *widen the tolerance* for colleagues with differing personalities and views, not to flatten out genuine differences and eliminate them. As such, the administrator is a teacher par excellence, educating his coworkers in terms of productive social relationships.

Although there are commonalities in organizational problems, there are also personal differences that may have an effect on the way the work is conceived and handled in the unit. Just as certain physical details of the educational environment can communicate symbolically to those who work in them, so too can the organizational and personal styles of the participants. Particularly important in establishing the tone of a bureaucracy is the "line" administrator who deals daily with the on-going problems of the unit itself and not primarily with "outside" groups—the elementary or high-school principal, college dean, etc. Regardless of the architecture, this person can often, through his own style of organization, have a considerable impact on the bureaucracy. Some of these administrative styles have been characterized as follows:

1. High communication style—stress on communicating with others.
2. High discussion style—high emphasis on face-to-face contact.
3. High compliance—follows suggestions made by others.
4. High analysis—much time spent in analyzing all factors to problems.
5. High relationship style—great concern with maintaining social and organizational relations, especially with superiors.
6. Personal organization style—emphasis on scheduling his own work.
7. High outside-orientation—perceives problems in terms of what they represent to groups outside the school.
8. High direction style—stress on giving orders to others.[16]

Obviously, these factors relate not only to administrators but also to teachers, students, and everyone else involved; they are types of human interaction which everyone maintains to some degree. A very interesting question in relation to organizational theory deals with the virtues of maintaining a consistent pattern of "style" throughout the unit. Although

[16] John K. Hemphill, "Personal Variables and Administrative Styles," in *ibid.*, pp. 178–98.

the notion of style consistency may be appealing at first (a whole school system composed of "number three's"), it raises many problems. For instance, if an entire system were composed of No. 3's, everyone would be following the suggestions made by others, but who would be making the suggestions? Clearly there should be (and must be, human beings being what they are) an interaction of various styles of organization.

One of the major difficulties in education was the stereotyped notion of the interaction of styles: the administrator initiated, the teacher complied; while with students, the teacher gave directions and the students complied. It should now be clear that leadership and organizational styles must be *situational;* there may well be times when a student or student group will serve the initiating function, while teachers and administrators may serve the compliance function. The next step would be to try to develop a chart showing what interactive patterns were most successful in which situations. Although interaction analysis has made some notable steps in the last decade, it is unlikely that we will in the near future be able to determine the ideal combinations of styles for all participants in a given interactive situation in advance. (Even if that were possible, it is not likely that organizational styles could be imposed on people.)

A further word needs to be said here about the concept of "mix" in educational bureaucracies. Although we firmly believe in the melting pot ideology and profess the virtues of having many different kinds of people interacting with each other, the reverse tends to happen very often in education. Within the faculty, new recruits are sought in schools and colleges who will share the prevailing view of the field and of teaching. (This is, of course, understandable. No one eagerly accepts as a colleague someone who will disagree—no matter how productively for all concerned —on the nature of the subject matter to be taught.) Many administrators feel (and practice) the notion that the most compliant, obedient teacher is the best one to hire, and the "ideal" school or college is the one made up entirely of such people. At the student level, personality tests are now available which will enable a college or private school to select its student body entirely from one personality type. (Many businesses are, of course, recruiting management candidates on the basis of personality inventories.)

It is here that the educational bureaucracy must differ from other enterprises. The "mix" of people one interacts with forms a vital part of the educational job or function, particularly in America, where social learning and skill is of great importance in the job of the schools and colleges. In a suburban school system like Park Forest in *The Organization Man,* the students have relatively little to learn from each other, because they are all appallingly alike.[17] A private school or college may also get into a predicament of having no "mix" at all. If human interaction is simply a necessary evil in a bureaucracy (like those described by Weber) then it should be made as smooth and efficient as possible by having interchangeable people, all exactly alike. As an aside here, it could be pointed out that in both *Brave New World* and *1984*, people's personalities are "produced" in accordance with the functions they will perform, to eliminate personal friction. Part of the horror of the books comes from seeing that it all makes sense, if arguing only from the bureaucratic criterion of "rational" efficiency. Because of the importance of "mix" to the goals of the educational institution, all participants in an educational bureaucracy should manifest different views, backgrounds, and personalities. A group of well-rounded students does not make a well-rounded school or college; the institutional sum is then only one student squared. Far better is the institution which seeks diversity at the individual level in order to provide balance at the institutional level.

the "Hawthorne Effect" and education

This failure of scientific management was the inevitable result of its assumption, most evident in "scientific" wage incentive systems, that rational economic interests alone govern the conduct of employees and of its neglect of social factors. To administer a social organization according to purely technical criteria of rationality is irrational, because it ignores the nonrational aspects of social conduct.[18]

It is clear that educational management, too, is becoming more "scientific" and efficiency-minded, at least according to the 1964 NSSE Yearbook.[19] However, "scientific" seems to imply the utilization of theory from the behavioral sciences, rather than the time and motion studies of a man like Frederick Taylor, who considered factory workers to be ma-

[17] William Whyte, *The Organization Man* (Garden City, N.Y.: Doubleday & Company, Inc., 1956).

[18] Blau, *op. cit.*, p. 59.

[19] But there is clearly a healthy divergence of views in this area. Three of the most interesting books on the topic are John D. Millett, *The Academic Community: An Essay on Organization* (New York: McGraw-Hill Book Company, 1962); John J. Corson, *Governance of Colleges and Universities* (New York: McGraw-Hill Book Company, 1960); and particularly, Raymond Callahan, *Education and the Cult of Efficiency* (Chicago: University of Chicago Press, 1962). In particular, the testing movement (as "scientific" a sector of education as one can find) has taken a constant drubbing from humanistically inclined critics like Joseph Wood Krutch, Paul Goodman, and Banesh Hoffman. For an astute analysis of the organizational crisis at the college level, see Ross L. Mooney, "The Problem of Leadership in the University," *Harvard Educational Review*, 33 (1963), 42–57.

chines. The essential lesson to be learned from the Hawthorne experiments was that the way to increase production was to increase the ego-involvement of the worker in his work. The worker does not leave his personality at the door. If we can make the worker think that he is an important part of a new plan, that the success of the new plan will depend in large part on him, and that his feelings and opinions about the new plan are very much needed, then the chances are good that the worker will produce at a high level.

Similarly, it is when things are new—a new building, a new curriculum, etc., that educational bureaucracies seem to function best. Perhaps the reason for this is that the whole enterprise is clearly visible for all participants—the new carpet must be kept clean because it is part of *our* new school. After a few years, the command becomes, the new carpet must be kept clean, period. The sense of the whole enterprise is lost. At the same time, practices and procedures have become codified, and the workers in the educational institution have become ego-involved in their daily practices, not in the ends or goals toward which these activities are supposed to lead. Educational means have become personal ends.

One of the most difficult problems for any educational institution is keeping the "Hawthorne Effect" alive, once it has been initiated. This problem will be discussed in greater detail in the section on social change, but it is worth considering here in the context of bureaucratic organization. We cannot be turning educational structures upside down every year just to gain the "Hawthorne Effect." People need some institutional stability, some organization that will make their work easier and more effective, be they teachers, students, administrators, or maintenance men.

At a general level, we can say that there is a way this can be done. The structure of the educational bureaucracy must take into account the fact that the lives of all the participants are constantly changing, even if the programs and practices of the institution are not. If change can be seen in the context of personal growth for every participant, then we will be on the way. This type of educational bureaucracy demands flexibility, and above all else, the possibility of treating the individual differently as he changes. One thinks of many examples of this type of organization. The ungraded primary school is designed to maximize, in a flexible way, the student's growth in different subjects at different rates of speed. It is a school built around the context of student *development*. In American education, student growth is seen basically as an annual phenomenon, as once a year we insert the student into a more advanced program. The ungraded primary assumes that student development is a continuous thing. Similarly, the group of American colleges referred to as the "experimental colleges" (Antioch, Bard, Bennington, Goddard, Sarah Lawrence,

Reed, and some recent joiners) have for years tried to design educational institutions based on the notion of continuous student and teacher growth. It is in the tutorial, the seminar, independent study projects, that the growth of individual students can be most effectively produced and supervised by the teacher. These devices, evolved in institutions that were intentionally kept small enough to keep student development visible and subject to continuous check, have lately become widely used—often in institutions so big that the individual student gets lost by the *institution*, even though one professor may keep track of him in a seminar.

It is clear, then, that experiments are under way to make sure that the "Hawthorne Effect" is achieved and maintained through the constant concern with student growth. But our original thesis was that all members of the educational institution should be made aware of their personal and intellectual growth. How about teachers? To a degree, of course, the system of automatic increments in public schools allows the teacher to realize that he is getting older and slightly richer, but is he getting any *better*? With students being evaluated and tested almost daily for growth, it is interesting that we have worked out few institutional patterns that take teacher growth into account. The "merit rating" systems tend to emphasize the teacher's current skill development, rather than looking at the past and future as well. At the college level, the promotion hierarchy from instructor to assistant professor, associate and full professor may function as a reward for teacher growth after it has happened, but it seldom serves as a mechanism for initiating teacher growth. Again, it assumes that the growth interval which is significant for teachers is between four and six years. At all educational levels, much more needs to be done with the beginning teacher, since it is there that maximum growth can be initiated. The internship concept is designed to do precisely this, both for teachers and administrators. Working with an experienced person is, of course, an extremely effective way to spur development in the neophyte. But in a year, the internship is over. Then, the recruit falls into the huge kettle consisting of *all* teachers, or all administrators, and the recognition of growth ceases. Much remains to be done in terms of introducing the concept of personal growth and development into the teaching and administrative organizational structure of educational bureaucracies.

conclusion

Much has been said here about the nature of educational bureaucracies, and more will be said in the chapter dealing with social change. It should be noted, however, that social institutions exist to further the wishes of those who participate in them. Bureaucracies are, as patterns of human social organization, *neither* good nor evil, no more than an axe is good because it was used to build a house, or evil because it was used to kill someone. It is a tool whose *use* can be good or evil, but not the tool itself. In fact, if more attention were given to the human needs of the participants and less to time and motion studies, it might well be that we can develop flexible, effective bureaucracies in education, which will provide for more meaningful personal involvement (and perhaps some new forms of freedom) by using individual growth as one central organizing concept. Certainly, we must not take Weber's position and assume that the vast network of educational bureaucracies cannot be changed. But we must first develop new organizational patterns that will allow each participant to attain his own highest level of growth.

3: the problem of functionalism*

Of all the theoretical issues which divide social scientists, the questions raised by the functionalist controversy have been the most persistent and devisive. It is partly for this reason that we turn our attention to these questions, and partly because the discussion may shed some interesting light on the operation of educational systems (and *nonsystems*—the distinction will become clear as we go on).

One's initial response to the functionalist argument is that it is absurd —of course, the function of a thing means what a thing *does*. But if we consider a very simple example, "The function of the engine in a car is _____," the problem becomes clear, because the engine is doing an

* *Sociologically inclined readers may observe that references to the* General Theory *of Action of Talcott Parsons are conspicuous by their absence. Although Parsons is a functionalist, he devoted little time to questions of function per se, and is, therefore, relegated to the bibliography in this chapter. More on this will be said in the chapter on social stratification, a subject on which his theory is more clearly applied by other sociologists.*

48

incredible variety of things, *all simultaneously,* from generating heat to creating a vacuum for the windshield wipers to providing torque which the rear wheels (after its being transmitted through gears, universal joints, drive shafts, etc.) apply to the road to push the car forward. The way we phrased the statement in quotes here is clearly misleading, since it suggests the engine of a car is a meaningful whole, or entity, which we can make statements about, while the truth of the matter is that the engine is only a small part of a larger system called an automobile, which exists as a component of a larger system called transportation vehicles. Thus, the function of any thing is dependent upon (a) the smaller units of which it is composed, and (b) the larger systems of which it is a subcomponent. Note that, as we move out to larger and larger "systems," our terminology becomes more abstract.

Function, therefore, is almost always *plural,* and the selection of some purposes and actions to be reported is largely *in the eye of the beholder.* It should also be clear that a statement of how the thing got to be that way is not the same as a statement of how it acts, and that both of these differ from a statement of the uses to which the thing can be put. Thus, function, purpose, and cause have a tendency to run together. Aristotle put it well when he said, "The house is there that men may live in it; but it is also there because the builders have laid one stone upon another." [1]

Such statements tend toward teleology, or the definition of a thing by a justification of its existence. As Hempel puts it:

> Historically speaking, functional analysis is a modification of teleological explanation, i.e., of explanation not by reference to causes which "bring about" the event in question, but by reference to ends which determine its course. [2]

For example, Socrates is reported to have said that God put our mouth just under our nose so that we might enjoy the smell of our food. Ben Franklin, a pragmatist if ever there was one, once declared that "God wants us to tipple, because he has made the joints of the arm just the right length to carry a glass to the mouth without falling short or overshooting the mark: Let us adore, then, glass in hand, this benevolent wisdom; let us adore and drink." [3] There is to be seen in this kind of talk, praise for that which *is,* simply because of the "purposes" for its existence.

[1] Quoted in George C. Homans and David Schneider, *Marriage, Authority, and Final Cause* (New York: Free Press of Glencoe, Inc., 1955), p. 17.

[2] Carl Hempel, "The Logic of Functional Analysis," in L. Gross, ed., *Symposium on Sociological Theory* (Evanston, Ill.: Row, Peterson & Company, 1959), p. 277.

[3] R. Merton, "Manifest and Latent Functions," in *Social Theory and Social Structure* (New York: Free Press of Glencoe, Inc., 1957), p. 38.

manifest and latent functions

When we apply these various types of functional statements to *human* behavior, the problems are much compounded. First of all, self-consciousness enters the picture. It is of no importance whether or not the car engine is aware of what it is doing, but it is of tremendous importance to know whether or not *people* are aware of the functions of what they do. For example, consider Merton's analysis of the Hopi rain dance, a custom which most of us would consider simply superstition. If pressed, our defense would probably be that the rain dance seldom achieved its objective of *bringing rain*. We are thus applying a *meteorological* criterion to the problem, which may be totally incorrect. The rain dance may also provide for a meeting of otherwise scattered families, the renewal of collective identity as a tribe, the chance to relieve frustration and aggression against the gods who refuse to let the rain come down, etc. These *social* functions, based on the social consequences of the rain dance for the participants, are a different order of phenomena from the car engine.

For example, the rain dance may be meeting many needs of the participants, with no *awareness* on the participant's part that these needs are being met. Merton speaks of these as *latent* functions, as opposed to the *manifest* functions of which the participants are aware. One simply cannot make these distinctions about car engines, as the question of whether or not the engine is conscious of what it is doing is absurd. Social "facts" are, therefore, different *in kind* from physical "facts," since what the person *expects* to happen may have important bearing on what actually *does* happen.[4] Because we humans are to a large degree creating our environment as we go, we all tend to become self-fulfilling prophets. (What teacher has not discovered that, when he *expects* his teaching to go badly, it does?) It is this reciprocal problem of human awareness that makes any discussion of social function so difficult. For example, individual A, who owns a new Cadillac car may explain this to himself by saying that he got it to use as a status symbol in his war with his neighbors, while Mr. B may just as sincerely say that his new Cadillac was purchased because of its mechanical structure, durability, and high resale value.

It is the relationship *between* manifest and latent functions of social

[4] *Ibid.* On the matter of the distinction in kind of social and physical "facts," see Stephen Strasser, *Phenomenology and Human Sciences* (Pittsburgh: Duquesne University Press, 1963, especially pp. 116 ff.

events that is of interest here. For example, does the car-owning *behavior* of A differ from that of B, just because he ascribes different functions to his owning of a certain kind of car? In this example, we probably have a tendency to think of A as being an (overly) honest man, while B, we think, is simply kidding himself. We therefore, with a perfectly clear conscience, posit certain *latent* functions of B's owning a Cadillac, feeling that his pragmatic justification may be just a cover-up for his "real" underlying psychological reasons for owning the car. In fact, the whole field of motivation research is postulated on the premise that, in order to sell products, one must find the *latent* functions these products serve for people. For example, in Ernest Dichter's treatise, aptly titled *The Strategy of Desire*,[5] the old war horse of the convertible is used again, the author contending that the convertible symbolizes the mistress, while the poor sedan represents the somewhat frumpy wife. (The convertible owner is, therefore, having a symbolic love affair without ending up in the divorce courts—at least Mr. Dichter *says* that is why men buy convertibles.)

A somewhat amusing, yet central, question can now be asked. What will happen if all potential convertible owners read Dichter's book? What will be the consequence of making a *latent* function (if it really exists) into a *manifest* one? (Several recent studies have suggested that men are becoming embarrassed when they walk into an auto showroom and announce that they wish to buy a convertible, because this is a declaration that they want a mistress, that they have an unhappy marriage, or both.)

Dichter's original job was to help car makers sell more convertibles; if his book sells well enough, he may accomplish the reverse. Or, to return to the Hopi rain dance, what would be the result if the observers went up to the dancers and stated that, although the ritual did not bring rain, the reason for the perpetuation of the activity was that it provided group reinforcement, the safe expression of anger against the gods, etc.? In *writing* about latent functions, it may well be that the self-fulfilling prophecy becomes the self-falsifying assertion.[6] As Clyde Kluckhohn put

[5] (Garden City, N.Y.: Doubleday & Company, Inc., 1960), p. 36. The most heart-filled critique of the motivation research school is still Vance Packard, *The Hidden Persuaders* (New York: David McKay Co., Inc., 1957). Dichter's defense against Packard's charges can be found on pp. 16 ff. of his book. Mr. Dichter certainly joins the ranks of the functionalists on that page in his defense of his trade: "Strictly speaking, a new car, a color TV set, cigarettes, beer, or French wines are not necessities. But they all represent aspects of a full life." Whether or not people, persuaded to want these things, are thereby leading a fuller life is certainly not a scientifically verifiable conclusion.

[6] This happy phrase comes from Ronald Dore, "Function and Cause," *American Sociological Review*, **26** (1961), 845–53.

it, "The scientist of human affairs needs to know as much about the eye that sees as the object seen." [7] Any description of a *latent* function is as much a description of the observer as the observed.

equilibrium and conservatism

Another aspect of the complexities of functionalism is brought out when we ask why Merton felt that the rain dance had to be explained at all. The answer is simple—a functionalist premise: the ritual kept on happening on a regular basis; *ergo* it must be part of a system, it must be *serving a purpose*. The anthropologist Malinowski put it clearly: "The functional view of culture insists, therefore, upon the principle that in every type of civilization, every custom, material object, idea and belief fulfills some vital function." [8] Thus, for the early functionalist, if somehow a bit of culture no longer served any purpose, it would instantly disappear from that culture. The position has been modified considerably since Malinowski's time, but the notion of a culture continuously perpetuating itself as a system still remains a dominant mode in the social sciences.

From reading the early anthropologists, it becomes clear that they were in the main rather well trained in biology, and most of their ideas of system and function came from biology (e.g., the *"organic"* nature of society). For a long time, the analogy of human society to the human body was believed to be a valid one—even Plato's *Republic* was to be a unity of head, heart, and stomach; Hobbes makes reference to the analogy of human and social "organs," and Adam Smith's use of the notion of the "invisible hand" makes the point. But the analogy is clearly misleading. The human body is possessed of a single center of consciousness, the society is not. Certain segments of a society may rebel and engage in conflict with the rest, but the fingernails do not rebel against the wrist.

In a way, this organismic model is the cause of many of our difficulties, since it is through the human analogy that we come to the notion of "homeostasis," or the inherent tendency of a system to maintain itself. The term was first used by a biologist named Cannon in 1932. In biological thinking, the maintenance of a system of organs in a given relationship to each other and the environment was what allowed the organism to survive (a good thing); therefore, homeostasis was a *good* thing. When we look at societies this way, we think of them as "striving" for homeostasis,

[7] *Mirror for Man* (New York: McGraw-Hill Book Company, 1944), p. 11. (This is probably the first, and finest, anthropological treatise for the layman.)

[8] B. Malinowski, quoted in Dorothy Emmet, *Function, Purpose, and Powers* (London: Macmillan & Co., Ltd., 1958), Chap. 4.

and because they *do* generally perpetuate themselves, we think that the human behavior which collectively makes up the society must be continued, *unchanged in form,* in order to "maintain the system." [9] (However, it is clear that the disruption of homeostasis in a human body may mean death, while the disruption of "social homeostasis," as in 1776 and the French Revolution, simply means that the social system is altered to meet the changing wishes of men.)

There is thus a conservative bias in functional statements, since they tend to interpret a society as a system (like the human body) which works, above all else, to maintain itself *as it is,* or dies. Teleological statements likewise furnish a handy rationalization for the present, by postulating that if God put it here, it must be good, as can be seen in the earlier examples from Socrates and Ben Franklin.

These functionalist statements and the early biological assumptions on which they rest virtually ignore the process of *change through time,* which is characteristic of both societies and organisms. For example, social *conflict* may have certain important benefits to certain societies at certain times.[10] Nagel points out that, once the time dimension is considered, it is extremely important to the organism that certain organs *do not* function at certain times, and that their *non*function is a definite part of the "system" of the whole organism.[11] The lowly hiccough, for example, still mystifies the medical profession, especially when it continues "functioning" when it is not *supposed to,* resulting, occasionally, in death. It seems, also, as if doctors would be happier if people had no appendixes, as they are hard put to find a "function" for them.

[9] Cannon, *The Wisdom of the Body* (New York: W. W. Norton & Company, Inc., 1932), p. 24. See particularly the last chapter, "The Relation of Biological and Social Homeostasis"; also the Epilogue. The temptation to apply generalizations to an unfamiliar field was too much for Mr. Cannon, who was a fine biologist but a rather poor sociologist. For example, he makes a relationship between a simple one-celled animal, completely dependent on the environment with no division of labor, and a "primitive" tribe. The fluid system around our cells, says Mr. Cannon, is like the human social system of production and distribution (highways, railroads, etc.).

Just as the circulatory system first warns the organism of disruptive danger, so it is the social distribution system that does the same thing. (Apparently, he would make an analogy between a traffic jam on a main highway and coronary thrombosis.) But the most dangerous statement he makes is on p. 299: "The organism suggests that stability is of prime importance." It is in the methods of adapting to the environment that the physiological and social parallel breaks down.

[10] On this point, see Lewis Coser, *The Functions of Social Conflict* (New York: Free Press of Glencoe, Inc., 1956). One must make a distinction, however, between the conflict itself and the *resolution* of the conflict. Many other social theories, such as those of Marx, Freud, Hegel, and Darwin, are based on conflict of one sort or another.

[11] Ernest Nagel, "A Formalization of Functionalism," Chap. 10 of *Logic Without Metaphysics* (New York: Free Press of Glencoe, Inc., 1956), p. 250.

We should also point out here that there are at least several ways of conceiving of a "stable" social system. First, there is the nonadaptive system, which maintains itself without change or adaptation—ancient China is the most obvious example. These systems are characterized by a very high degree of autonomy and an intentional isolation from the forces outside the system that work for change; e.g., the Berlin Wall, the highly isolated socialist communities in early America, the Indian reservations, etc. In a time of rapid and pervasive social change outside the system, this type of equilibrium is often threatened, because the equilibrium is entirely internal. We can speak of this type as a closed system.

A much more flexible model is the adaptive system—here the equilibrium is dynamic rather than static. The social system is constantly modifying itself in order to be in reciprocity with forces outside itself. Rather than isolation from the "outside," the desired end is to have constant contact with the forces outside the system that will have to be dealt with. Internally, as well as externally, the system is geared for change. This kind of system we refer to as an open system. Open systems are reciprocal; that is, as they are responding to external forces, they are also modifying these forces, usually through a system of feedback. For example, a thermostat is designed to take action when the air gets too cool by turning on a heating unit. This action is followed by reaction, when the air warms enough to shut the thermostat (and therefore the heater) off. The system is maintained, but only through internal action which responds to external changes. In the social realm, open systems will resemble the political party, while closed systems will resemble the hospital.

reciprocity and autonomy— the parts and the "whole"

Another interesting aspect of functionalism is its concern with the relationship of the parts of the "system" to the whole—the arrangement of *reciprocity* and *autonomy*. Some have contended that the tension between the part desiring autonomy, and the pressure from the system as a whole to control all the parts, is the basic driving force in all social systems.[12] Notice that here, once again, we are in the realm of applied biology, since the biologist has been more concerned with the parts-whole relation than have other scientists.

With the growth of awareness of the great complexity of the cell, new problems arose. If the body is really made up of billions of semiautonomous cells, how do they "know" what the "whole" organism is like, i.e.,

[12] See Alvin Gouldner, "Reciprocity and Autonomy in Functional Theory," in Gross, *op. cit.*, pp. 241–70; also Coser, *op. cit.*

when to form a scab over a wound? When a starfish egg is cut in half, how does each half "know" it should grow into a whole starfish? How does a lizard "know" that when its tail is cut off, it should grow a new one? How does the queen bee "know" that, when a large number of drones have been killed, she should lay more of these eggs to bring the hive population into balance?

These are fascinating questions, the answers to which are still not known, although DNA research in the chemistry of genetics is getting closer than we have ever been. However, an earlier group of biologists, writing at about the time of the first sophisticated anthropological research, were sure that an "awareness" of the whole must be within each part. These biologists, called vitalists, postulated a force which they called "entelechy," that gave (through a mechanism never made quite clear) a "vision" of the whole organism to each part.[13] It was thought of as a kind of "missing link" between the cell and the creature. Note that the development of the concept of entelechy was not based on any observable evidence that such a force existed; they felt that in order for organisms to work systematically, there *had to be* such a force, to relate the parts to the whole—the more entelechy, the more stable the system—entelechy was a *necessary* concept.

This sort of thinking can be seen far too often in the social sciences. Arnold Green's first edition of a sociology text states, "Stratification is universal because it is *necessary.*" In the second edition, he simply says, "Stratification is universal," thereby leaving the functionalist camp.[14] In an excellent critique of the work of the anthropologist Lévi-Strauss, Homans and Schneider point out this teleological tendency:

Why, the reader may well ask, does Lévi-Strauss consider so important the linking together, through marriage, of the different groups within a society? Why do they *have* to be linked? We can best answer this question by trying to answer another one: Why does he consider matrilateral cross-cousin marriage a step forward in human marriage arrangements?

[13] The most fascinating of the Vitalists (a theory of biology which was related by its supporters to philosophy, ethics, and parapsychology) was Hans Adolph Driesch. See particularly his *The History and Theory of Vitalism*, trans. Ogden (London: Macmillan & Co., Ltd., 1914); and his *The Science and Philosophy of the Organism* (London: Adam and Charles Black, Ltd., 1939). See also Edmund Beecher Wilson, *The Cell in Development and Heredity* (New York: The Macmillan Company, 1925). The best and most interesting summary of this material is by Emmet, *op. cit.*, Chap. 3, "The Notion of Biological Functionalism," although she attributes Wilson's work to Driesch. See also Nagel, *op. cit.*, Chap. 10.

[14] Arnold W. Green, *Sociology* (New York: McGraw-Hill Book Company, 1956), p. 217. Mentioned in Walter Buckley, "Social Stratification and the Functional Theory of Social Differentiation," *American Sociological Review*, **23** (1958), 369–75, pp. 369–70.

The answer is that he holds generalized exchange to be *better* than restricted exchange from the point of view of the organic solidarity of the society. . . . The greater the marriage specialization of each of the kin-groups in a society, the greater the dependence of each upon all, and hence the greater the organic solidarity.[15]

functionalism and values

Even worse, Lévi-Strauss assumes that human consciousness is a sort of entelechy, in that people are *aware* of the relationships between themselves (cells) and the society (organism), and that they *know* somehow which social mechanisms are better and which are worse:

He (Lévi-Strauss) has a high opinion of primitive man—or some of them —as thinkers, and he holds, if we understand him aright, that the members of some societies chose matrilateral cross-cousin marriage because they could "see" in much the same way that Lévi-Strauss himself could "see" that it was better than other forms.[16]

It should be clear from these examples that the functionalist (particularly when concerned with latent functions) is going to be working in the realm of value judgments. Some followers of the school accept this fact bravely, saying that "To ask for the function of any social arrangement is to call for its justification—or alternatively for its condemnation," that the evaluation involved in functional analysis is "objective and needs no apology." [17] But to assume, for example, that systems of stratification are universal because they are *necessary* should not mean that any *particular* system of stratification (such as the segregation of the Negro) is either necessary or good. Certain social systems should not be *allowed* to continue to function because of their debilitating effect on the individuals involved. To say that Hitler was a failure only because he could not *perpetuate* the system he created is to miss the moral point.

The value judgment contending that the more orderly, regular, and systematic a social subsystem is, the "better" it is, should be questioned also. During World War II, for example, great consideration was given to the problem of how to send Allied bombers over Europe with the

---

[15] Homans and Schneider, *op. cit.*, p. 10.

[16] *Ibid.*, p. 19. Waller and others of course contend that we act first and think later, which seems more sensible than the rationalistic fallacy. How many of us are monogamists because we have consciously rejected polygamy as being an *unstable system?* How, for instance, would Lévi-Strauss's natives know what other systems were possible? (There may be many marital systems possible which have not yet come into existence.)

[17] Both from Harold Fallding, "Functional Analysis in Sociology," *American Sociological Review*, **28** (1963), 7.

greatest efficiency (greatest number of hits, fewest pilots and planes lost). It was discovered, after much experimenting with number of planes leaving together and frequency of their runs, that the most efficient "system" was a completely *random* one—a nonsystem. Any systematic, orderly plan for the dispatching of the planes would, of course, be quickly detected by the enemy, but if they were sent on a random basis, there would be no plan for the enemy to detect. Another example would be the "formula" boxer, who always does things the same way, and generally gets beaten by anyone who can detect the system.

Another value problem here is the inability of the functionalist to look at those disruptive elements within a society that *also* manage to maintain themselves, such as crime, strikes, divorce, drugs, etc. These "bad" subsystems of our society (which are probably as universal as the "good" systems of stratification) have remarkable adaptability and permanence, yet most functionalists will only speak of their disruptive effect upon the *whole*, rather than their internally systematic aspects. To say, for example, that the liquor industry ceased *functioning* with the advent of Prohibition just because its activities were no longer legally sanctioned is a serious misreading of American history. It has been estimated that there are two prostitutes for every doctor in America, which puts the functionalist in a cruel dilemma. He would like to dismiss the prostitute as being *disruptive* for the marriage system, but it is obvious that prostitution is a very stable subsystem and, as such, must be serving some vital function! (Perhaps they are more vital than organized medicine, because they outnumber doctors two to one.) [18] In these cases, the functionalist has no right to dismiss the "underworld" as irrelevant or immoral, particularly since they meet his major criterion of stability.

The functionalist's judgment that these systems are disruptive to the mainstream is certainly difficult to prove. Is divorce itself a disruptive system, or does it provide a socially approved way of eliminating "nonfunctional" marriages, thereby allowing the institution of *marriage* to perpetuate itself? It may well be (this is a guess) that the existence of the social institutions we think of as immoral may be necessary for the continued existence of those we think of as moral, that their relationship is not competitive but *reciprocal*. (Actually, as on the tennis court, a great deal of reciprocal agreement on rules, etc., is necessary before meaningful competition can occur.)

The major point here is that no society, at least no modern industrialized society, can be viewed as a *single system*, all subsystems of which are moving smoothly together toward the same goal.

---

[18] Estimates (for 1950) from Merton, *op. cit.*, p. 81.

Life is labor *and* management, church *and* state, rural *and* urban, Democrat *and* Republican. We are arguing that the tension created between conflicting subgroups in a pluralistic society can be very productive and should be encouraged. Particularly in a time of rapid social change, such as our own, no group has *the* answers, and the idea that yesterday was a failure may be a success tomorrow. It may well be that the most efficient social system for us is not the monolithic machine, but a flexible, adaptable system of checks and balances, in which a maximum number of people *understand each other's position.*

A corollary here is that, before we pronounce a given social institution as "dysfunctional"—therefore, evil—and begin to eradicate it, we should give thought to what it was doing there in the first place and what will be a satisfactory *substitute.* As Merton put it:

> To seek social change without due recognition of the manifest and latent functions performed by the social organization undergoing change, is to indulge in social ritual rather than social engineering.[19]

To say (as Lévi-Strauss might have said) that divorce should be eliminated because of its dysfunctional consequences for American society *as a whole* is to commit a major error by focusing attention only on the whole and ignoring the part. Likewise, before condemning racial segregation as being beneath our attention because of its disruptive aspects on society *as a whole,* we should first consider the problem of why the white Southerner believes in it and responds to it. We are then in a position to try to develop substitute structures that can accomplish some of the same ends without exploiting an entire race. If this is not done, and suitable substitutes are not found (the need for a person to feel superior to someone else, the need for in-group solidarity, the release of personal tension through some kind of aggression), then *efforts toward integration may go the way of Prohibition.*[20]

The conclusions of our argument, therefore, are about as follows:

1. Society is best viewed as a kaleidoscope of shifting group structures, now cooperating, now competing, with a vast assortment of other groups, but inevitably changing through time. There is no single monolithic arrangement of *social* subsystems, internally compatible, producing a consistent hierarchy of action.

[19] Merton, *op. cit.,* p. 81.
[20] Alexander Bickel, "Much More than Law Is Needed," *The New York Times Magazine,* Aug. 9, 1964. Bickel's position, that we must convert the white Southerner would be enhanced by a discussion of what the present system does for the Southern white.

2. The term "function" may refer to the antecedents, causes, purposes, processes, effects, or consequences of a thing, or to any combination thereof. The term "function," without any qualification as to what aspect is being considered, can be misleading.

3. The assumptions of a person making observations about society are as important as the observations themselves. Although this gets one into an infinite regress (the assumptions of the *reader* of the observations, etc.), it is the only answer to the central question, "How can man as a person make man as a person the object of an empirical inquiry?" [21]

4. The "rationalistic fallacy," that people are clearly aware of the reasons for their social institutions being as they are, that they engage in one marriage pattern because they can "see," with a vision of the whole, that this is the most "functional" pattern, is clearly a fallacy. We act first, analyze later. Just as the individual cell does not "see" the whole body (entelechy), so the individual person does not "see" the *whole* society.

5. To say that a given social institution is disruptive to the whole and should *therefore* be eliminated will be totally ineffectual, unless attention is focused on the *institution,* not the whole, to see what the consequences of its elimination would be and what substitutions might be made.

6. When a supposedly latent function, even if only the product of the observer's imagination (the convertible owner wanting a mistress) is made manifest, a *reversal* of the expected behavior may occur. Self-consciousness of "function" by participants may alter the nature of the social institution.

7. Consistency, reliability, stability, permanence, continuity, and integration are not necessarily the only characteristics of "good" social systems, although they are characteristics of a "good" auto engine. These are two different uses of the word "good."

8. Social institutions may appear to be working against each other (marriage and divorce), yet a reciprocal or symbiotic relationship may actually be going on, just as certain small fish, in return for protection, clean the scales or teeth of the larger fish. In our perspective, some social waste or "garbage" is bound to be created if conflicting groups are allowed to interact, and some social institutions do something about it. The elimination of divorce ("marriage garbage collector") might have serious consequences for the institution of marriage.

---

[21] Strasser, *op. cit.,* p. 7.

9. Instead of arguing about whether structure determines "function" or "function" determines structure, we will take the interactionist position on the issue: structure and "function" (however defined) are two sides of the same coin, like heredity and environment, and culture and personality. This is the only position to take if one is willing to admit that people and societies exist *in time*, and that static conceptions, of people or groups, cannot take account of change:

> Social structure merely defines some pattern picked out at one moment from the endlessly continuing process of social interaction. There is nothing static in either concept, system or structure, except in the sense that all process is assumed to have an analyzable structure at any moment in a time series.[22]

10. When we argue about the "function" of THE human heart (its processes, purposes, and effects) we are pretty much in agreement on the generalized statement about what all human hearts are like, but when we talk about the "function" of a *social* institution, such as kissing, people may (unlike hearts) vary widely in processes, purposes, and effects. Thus, it is very dangerous to abstract, for analytical purposes, a social institution past the level at which it can still be translated into the *specific activities of specific individuals*. (As critics of Talcott Parsons have put it, his General Theory is supposedly about action, yet no *person* ever *acts*.[23] His interest stops after overly generalized descriptions of how people decide *what* to do—the actual *doing* is of no concern. This lack of interest may, of course, be due to Parsons' awareness that his theory, which violates conclusion number 10, *will not predict* what individuals will do.)

functionalism and education

In trying to apply this analysis of functionalism to the contemporary educational scene, one thing becomes apparent: education (in the sense of socializing the young) is, to a very high degree, invested in a single specialized institution, composed of all the buildings and people who constitute schools and colleges. This increasing specialization means that other institutions, particularly the

[22] Bernard Barber, "Structural-Functional Analysis: Some Problems and Misunderstandings," *American Sociological Review*, 21 (1956), 133.

[23] Chandler Morse, "The Functionalist Imperatives," in Max Black, ed., *The Social Theories of Talcott Parsons* (Englewood Cliffs, N.J.: Prentice-Hall, Inc., 1961), p. 107.

home and the church, are declining in their educational influence on youth, although they have had a major responsibility in this area. The school has thus become a focal point for *all* youth services, and is steadily extending the number of years it has youth under its influence, from pre-kindergarten to postgraduate school. There is now almost universal agreement that everyone should possess a high-school diploma, and there has been a steady procession of pamphlets arguing that everyone, *regardless of ability*, has the right to a college education of some kind, particularly on vocational grounds. This means that every young person has, as a birthright, a place in some college or university.

We are clearly centralizing our educational concerns within the variety of systems we call educational. In previous times, this was not the case, since one learned adult roles by *performing* them, by imitating the work of adults. The learning of tasks was accomplished by doing them. This was often done in a very casual way—the boy, watching his father build a canoe, simply picks up a chisel and begins to cut, while the father proceeds with his own work. That is, the father *does not cease his work to become a teacher;* the responsibility for learning is largely on the boy. As he imitates, he identifies with the values of the father, again, without much formal, or even conscious, instruction. The more the culture allows the expression of values through direct action, the easier it is for the young to identify with the parent by imitating his actions.[24] Thus, the actions of building a dug-out canoe can be full of religious, aesthetic, philosophic, and tribal significance, and these values are transferred to the young not by memorizing lists of words which describe the values but by allowing them to perform the *actions in which the values are made manifest.*

This sort of imitation is difficult in our society, particularly for a male child, as relatively few male children in our society know exactly what their father *does*. A revealing incident on this point involved a group of kindergarten children in a pseudo-experimental situation who were asked to "play mommy or daddy." The girls went immediately into the play house, went to the kitchen, and busied themselves with the tasks they had watched their mothers do. The boys were stymied, except for one little fellow who got on his tricycle, left the play house, went around the corner, hid for a time, then reappeared saying, "It's five-thirty!" went into the play house, and collapsed with a sigh before the television set. When asked to play his father on weekends, he did precisely the same

[24] Dorothy Lee, *Freedom and Culture* (Englewood Cliffs, N.J.: Prentice-Hall, Inc., 1959). This is a beautifully written book, particularly the discussions of the Hopi Indians.

thing, but carefully added some golf clubs on the back of his tricycle. From his point of view, this was a good performance from a very limited script, as the father's essential occupational activities took place outside his son's environment.

educational functions—
manifest and latent

One of the items for functional analysis in Merton's paradigm [25] concerns the relationship of structure to function. Although the relationship is to some extent reciprocal, we can look at structure as having a limiting effect on function—a small sports car, because of its size, cannot be used for transporting elephants. Therefore, one way we can get to the question of the functions of education, is by considering its structure to see what limitations the structure places on the functions that can be performed.

One obvious thing about educational structure is its visibility. Clearly, "education" is not something which is allowed to take place by chance in our culture. (There are, of course, other cultures in which there is no formal educational structure at all.) If one tries to look at this structure as dispassionately as possible, the first thing that is likely to emerge is the great importance placed on conflict in the form of highly structured individual competition. One can see, at almost any level, students (learners, presumably) being evaluated in terms of the performance of other students. Yet the formal documents of educational institutions seldom make reference to competition, except perhaps in athletics. Thus one of the latent functions of education would seem to be the inculcation of norms regarding competition. Because open aggression is universally frowned upon, the student is called upon to compete with his fellows and be pleasant to them at the same time.

One might now ask why the educational structure seems so consistently established to perform this (latent) function. With all the variation one can find in American educational systems, this commonality is even more striking. One can infer from this analysis that two central concerns of our culture involve aggressiveness (getting ahead) and sociability (getting along with the people you are trying to get ahead of). Both

[25] From *Social Theory and Social Structure* (New York: Free Press of Glencoe, Inc., 1949), pp. 49–61. To a large degree, this author has attempted to follow Merton's paradigm in this discussion of structural-functional relationships and their application to education. For the original (and still best) formulation of the manifest-latent function distinction, see pp. 21–61 of this volume. See also the excellent summary, *Functionalism in the Social Sciences*, Monograph No. 5 (Philadelphia: American Academy of Political and Social Science, 1965).

concerns are vitally important; aggression, because of our culture's constant need for mobile people with new skills to get to "the top" so that the best people are doing the best job (which is, after all, a highly disruptive activity, creating imbalances in social systems and tending toward "disorder"), and sociability, because of the need for some stabilizing force, a stability to counteract the disruptions caused by social fluidity, competition, and mobility.

To investigate the socializing function of education, Jules Henry spent many months as an anthropological observer in a typical middle-class suburban school.[26] In this elementary school, the principal delivers a brief homily every morning over the intercom (which allows him to speak to any room or listen without being observed). Part of the ritual, which stresses love and friendship, is the daily award of kisses (delivered by the intercom) from the principal to any student whose birthday it was:

> Boys and girls, for this month our new theme is "Always Friendly." The word I want you to learn for today is "friend." . . . One thing that helps you to be friendly is your smile. . . . You have to feel friendship. How do you keep friends? How do you behave in a friendly way? . . . The best way to have friends is to be a friend. A girl is kissed for her birthday ten times over the intercom by the principal and is asked the question, And do you know how to be happy, Marilyn? Marilyn says, Make others happy.

Mr. Henry's role was to be an unobtrusive observer, keeping a careful running account of what was going on in a particular class. He had no personal contact with the students in this class, outside of a perfunctory greeting. One day, completely unknown to Mr. Henry, the teacher asked the children to write a letter to Mr. Henry. *At no time* did the teacher make any statement as to what the content of the letters should be. Yet, even without direction, the letters all sounded alike:

> Dear Mr. Ryan (*Henry's "alias" to the children*),
> I like you and hope you like your job. I hope you can come to school every day.
> Love,
(boy)

> Dear Mr. Ryan,
> I am very happy that you come and watch us and I think that you are very nice.
> Love,
(girl)

---

[26] "Working Paper on Creativity," *Harvard Educational Review,* **27** (1957), 148–55.

Dear Mr. Ryan,

In my heart I have all of your words and I have wonderful thoughts about you. Love to your family.

Love,
(*boy*)

Dear Mr. Ryan,

I love you very much and I hope I can come and visit you at University High.

Love,
(*boy*)

Dear Mr. Ryan,

I hope you are blessed by God. I am glad you come to see us, you are very handsome. I love you. My heart has very much room for you.

Love,
(*girl*)

Dear Mr. Ryan,

I hope you like and love Ratoncito (the class's pet white rat), and I hope you like and love me too and I hope you never die because if you do I could just cry. I hope you and I will be very good friends and hope when you are a father I will love you.

Love,
(*girl*)

Henry explains what has happened as follows:

> It will be seen that expressions of love and euphoria are always present and form the underlying verbal matrix within which the letters are written. Thus there is a clear chain-of-command from principal to child which determines that even in spontaneous letter-writing, where no content instructions are given, the iron verbal matrix shall not be broken. In this school situation the principal, as a cultural relay, transmits over the intercom the stereotypes that come to verbal expression in the children's work.

This example makes clear that, even though the *formal* curriculum of this school makes no mention of teaching students the "right" behavior in terms of loving everyone, the principal has been conducting a catechism which has produced precisely that. (In fact, the children even *compete* in terms of how much they love each other!) Granted that the parents of these children probably for the most part share the principal's view, we still have established as a latent effect (or function) of the school program the *collective affirmation of a value* not included in the curriculum.

Strong pressures are brought to bear to keep the structure of competition and sociability in parity. Thus, the nonaggressive student (who "doesn't try") is severely chastised, as is the overly aggressive student who openly hates his competitors. The teacher thus functions as a social thermostat, keeping the student's aggression alive, but within carefully controlled limits. To return to Goffman's language for a minute, the teacher runs a tension-management system. This system does not (and perhaps cannot) allow much cooperative student activity. It seems to function in terms of constantly focusing the individual's attention on his own performance, both intellectual and social, in relation to some group norm. The provision in the structure for collaborative intellectual activities—students working together on a single academic task—is so small as to be nonexistent.

This conscious attention to the evaluation of individual student performance suggests another very important function, that of a measuring and selecting agency for the culture, particularly its occupational structure. Increasingly, the possibility of a person's achieving a certain occupational level is dependent on his reaching a certain educational level. This "filtration" function seems well suited to the educational structure, at least in an obvious sense: all children can be "filtered," at least at the elementary and high-school levels, since education is compulsory. However, this filter structure needs to be looked at carefully.

Ostensibly, the function of this filter is to make sure that only the "best" get through to important positions in our society. Therefore, one assumes that "merit" is what passes through the educational filter. The problem seems to be that the filtering system acts to the advantage of young people from wealthy socioeconomic areas, because they are represented far more often than one would expect at higher educational (and occupational) levels. There is no reason to assume genetic superiority in upper-class membership; therefore, there must be environmental advantages for the upper classes that slip through the educational filter.

Here again we find the educational system fulfilling two contradictory functions: selecting only the "meritorious" for high positions in our occupational and social structure, and simultaneously maintaining the built-in advantages of the wealthier sectors of society. It is always difficult to "check out" how well an institution is performing a given function, but the problem is particularly difficult here. Is the educational system structured to perform adequately the function of filtering out the "best"? Is there a clear-cut description available of what "the best" means in operational terms? Is the schools's "best" the same "best" that can work most effectively in adult society? [27] There is no simple way to evaluate this function due to our inherent disagreements over what is worth an "A" in adult behavior. It is difficult, but we may have to get used to the notion that, in both structural and functional terms, educational systems are working to destroy societal inequities and to maintain them at the same time.

curricular functions

Formal "education" happens, in the broadest sense, by a process of exposing the student to something—it may be a book, a picture, a record, a teacher lecturing, etc., so that the student may absorb it (remember it) or reflect on it (think about it). The main justification for imposing content on the student is that it is necessary (the student cannot "function" well in society without it, or he cannot function at the next level of education). The structure of curriculum is basically hierarchical; that is, it begins with "simple" or "basic" material, and works up to "complex" material. This structure is designed to perform the function of developing the student's powers of thought through the same hierarchy.

The structure of curriculum, then, predisposes a hierarchical structure of knowledge; that there are simple ideas and complex ideas, and that the way to the complex is via the simple. This curriculum structure also predisposes a model of the human brain, which "learns" in the same way, moving from simple to complex. There is today a very exciting debate in many circles as to whether or not human learning moves through this sort of hierarchy or not. It may well be, as an alternative, that any student at virtually any age can be taught any material. Should this prove to be substantially correct, the structural and functional assumptions behind our present notions of curriculum will be stood upside down, and we will have a genuine educational revolution on our hands. If, for example, we realize that there is not one way "in" to a subject, but a million, then the hierarchy vanishes, and new structures of a much more flexible nature become possible. This is one of the most exciting possibilities in all of education.

Another aspect of our earlier analysis that can be applied to education concerns the overemphasis by the functionalist on the "systematic" aspects of social institutions. Particularly at the administrative level, in the implementation of the curriculum, there is a considerable body of

---

[27] For a humorous but helpful account of what a society *would* be like if those with merit always got to the "top," see Michael Young, *The Rise of the Meritocracy* (Baltimore: Penguin Books, Inc., 1961).

feeling that a good educational institution is one which resembles the car engine with which we began this chapter—consistent, reliable, stable, unchanging in performance, with all elements smoothly meshing together.

We might ask, however, if this pattern of organization is necessarily related to student *learning*. Do students learn more in a school in which the administrative reins are tightly held? In terms of the latent learning we mentioned earlier, what view do students get of the outside adult society in such a school? Do they assume that in adult life in a pluralistic democracy they should continue the pattern of blind obedience to those in positions of power? We might also ask whether or not a "functional" school is the best environment in which faculty members can develop their creative skills, attitudes, and commitments to the fullest degree.

As an obvious example of the misuse of "systematic" aspects of education, consider the problem of every administration, The Schedule. Some of the assumptions used in making The Schedule are as follows:

1. All subjects should be taught in classes of the same length. (English in 40-minute periods, history in 40-minute periods, etc.)

2. All periods of each subject should be the same length. (Monday English is 40 minutes, Tuesday English is 40 minutes, etc.)

3. Classes should occur at the same time each day. (Monday English 9:15, Tuesday English 9:15, etc.)

4. Teachers may not go over the designated period with a given class, since this would disrupt The Schedule.

5. If a teacher's room is noisy (unsystematic), no learning is going on; if a teacher's room is quiet (systematic), learning is going on.

6. All students coming out of a given class should know the same things.

7. All teachers teaching the same subject should teach the same things.

8. The best way to set up a bunch of students for teaching purposes is by *age*—therefore, for purposes of The Schedule, all twelve-year-olds (or eighteen-year-olds) are alike.

The reader, from long experience, can probably add to these eight cardinal principles of scheduling. There is no question that following these eight assumptions is the easiest way to set up The Schedule—but what evidence is there that this is the best way for students to learn? (It might also be interesting to find out what sort of latent learning this organizational pattern produces in the students.) The alternatives of flexible scheduling techniques are much more difficult, but they do allow for increased teaching and learning possibilities. Study halls are almost universally agreed to be of little use (certainly, according to Bruner's notion of self-discovery, nothing could be worse!), yet they exist, due to the fact that there are more periods in The Schedule than students have classes. Instead of building the educational program around The Schedule, it would be interesting to try the reverse.

Along with these manifest structural-functional relationships, there are other ways of looking at curriculum. There are latent functions in certain kinds of material as well, for in the act of "learning" them, we are supposed to be somehow transformed as persons at the same time. The study of classics is supposed to "quicken the mind," the study of philosophy is good for the soul, etc. This latent or transformational aspect of certain kinds of curriculums seems to occur most often in content that is not easily applied to real problems. Many writers have pointed out that curriculum does not keep pace with social change, and that if it cannot be justified on pragmatic grounds, it tends to be justified as the "wisdom of the ages" or the "backbone of our Western Tradition."

One can even justify teaching the New York City telephone directory in this manner.[28] The formal curriculum then represents an educational "closed system," in that there are few structural patterns whereby the society can gain access to curricular decision making. Likewise, educational institutions are not well structured to ascertain the value of various curricular patterns in the lives of individual students on a continuous basis. Due to this absence of structure, we can say (with some temerity) that there is little reason for commitment to the curricular function of having a significant impact on students' lives, because the educational structure provides no machinery for manifesting, or evaluating, this function.

the "two cultures" in education— the curriculum and the fun culture

Although this "formal" curriculum and its structure do not often seem directly related to immediate student needs, there is (again, at all educational levels) a second, informal, or "latent" curriculum. Our use of "latent" here should not be

---

[28] M. Harmin and S. Simon, "The Year the Schools Began Teaching the Telephone Directory," *Harvard Educational Review*, 35 (1965), 328–31. In the same genre, see W. Sayres, "The Singular Society of Loscho," *Harvard Educational Review*, 27 (1957), 301–9; and Harold Benjamin, *The Saber-Tooth Curriculum* (New York: McGraw-Hill Book Company, 1959).

interpreted to mean unorganized, since often this structure is more meticulously detailed than the formal curriculum. Rather, these are activities which are not considered by the participants as being of a formally educative nature. Because this curriculum exists without books and other devices, it tends to be implemented through social interaction. For this reason, we can speak of it as a subculture.

For want of a better term, we can speak of this subculture as the fun culture of education.[29] It includes all extracurricular activities that take place in the school, whether formally organized by the educational administration or not. In general, we can differentiate between formally organized patterns—such as interschool athletics, school dances, student clubs, etc.—and those patterns which are not formally organized, such as student fads (hula hoops, frisbees, troll dolls, unusual clothing, and beards and unusual haircuts; as well as the pattern behavior of dancing, necking, petting, and other obvious expressions of interest in sex).

This second curriculum is very definitely an "open system" in education and seems to be communicated with amazing speed to other educational systems at that level (high schools, colleges, etc.). The mass media have something to do with this communication, but not a great deal. For example, that which is portrayed on television as being "in" with high-school or college students is fiercely resisted. Conversely, frisbees, long hair, troll dolls, or "Wishnicks," and hula hoops received almost no attention in conventional advertising media, and if they had, sales might well have declined. (Here again, the making of a latent function manifest would have reversed the result.) These fad items (in a way, the curriculum of the fun culture) are communicated entirely through personal interaction. The fact that one of these fun culture items can be transmitted to twenty million children throughout the nation in a week or so with no mechanism other than word of mouth should give us food for thought.

[29] The evolution of the notion of a fun subculture is interesting. Besides the obvious reference to Veblen's leisure class theories, the interested reader might also consult Willard Waller, *The Sociology of Teaching* (New York: John Wiley & Sons, Inc., 1932); Lerner, "Comfort and Fun: Morality in a Nice Society," *American Scholar*, 27 (Spring, 1958), 153–65; Fred Katz, "The School as a Complex Social Organization," *Harvard Educational Review*, 34 (1964), 428–55; David Riesman, *The Lonely Crowd* (New Haven, Conn.: Yale University Press, 1950); Burton Clark, *Educating the Expert Society* (San Francisco: Chandler Publishing Co., Inc., 1962); Wayne Gordon, *The Social System of the High School* (New York: Free Press of Glencoe, Inc., 1957); James Coleman, *The Adolescent Society* (New York: Free Press of Glencoe, Inc., 1961), and at the college level, George Stern, "The Intellectual Climate of College Environments," *Harvard Educational Review*, 33 (1963), 5–41. The relationship of the fun culture to the consumer role comes from Alvin Toffler, *The Culture Consumers* (New York: St. Martin's Press, Inc., 1964).

The structure of this subculture is difficult to ascertain, since it is deliberately kept from the eyes of prying adults. (It would be possible, however, to spot potential fads and follow up their machinery of transmission.) Because of this vagueness of structure, it is also difficult to deduce possible function from it. Because of the uniformity of the fun culture at any given time, and the conformity to its norms and behaviors on the part of young people at the relevant age, it is reasonable to assume that this is a system of identity management. Ours is a very youth-oriented culture (judging from advertising, the "good life" seems to occur at about age 20), both because youth are the future, and we are interested in the future; also because almost half of our citizens are under 25. One consequence of this emphasis on youth is that there are few adult models to which teen-agers can aspire—sports figures and popular singers tend to "peak" early, leaving no 40-year-old heroes in the fun culture. Therefore, as long as more mature adult society has in a sense defaulted, the fun culture has no alternative but to create identity models for youth as they are, not as they might become.

The fun culture has no finely graduated divisions as to age: eight-year-olds seem to be very much a part, doing the same dances of those twice their age. One very curious thing about this subculture is that it pays almost no attention to one of the most important facts in a person's life: the onset of puberty. In almost every other society, the onset of sexual maturity brings with it some indication that the youth is ready to be inducted into adult society. American culture makes no distinction between youth and adult stature; therefore, no initiation into adult culture is necessary or possible, since the predominant mode of the culture *is* youth, not adulthood.

One could hypothesize that the fun culture is necessary to provide some identity models for youth when adults do not or cannot do it for them. (One could also hypothesize that in a culture in which adults are constantly exhorted to think, act, and feel young, the fun culture provides *adults* with identity models as well. If one is supposed to act like a kid, one might as well find out what the kids are doing.) This second hypothesis is a trifle risky, but doubters should look for themselves at, for example, Cadillac advertisements from the late 1930's down to the present. One finds, at about the beginning of the 1960's, a sharp drop in the ages of the owners pictured in the ads. No longer could one sell cars by saying (symbolically) that when one was 55, one arrived at the good life by buying a Cadillac—by 55, one was long "over the hill." As support for this notion, the Crestwood Heights study, which will be referred to in detail later, surveyed a large number of intelligent and influential members of a wealthy community, to find that they felt that the "ideal age" for a woman is 24, while the "ideal age" for a man was only 33.[30] There is, therefore, some support for the thesis that the fun culture provides models for adults as well as children.

We can turn now to the more organized part of the educational fun culture: football games, band concerts, dances, etc. Because the structure is clearer here, we can perhaps speak more knowingly about possible functions. Again we note the tendency toward aggressive competition mixed with sociability, be it the Saturday afternoon football game, the state basketball tournament, or the massed chorus competition. These extracurricular activities are particularly "open system" activities, since they allow the local community to participate, which seldom happens in the "closed system" activities of the formal curriculum.

The structure of competition is of particular interest, in that group sports tend to be those most widely attended. I have suggested before that the football or basketball team represents its constituent community in a very important way, a way in which no individual track star could.[31] When the football team wins, it is a collective effort, and the collectivity symbolically represents the constituent community very well. Thus, when Middletown High plays Hillsdale, the teams truly represent the towns, as when Iowa plays Wisconsin, the teams represent the states. The track or swimming team could never do this, since the structure of competition is basically individual—the teams are teams only partially, never working together simultaneously as a unit.

Although we tend to think that these activities work at cross purposes with the formal curricular structure, the relationship may actually be a symbiotic one, as with marriage and divorce. For example, Waller has shown that this sort of competition has the unifying effect that war can produce by uniting a population in a common cause. Thus, it is a centripital force, acting to pull the school together. Not only does it give the school a sense of closeness and unity; it also provides for a close unifying link between the educational institution and the community, a link which is hard to forge any other way. It provides a medium of communication *between* communities which all can understand. If it is true that aggression is indeed innate, we have here a pattern that allows aggressive impulses to be released in a reasonably harmless way.

This release of aggression may help the formal curricular program in another way, in that it drains off a great deal of energy (from both participants and spectators) which might otherwise be used in activities

---

[30] J. R. Seeley *et al., Crestwood Heights* (New York: Basic Books, Inc., Publishers, 1956).

[31] *Education in Social and Cultural Perspectives* (Englewood Cliffs, N. J.: Prentice-Hall, Inc., 1962), pp. 37–40.

the adult community considers evil. It also provides reasonably healthy adolescent models for the younger children to imitate. This large expenditure of energy, then, may be very useful in the educational enterprise. It also can increase social mobility by providing access to higher education (and to professional sports levels) for those who otherwise might not be able to afford it. There are times when it appears that the amount of energy expended by youth in the fun culture would leave little for "education." (In fact, the dances of the twenties and sixties suggest that these are affluent eras in which the disposal of excess energy represents a major social problem.) In an era in which occupational skills are highly specialized and not much in public view, we have in sports an easily understood system that the audience can share as an exhibition of skill. To support the thesis, it could be pointed out that the television schedules increase their component of sports events constantly.

It is a commonplace today to say that many noneducational institutions perform an "educative" function, in that they formulate or revise the perceptions of the young. These institutions often stoutly deny that they have any impact on, or responsibility for, youth; yet the influence of comics, glamour, movie-star and "love" magazines, radio and television programing and advertising seems undeniable. Many industries have realized the importance of early induction into the product's use—if the *first* time a youngster drinks a bottle of soda, smokes a cigarette, uses cosmetics, he uses your product, you may have a customer for life (and his life will last another 60 years!). Thus, manufacturers and advertisers have tried for years to carefully manipulate the fun culture so that their product will be used on the "first try." Their efforts have not been entirely successful, for some of the reasons we have already pointed out.

However, the future may be promising for manufacturers who wish to manipulate the fun culture. Not only are methods of persuasion and influence getting more sophisticated; also, young people may be increasingly aware of the fact that the fun culture will be a major part of their *adult* lives as well. Sociability, consumership, and skillful use of leisure are areas of the fun culture in which age makes no difference at all. These areas are for the most part outside of the "closed system" of the formal curriculum, yet they increasingly represent major areas of adult life, of great importance in terms of hours spent in them and as a medium of self-expression. College students reading this book will themselves come to know the twenty-hour work week. In this era, the average worker will have about 96 hours a week of waking time to spare, time which will, for the most part, be invested in the fun culture.

It is perhaps time that the formal curriculum structure at least acknowledged the existence of the fun culture, yet the pressures not to do so are strong. (Even in sociology, study of fun culture artifacts is seen by some as "nonacademic," and therefore not worth intensive observation.) The main drawback to the fun culture is its definition of fun. American culture combines romantic and pragmatic elements—we marry for love and work for money. The fun culture is heavily romantic in appeal, and the romantic has always been of short duration, tending toward the search for Instant Bliss. (One product, called "Instant Sex," is now on the market. It comes in a pressure spray can.) Those who come to accept the message that fun comes in a cigarette or a can of beer are bound to be disappointed. There is a great deal of fun inherent in the formal curriculum which is never communicated to students, due largely to our conviction that "learning is a serious business."

Joy is forever beyond the fun culture, yet every teacher has seen, at some time, the exhilaration that students can know in the use of their minds. This type of fun is of a deeper and longer nature. The arts, the world of ideas, sensitivity and wisdom are rich enough and varied enough to provide any person with a lifetime of enrichment and joy. It requires some expenditure of effort on the person's part, but this effort is amply rewarded. It is impossible to imagine either Schiller or Beethoven writing an Ode to Fun.

We are suggesting, therefore, that the structure of the formal curriculum be revised in order to provide a new function: a genuine alternative to the fun culture. To do so would not be necessarily to throw out the existing curriculum but to change the approach to it. The present structure is so highly organized in the area of intellectual competition between individual students that there is little time to savor, reflect on, or enjoy the curriculum for its own sake. When one thinks of the way small children of any race, creed, nationality, or social class take to painting, dancing, singing, telling stories, or finding out about the world around them, one realizes that there is no inherent reason for the almost universal hostility students show toward the formal curriculum. The structural problem rests with the monolithic importance given to individual competition—there must be parts of the curriculum which can be enjoyed (perhaps after hard work) *together*. One of the reasons so many graduate students at the last stages of doctoral work become cynical and disillusioned is that they have for years used their intellectual skills in the competitive battle for academic status, rather than enjoying them for their own sake.[32] Our somewhat ill-advised Protestant heritage tells us that hard work and effort are not to be enjoyed—enjoyment suggests the life of ease and wantonness. But there clearly is a joy in the acquisition

[32] Suggested in conversations with Max Wise of the Danforth Foundation.

of new skills and new awareness that all people of all intelligence levels can feel. If the curriculum were designed to perform this function, most of the problems of the encroachment of the fun culture would solve themselves.

inadvertent learning

A very important subheading under "latent function" concerns the student response that is encouraged or reinforced by the teacher without his being aware of it. Many times, the teacher unwittingly operates to perpetuate student behavior he would like to eliminate. One way this can happen is by the establishment of a self-fulfilling prophecy by the teacher; for example, one high-school teacher began a class by saying, "All right, we'll just wait until it's quiet." Forty minutes later, he was still waiting. Teachers are prophets, also, in regard to the success or failure of certain students—by saying in class that a certain student is probably going to fail, the student's morale can be shattered enough to create the consequence.

As another example of latent learning (*and* teaching), consider the following event. The author was sitting in on a fifth-grade class which was to have a game of spelling "baseball." In this game, there are two teams; the "pitcher" throws a word to the "batter," who goes to first base if he gets it right, etc. It was an intense contest in which the children obviously were very much involved. The author (who was known to the children only as a casual visitor) then asked the children to write down *everything* they had learned during the game. Some of the answers were as follows:

> It is wonderful to be chosen captain.
>
> It is a terrible thing to be chosen the last man on the team.
>
> The pitcher gets lots of attention. I want to be the pitcher the next time.
>
> In the third inning the teacher forgot and gave our team four turns at bat instead of three.
>
> I made Johnny miss his word by tapping my pencil next to his ear.
>
> Bill is the worst speller in our grade.
>
> The teacher gets mad when we cheer too loudly.
>
> I like to be on the team that wins.

Surprisingly enough (at least to the teacher), no one mentioned spelling! To check this, each student was given, the next day, the words he had missed on the previous day's game. No improvement at all was observed. Clearly, what the teacher thought she was teaching and what the students were actually learning were two different things.

One major reason for inadvertent learning is that in a "democratic" institution like a school, everyone is supposed to succeed; and we therefore spend a maximum of our counseling and advising time on the bottom level of the student ability distribution in order to get all students up to a passing level. Particularly at the elementary-school level, teachers will tend to give more rewards, time, and attention to the student who gives the wrong answer than to the student who gives the right one. If the status system is such that students are judged by their peers on how much of the teacher's time, attention, and concern they can get, then the student who gives the wrong answer and gets much of the teacher's time (both to make sure he gets the right answer, and to try to prevent the student from being "damaged" by the trauma of being wrong) may be inclined to give more wrong answers to get more of the attention of the teacher.[33]

There are also individual differences in students' perceptions of teacher's praise—some avoid doing exceptionally good work because they cannot stand the embarrassment of being singled out for group attention. This situation also exists in other cultures:

> Related to this is the Hopi reluctance to stand out, to be singled out from the group. Teachers in Hopi schools have reported discomfort and even tears as a reaction to praise in public. It appears that what is in fact disturbing is the comparative evaluation that results in singling out and praising. . . . Children cannot be persuaded to compete in school, classwork, or in playing games. One school reported that the children learned to play basketball easily, and delighted in the game; but they could not be taught to keep score. They played by the hour without knowing who was winning. Without emphasis on the score, the structure of the game, with everyone doing his utmost within his established role, is in a simplified way similar to the kind of structure we find in the Hopi group.[34]

There seem to be many American students who would share the Hopi view. The teacher who inadvertently stresses competition and individuality as a motivating factor may be producing a reverse effect in some students. The same holds, of course, for the administrator who, in order to get his faculty to "produce" to the utmost, plays one off against another in meaningless competition.

[33] Henry, *op. cit.*
[34] Lee, "Personal Significance and Group Structure," *op. cit.*, p. 20.

Even at the college level, if the instructor has a class of 100 students, there may be one "troublemaker" who always asks nasty or difficult questions in class and seems to be bent on disrupting things. By taking him seriously and responding to his questions with concern and patience, he becomes removed from the anonymous category of his 99 peers; the instructor has to recognize this one person as a person, thus giving him rewards which are not (and perhaps cannot be) given to the other 99 students. For just this same reason, foremen in factories have been known to promote the troublemaker or clown to a higher position, both because it will make the foreman's job easier, and because the clown has visibility —he may be the only worker that the foreman knows.

reciprocity and autonomy
as functions in education

Part of the difficulty in doing a functional analysis of American education involves the relationship of the almost limitless number of "parts" to the "whole." The "whole" is so diffuse, so unsystematic, that it defies description, much less analysis. One of the major reasons for this vagueness in our conception of "American Education" is the tremendous amount of autonomy and the corresponding lack of reciprocity between the subsystems in education. Each school system, each college and university, is structured to operate as if no others existed. Within the individual educational system, some reciprocity is provided between the governing, administrative teaching, and student sectors, at least enough to keep the enterprise going. Similarly, in undergraduate admissions, the system of "Carnegie Units" provides a minimal base or unit of exchange between high schools and college (although it must be said that the Advanced Placement courses have made the evaluation of a high-school record much more difficult and the "unit" system less useful).

Working toward more reciprocity in the system are the state boards of education with a chief executive, the regional accrediting bodies, and the federal government working chiefly through the U.S. Office of Education. These relationships are tricky, causing emotions occasionally to rise, due chiefly to our commitment that freedom and autonomy are the same thing. The autonomous school is, therefore, the free school. We also used to think that the town that was totally independent from all other towns was free. However, communication, travel, electric power, and food supply would be impossible without a system of reciprocal coordination between communities.

If we accept for a moment the distinction between freedom *from* and freedom *to*,[35] we can say that the autonomous system may have freedom from (oppression by outsiders, coercion, and persuasion), but not the freedom to do, to grow, to become something new. The autonomous community (or school) is thus a "closed system," and its freedom is confined to current activities *within* the system. The "open system" of reciprocity provides far more potential for growth, change, and adaptation—it is limited only by the quality and quantity of reciprocation. It is strange but true that autonomy (which did provide freedom in a static culture) may work against freedom in a rapidly changing culture, such as our own.

However, these reciprocal relationships between educational subsystems must be voluntary, not coerced, if the individual institution is to retain the right to decide what it wants to become. Thus, more reciprocal relations in education could (and indeed should) result in more, not less, diversity. The specter of a monolithic educational system, with every movement of every teacher controlled by a single central authority (Washington, probably), is really not very likely. What should be worried about is the totally autonomous local educational institution, which does control every movement of every teacher, which is totally closed to new ideas, which makes no effort to change or improve, which wishes only to maintain a "steady state" of that which it is now doing. Totalitarianism can, after all, occur in individual subsystems as well as in aggregates. The institution that knows the directions in which it should move has nothing to fear from reciprocal relations with other institutions. The greatest danger is with those institutions which wish only to continue what they are presently doing, without knowing why.

conclusions

The structure and functions of American educational institutions are extremely diverse. Within this diversity, we are doing many things to students we do not wish to do. Diversity (in the sense of insularity) is not an unqualified virtue, unless the diversity is assisting the institutions to improve. Reciprocity is vital if we are to find out what other institutions are doing. If every scientist had to discover every scientific law for himself, we would be back in the Stone Age. Yet, the dissemination of new developments in education is often extremely poor, due largely to the resistance of the autonomous institution to anything which comes from "outside."

[35] Erich Fromm, *Escape from Freedom* (New York: Holt, Rinehart & Winston, Inc., 1941), as well as his later works.

We spend, in education, considerable time formulating the functions we wish the schools to perform. Every college catalog, every high-school brochure gives a very clear, often noble and inspiring view of the functions that school or college performs. What is being suggested here is that the educational structure may not be well adapted to meet these functions. There is a real dearth of thinking about alternative ways of structuring educational institutions so that they might fulfill, in a more genuine, effective way, the functions we now say (and fervently hope) they do.

We also must take seriously Merton's warning that to change a social structure without being aware of the latent functions being performed by that structure may be extremely dangerous. We need to give thought to both structure and function, realizing that new functions may well require new structures. (As an example, a slum school and an upper-middle-class suburban school may have very different functions, but as structures, they are often identical. What sort of alternative structures might better fulfill the functions of *particular* schools? The question deserves consideration.)

EXTRA BIBLIOGRAPHY ON FUNCTIONALISM

Probably the major writer in this category today is Talcott Parsons. He is very difficult to read. Most important are *The Social System* (New York: Free Press of Glencoe, Inc., 1951); *Essays in Sociological Theory* (New York: Free Press of Glencoe, Inc., 1954); *Structure and Process in Modern Societies* (New York: Free Press of Glencoe, Inc. 1961). As examples of the application of theory to practice, see his "A Revised Analytical Approach to the Theory of Social Stratification," in Bendix and Lipset (eds.), *Class, Status, and Power*, (New York: Free Press of Glencoe, Inc. 1953); and more concretely (and less effectively), "The School Class as a Social System," *Harvard Educational Review*, **29** (1959), 297–318.

Criticisms of Parsons abound. Most of the best can be found in Max Black, ed., *The Social Theories of Talcott Parsons* (Englewood Cliffs, N.J.: Prentice-Hall, Inc., 1961). Also good are Daniel Foss, "The World View of Talcott Parsons," in Stein and Vidich, eds., *Sociology on Trial* (Englewood Cliffs, N.J.: Prentice-Hall, Inc., 1963); and the devastating remarks of C. Wright Mills, "The Grand Theorists," in *The Sociological Imagination* (New York: Oxford University Press, 1959).

The argument over functionalism was so decisive that Kingsley Davis, president of the American Sociological Association, devoted his presidential address for 1959 to it, "The Myth of Functionalism as a Special Method in Sociology and Anthropology," *American Sociological Review*,

24 (1959), 757–71. Davis (who is one of the major exponents of the functionalist theory of stratification) tried to call off the debate by asking what *non*functionalism was; then, satisfied that there was no answer, proclaimed that everyone belonged in the functionalist camp. In 1961, Ronald Dore answered, stating that Davis had neglected important differences in sociological analysis: "Function and Cause," *American Sociological Review,* **26** (1961), 843–53.

The references cited as footnotes in the text, plus this bibliography, should provide the reader with a range of information on the topic.

4: social stratification— systems of closure

As we will discover in the chapter on creativity, words have an inherent tendency toward disclosing part of "reality" to us, while at the same time blinding us to the rest. When we think of "stratification," "stratify," or "strata," our minds conjure up an image something like a sedimentary

rock formation: ▦ . If we were to take our rock and turn it on its

side thus:▕▏▎▏▕ , we might conclude that the perspective was in error,

since rocks generally form in *horizontal*, not vertical, layers. There is a

vitally important difference between the two diagrams. If we drilled

a core out of the first: ▦ , there would be a definite difference

between the "top" and "bottom" of the sample, while if we took a core of the second: ⌷⌷ , all parts of the core would be virtually identical. This

little excursion into geology has a purpose: when we speak of *social*

strata, we again, because of our inheritance of perceptions from the world
of rocks, think of a basically *horizontal* set of layers of people—if "cored,"
containing a "top" and "bottom" layer.

This predisposition blinds us to other arrangements that layers could
take. The usual circularity of the dictionary definition extends us no help
on this problem; *Webster's Third International* tells us that stratification
is "the act or process of stratifying or state of being stratified: disposal
or growth in layers." For instance, a cross section of a tree will reveal a

pattern of layers: ◎ , but these layers are *circular* and *vertical*, while

those of rocks are *straight* and *horizontal*. A tree trunk does not reveal

its pattern of stratification: ▯ ; its layers have an *inner* and *outer* di-

mension, rather than *top* to *bottom*. Thus we have difficulty in thinking

that trees are (as is the case) stratified.

It may well be that for the analysis of human patterns of social stratification, the tree cross-section model, suggesting inner dimensions, would
be at least as productive as the top-and-bottom analogy we get from
the rock example. For instance, if there is a ruling "establishment" in
America, as Rovere and others have suggested, it might be more useful
to think of it as the central, or "inside," strata, rather than the "top."

Leaving the problem of models aside for the moment, it is clear that
some "layering" or differentiation between people is characteristic of
virtually all human societies. This differentiation may take many forms,
but two of the major ones are those of *role* and *status*.[1] As we said in
Chapter 2, role refers to the parts we play in the drama of life (such as
mother, father, son, daughter), while status refers to the amount and
kind of regard others have for us as persons and for the activities we
perform.

The early functionalists, seeing that stratification was present in all
human societies (and many subhuman ones as well), proclaimed that because stratification was *universal,* it must be *necessary,* and proceeded to
seek out *the* "function" (note the singular) of *all* stratification systems.

---

[1] These terms were first used by Ralph Linton in *The Study of Man* (New York:
Appleton-Century & Appleton-Century-Crofts, 1936).

Marxist theory, which emphasizes the importance of conflict between the layers, and the resultant confusion and disorganization, was not a very appealing model for those who were trying to describe human society as *system*atic. What was needed was something once described by Veblen as a germfree system of knowledge, to be kept in a cool, dry place.

At approximately the same time, two different explanations of (or rationales for) systems of stratification were developed. Both have been the subject of vigorous debate within the field of sociology since their inception between 1940 and 1945. The first of these theoretical positions was taken by Davis and Moore, who saw a system based largely on differentiation of social *reward* or status. Some members of a society clearly have more of this status than others—it is a form of social currency, almost like a monetary system, a medium of exchange.

Like Adam Smith some years earlier, Davis and Moore saw this "system" as operating in an autonomous fashion, guided perhaps by some sort of "invisible hand," if we may continue with the economic analogy. They assumed, as functionalists generally do, that in order to attain maximum "efficiency" in a social system, those who have the best qualifications for the jobs which "must be done" in the society if it is to survive must be guided to those jobs (or roles) they can do best. Assuming that people operate on a "what's in it for me" approach, they postulated that a system of unequal social rewards (status) was "necessary" in order to lure the right man to the right job. (Job is being used here in the sense of role: *any* activity, not specifically occupational activity. One of the "jobs" of women, in this sense, is the production and nurturance of children, whether they get paid for it or not.) As Davis and Moore have put it:

> Social inequality is thus an unconsciously evolved device by which societies insure that the most important positions are conscientiously filled by the most qualified persons.[2]

Two factors were set forth which would determine the amount of status (social reward) given the performer and the task: first, relative scarcity of personnel able to do the job; second, the "functional" importance to the society of getting the job done. Based on an index of these two factors, the society, in some unexplained way, rewards people differ-

---

[2] K. Davis and W. E. Moore, "Some Principles of Stratification," *American Sociological Review*, **10** (1945), 242–49. Also K. Davis, "A Conceptual Analysis of Stratification," *American Sociological Review*, **7** (1941), 309–21, and K. Davis, *Human Society* (New York: The Macmillan Company, 1949), especially pp. 365–70. For a good critique of their definitions and method, see M. Tumin, "Some Principles of Stratification: A Critical Analysis," *American Sociological Review*, **18** (1953), 387–94.

entially, luring the "best" people into the most "important" tasks or activities. Thus, for a society in which food is plentiful, the role of Hunter would not be overloaded with status, while in a society with a scarce food supply, he who supplies food should be heaped with power, honor, glory—status.

This view, which has strong undertones of our notions of free enterprise capitalism, contains some interesting assumptions: first, that people are *equally* interested in social status; second, the status which the person inherits from his parents at birth (ascribed status), coming not from his skills but from his progenitors, is left unaccounted for. (It would seem that ascribed status is working *against* the Davis-Moore position, as it often works to make sure that the best-qualified person does *not* get the job. The son of the chief has a very good chance of being chief, even though he may not be the "best man." Mark Twain's story of the visitor to heaven is relevant here. The visitor told St. Peter that he wanted to meet the greatest general who ever lived. St. Peter pointed out a small man with wings, at which the visitor cried out, "But I knew that man in life, and he was only a simple shoemaker!" "Yes," replied St. Peter, "but if he *had been* a general, he would have been the greatest.")

Every society, through its system of social stratification, holds back, or reduces the life chances, of certain members of the society. (I have come to call this index the "garbage factor" of a society.) If any members who are held back are those with the greatest potential, then the stratification system obviously defeats itself, at least in terms of the Davis-Moore thesis. The thesis also has an elitist ring to it. T. S. Eliot, for example, said earlier in *Notes Towards the Definition of Culture:*

> However moderately and unobtrusively the doctrine of elites is put, it implies a radical transformation of society. Superficially, it appears to aim at no more than what we must all desire—that all positions in society should be occupied by those who are best fitted to exercise the functions of the positions.[3]

Another assumption of the Davis-Moore view is that the society functions essentially like an organism, that the society has a life of its own, distinct from the existence of the people who comprise it. Thus the system of status rewards is intentionally controlled or manipulated by the "society" to lure the "best" people to the "most important" tasks. In the chapter on functionalism, we have discussed some of the obvious dangers of this point of view.

[3] T. S. Eliot, *Notes Towards the Definition of Culture* (New York: Harcourt, Brace & World, Inc., 1949), p 35.

The major assumption of the Davis-Moore theory, and one most often criticised, is the notion that *only* with a system of social inequality (unequal status awards) can a society survive. Many writers have suggested that there are alternatives to inequality, even within the functionalist camp.[4] For example, Richard Schwartz has pointed out that in some societies, particularly in two Israeli settlements which he studied extensively, other devices besides inequality operate to bring talented people to the conscientious performance of vital tasks. B. F. Skinner, although a psychologist, has designed a rather effective plan for a modern utopia in which inequality in the *task* system has been virtually eliminated.[5] (Whether or not *Walden Two* will become a social reality or not is open for discussion.) Tumin, a frequent and perceptive critic of the Davis-Moore position, has stated more recently that there may be many forms of inequality in a society (such as hair and eye color) that never get incorporated into a system of *social* stratification (a system of unequal award of social status).[6]

There seems to have been some modification of the Davis-Moore view, at least as seen in a special issue of the *American Sociological Review*, and in an earlier article by Davis.[7] Many of the normative assumptions of their position have been noted, particularly the bias toward system maintenance and away from innovation and change. They still contend, however, that the total *elimination* of inequality represents a social impossibility. It is here that the arguments of Parsons, the other major theorist to enter this internecine struggle, are persuasive. In a rather oversimplified manner, we could say that Parsons bases his view on the inevitable possibility of evaluating human *activity* of virtually any kind in a normative way.[8] Any action we undertake can be said by others to have been done well or poorly, and we *may* get praise or rebuke for our action. (As

[4] See R. Schwartz, "Functional Alternatives to Inequality," *American Sociological Review*, **20** (1955), 424–30; R. Simpson, "A Modification of the Functional Theory of Social Stratification," *Social Forces*, **35** (1956), 132–37, and W. Buckley, "Social Stratification and the Functional Theory of Social Differentiation," *American Sociological Review*, **23** (1958), 369–75. More recently, see the special issue of the *American Sociological Review*, dealing with articles by Fallding, Tumin, and two by Moore, **28** (Feb. 1963), on the problem of functionalism and inequality.

[5] *Walden Two* (New York: The Macmillan Company, 1948).

[6] M. Tumin, "On Inequality," *American Sociological Review*, **28** (1963), 19–26. On the issue of social change and functionalism, see K. Bock, "Evolution, Function and Change," *American Sociological Review*, **28** (1963), 229–37.

[7] *American Sociological Review*, Feb. 1963. Also, K. Davis, "Reply to Tumin," *American Sociological Review*, **18** (1953), 394–97, in which Davis notes these criticisms of his view.

[8] T. Parsons, "A Revised Analytical Approach to the Theory of Social Stratification," in R. Bendix and S. Lipset, eds., *Class, Status, and Power* (New York: Free Press of Glencoe, Inc., 1953), pp. 92–128. See the bibliography on Parsons in the chapter on functionalism of this book.

an example of how this factor can be manipulated, consider the campaign of toothpaste manufacturers to set up in each family a status system based on how "well" each person brushed his teeth!)

To summarize this theoretical discussion, we can say that some kind of system of social stratification is present in virtually every human society. We cannot say that this system is functionally *necessary* for the continuation of society, but we can say that it seems to be a fact of human existence. This is due more to the ability of human beings to compare and evaluate performance than it is to the more elaborate and deterministic (and teleological) Davis-Moore position. (To point out the pervasive quality of human evaluation, one may point to the cartoon of two bums sitting on a park bench, one saying to the other, "Why, I'm *twice* the social failure that you are!")

The interactionist approach to stratification would indicate that in the dynamic processes of human interaction, *both* equality and inequality are involved. The stratification system defines and limits, while *at the same time* it provides mobility, to allow some people to pass through the barriers. Inequality—of position, reward, opportunity—points up those interactive processes by which individuals compare themselves with others, and compete with others for the good things they consider important. Equality is the other side of the *same coin*, suggesting human relationships that are cooperative and collective rather than individual, and in which individual gain may be sacrificed for the good of the whole. From the Greek Agora to the Trobriand Island culture, we can see that the interaction of these two components in some sort of *reciprocal* way is at the heart of all organized human societies. The functionalists, who have set up many dichotomies after "pulling these components out" for analysis, have not been able to put them back and see what happens. It is the interaction of systems of equality and inequality within a given social organization or society that should be the next target for sociological analysis. A meaningful theory of interactive stratification has yet to be formulated, but its value would be great.

the concept of social class— history

The notion that human societies are not only stratified but that the layers represent separate, very autonomous groups serving very different "functions" goes back to the beginnings of recorded history. Plato, one of the first to commit the anthropomorphic fallacy, felt that a society was a single man writ large. Just as the various *organs* of the human body perform various "functions," so the various social "organs" (classes) of a society operate:

> . . . if two things, one large, the other small, are called by the same name, they will be alike in that respect to which the common name applies. Accordingly, in so far as the quality of justice is concerned, there will be no difference between a just man and a just society.
>
> We decided that a society was just when each of the three types of human character it contained performed its own function; and again, it was temperate and brave and wise by virtue of certain other affections and states of mind of those same types.[9]

In a just society, says Plato, wisdom rules the elements of spirit and appetites. In similar fashion, he believes that all men have an *innate* tendency to be governed by one of these three elements: ergo, there are in his ideal Republic, three social classes: one concerned with physical appetites, one with spirit or patriotism, and the ruling philosopher kings in whom wisdom rules. The sorting and selecting of the people into their proper "class" was to be done by the educational system. With Plato's assumptions about the dominance of innate characteristics, the job of the educational system was very simple: at each level of increasing abstraction in the curriculum, those who were innately incapable of understanding things at that level would simply drop off and join their "proper" class. Environmental effects were of no concern to Plato, and thus were ignored in the educational scheme.

The realities of history tell us that some sort of system of social stratification has been operating since the cessation of nomadic tribes and the beginnings of town life, some seven or eight thousand years ago. Population concentrations, new agriculture and technology meant that some men could exist without devoting all their energies to the acquisition of food for themselves. Out of this division of labor came several specialized groups, particularly the priest and warrior classes. However, the vast majority of these early civilizations were peasants and slaves, on whose muscular backs rested the framework of the social class system (in Plato's own time, the "democratic" process of the Athenians was supported by thousands of slaves who were considered by the citizens to be subhuman animals). This essential dichotomy of rulers and slaves was supported and intensified by the various systems of writing, which gave to the ruling classes the gift of collective memory. Keeping the peasants and slaves as ignorant as possible was one important characteristic of a successful ruler.

With the breakdown of the feudal manors, the increase in the desire

[9] *The Republic*, trans. Cornford (New York: Oxford University Press, 1945), p. 131.

to explore the rest of the world, and the evolution of a sophisticated system of currency, the "third estate" of economically oriented entrepreneurs came into being. Here, in the development of a bourgeoisie, is a vital shift in thinking about social classes. The old split between rulers and slaves was broken, perhaps for the first and last time. When Luther gave to every man the right to know and understand the Bible for himself, the break in the social control of ignorance, particularly in terms of the printed page, sharply reduced the gulf between ruler and slave. Although the entrepreneur class was never cohesive and contained very disparate elements, it did drive a wedge that spelled the end of the estate system and the beginnings of a basically urban pattern of social classes which is still with us in contemporary life.

social stratification and social class

There is an important distinction we must make between a system of stratification and a system of social classes. We can stratify people by as many categories as there are ways in which people differ; if we include both attributes and actions, the number is infinite. However, if the differentiating characteristic is important to the people involved, and if they see themselves as being different from "the rest," if there is on their part a *consciousness of kind*, then we are in the realm of *social* classes. A statistical category is not a social class. For example, if we got together all redheaded people in our society, it is unlikely that they would be different from others in any other way *except* hair color—this attribute does not have the power of differentiation needed to produce a social class; redheads do not live in certain areas, hold certain jobs, make certain amounts of money, vote in certain ways, buy certain kinds of cars, join certain types of organizations, etc. Thus we have here a criterion by which people may be stratified, but we do not have the makings of a *social* class. The two necessary conditions for a social class are (1) a *consciousness* on the part of the individuals in the class that they are different in significant ways from the rest; (2) some differential *behaviors* which are not shared, at least not to the same extent, with the rest of society. If we were to change the criterion from color of hair to color of skin, it is clear that we would be in the realm of social class, if not "caste." The Negro-white distinction, for example, would yield both class consciousness and differential behavior; the latter particularly in terms of residence areas, occupations engaged in, earned income, voting rights, geographical spread throughout the country, etc.

These two criteria have made trouble for virtually every investigator who has attempted an analysis of the structure of social classes in the United States. The major difficulty concerns the lack of *direct* measurement of social class; it is of necessity symbolic, inferential, and arbitrary. For example, one researcher may use the occupation of the respondents as his index of "class," while another may use income, or type of house, or location of house, or educational level of parents, or of children, or number of major appliances owned, or "cultural level" of television programs watched, or number, year, and costs of automobiles owned, ad infinitum. The researcher is almost completely free to choose his own index of social class membership, with little opportunity to validate his choice. Thus, social class comes to mean that which the observer *thinks* it means, so that the sociologist often creates something he calls social class by using a certain set of categories. Other researchers, using different categories, may study the same people and come up with an entirely different conclusion regarding the existence of social classes. The need for empirically agreed-upon ground rules for the investigation of social class is obvious and urgent.

problems in measuring social class

In general, there have been four views of the social class structure that have dominated research done in this field. (There are about one thousand articles and books published since 1925 which deal with social classes in America, so that we are talking about a large segment of the field of sociology. The depression was probably the most important trigger for much of this research, since it caused most people to re-evaluate their notions of America as the land of opportunity in which hard work would inevitably get anyone to "the top," a land without social class restrictions.)

the assumption of discrete, closed classes

The assumption of discrete, closed classes was most often seen in the work of those who, particularly in the thirties and forties, investigated whole communities. This was, for the most part, a time when America was still a nation of small towns, and the vast urban and suburban migration so typical of contemporary American life,[10] had not

10 As often as not, the "small town" is not dying out but is expanding into a large city. Thus, the "death" of a small town is often due to growth into another category of size. But many local unincorporated towns are showing a decline in

reached anything like its present proportions. The notion of studying an entire community was one borrowed from the anthropological studies of "primitive" communities which were very much in vogue in the middle and late thirties; in fact, W. Lloyd Warner, the chief exponent of the community study approach, was himself an anthropologist. Under Warner's aegis, the so-called "Chicago School" completed a large number of intensive investigations of American communities which have codified much of our thinking about social classes in America. The importance of anthropological perspective was made quite clear by Warner in a "summary" book published in 1953, after he had finished the first four volumes of the prodigious "Yankee City" study: [11]

> For the last twenty years the author, in collaboration with social anthropologists and other social scientists, has studied American communities with techniques he had previously used in the investigation of Australian tribes. . . . In popular belief modern man seems far removed from his Stone Age kinsmen of aboriginal Australia; but, despite obvious differences, the fundamental core of life of each is very much the same. . . . From the beginning of the research on America I was struck with the basic similarities between the meanings and functions of American myth and ceremony and those of aboriginal Australia.[12]

As proof of his commitment to anthropology, Warner's first chapter consists of an analysis of an American "sacred ceremony," Memorial Day, while the second is subtitled "Social Anthropology and Modern Life." He is without question a fine anthropologist, particularly in his perceptive treatment of the "latent," symbolic meanings inherent in some of the events which we do not perceive. For example, his conclusion to the chapter on Memorial Day as a sacred rite is worth repeating here:

> The Memorial Day rite is a cult of the dead, but not just of the dead as such, since by symbolically elaborating sacrifice for the country through, or identifying it with, the Christian Church's sacred sacrifice of their god,

---

population, or at best a maintenance of past levels which, in an era of population growth, is indicative of a relative decline. See Glenn Fuguitt, "The Growth and Decline of Small Towns," *American Sociological Review*, **30** (1965), 403–11.

[11] All five volumes were published by Yale University Press:

1. *The Social Life of a Modern Community* (1941).
2. *The Status System of a Modern Community* (1943).
3. *The Social Systems of American Ethnic Groups* (1945).
4. *The Social System of the Modern Factory* (1947).
5. *The Living and the Dead: A Study of the Symbolic Life of Americans* (1959).

A one-volume summary of the series, titled *Yankee City* (highly recommended) was published by Yale University Press in 1963.

[12] *American Life: Dream and Reality* (Chicago: University of Chicago Press, 1953), pp. viii-ix.

the deaths of such men also become powerful sacred symbols which organize, direct, and constantly revive the collective ideals of the community and the nation.[13]

The mythical names given by Warner to the communities he studied, such as Yankee City, Elmtown, Middletown, Jonesville, have become household terms in the vocabularies of many Americans. It should also be said that by calling Newburyport, Massachusetts, "Yankee City," Warner was encouraging his readers to generalize the research results from the specific town to the nation. In the public consciousness, "Middletown" comes to mean not just one specific place but *every* town. As in the case of Kinsey's research in another field, it would be difficult indeed to measure Warner's influence on American perceptions of the nature of social classes, but it would seem reasonable to assume that the influence has been strong.

Warner's basic thesis was that a six-class system could be found in virtually any part of the United States, with very little variation as one moved. The six classes were arrived at by forming upper, middle, and lower horizontal layers and getting an upper and lower component of each; thus, the upper-uppers, lower-uppers, upper-middles, lower-middles, upper-lowers, and lower-lowers. It is very difficult to get at the assumptions on which this pattern was formulated in the first place. It is clear that in every study published, the researchers went in with techniques for finding a six-class system. Remarkably enough, they usually found what they were looking for. Warner assumed in selecting Newburyport for study as "Yankee City" that here was a firmly established "old-line" American upper crust community, yet a competent historian who has studied Newburyport for years has pointed out the fact that most of the supposed noble ancestry and long-term influence of the upper class in that city is pure myth.[14] (On the other hand, the Warner approach may still be valid, if people *act* as they would if the myth were historically valid.)

The Yankee City studies suggest that the American social class system is *roughly* as follows (the tenths are rounded):

upper-upper	1.4%
lower-upper	1.6%
upper-middle	10.0%
lower-middle	28.0%
upper-lower	33.0%
lower-lower	25.0%

[13] *Ibid.*, p. 26. It must be said that Warner was an extremely astute observer of the symbolic structures in cultural activities. Vol. V of the *Yankee City* series is extremely original and stimulating.

[14] S. Thernstrom, "Yankee City Revisited: The Perils of Historical Naiveté," *American Sociological Review*, 30 (1965), 234–42.

In each of the three main groupings, then, Warner felt that the upper class represented about 3 per cent of the total population, the middle class 38 per cent, the lower class 58 per cent. Thus, the class structure for Warner resembled a pyramid, with the lower class forming the base:

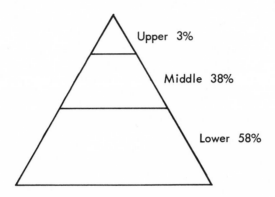

The devices used by Warner to place members of the community in their social classes were twofold: first, a measure of "objective" or material indications of class, such as type of house, occupation, income, and neighborhood (referred to as the Index of Status Characteristics, or ISC), and a measure of the individual's social participation in community affairs (known as Evaluative Participation, or EP). These techniques have been very clearly presented in a manual, now widely available for those who wish to make use of them.[15]

criticisms of the Warner approach

As one might expect, there have been a large number of critical appraisals of the contributions of the Warner school.[16] Many of these are technical and not worth exploring here, but certain major points should be made clear. First, Warner's methods were designed for the investigation of small, relatively closed communities, in which people knew each other and worked where they lived. The highly mobile population of today, with more than one car per family, living in a megalopolis, or urban sprawl, contains a far greater

[15] W. L. Warner, M. Meeker, K. Eells, *Social Class in America* (Chicago: Science Research Associates, 1949).

[16] E.g., H. Pfautz *et. al.*, "The Current Literature of Social Stratification," *American Journal of Sociology*, **58** (1953), also, R. Kornhauser, "The Warner Approach to Social Stratification," in Bendix and Lipset, *op. cit.*, pp. 224–54.

fluidity of movement, and a greater flexibility of status judgments than was the case in Warner's small towns. Small, relatively closed communities still exist, of course, and are still being studied,[17] but not as typical of America as a whole.

Warner was never able to establish a clustering or central tendency within each of his social classes, which would be necessary to support his belief in a system of relatively closed, autonomous social classes. In every case, on virtually every measure, people spread evenly over his class categories, making the cutting edges arbitrary indeed. Thus, it would appear that the community studies of the Warner school, although of great interest in a historical sense,[18] and rich in the symbolic analysis of American cultural traits, cannot support the central assertion that there exists in America a stable system of six finite social classes.

the assumption of social class as a continuum

The notion of social class as a continuum, although more difficult to deal with empirically than sorting people arbitrarily into six boxes, suggests that it is in the *overlapping* of class lines that we may look for clues as to how people work within a class system, if indeed they do. Two extensive studies, one of Danielson, Connecticut, and one of Columbus, Ohio, indicate that most people do operate on perceptions of status differences in the people around them, but that no *fixed number* of classes exist.[19] Many of the same criteria used by Warner (occupation, type of house, dwelling area) were used here, but the conclusion seems warranted that any division of the sample into a finite number of classes would be an arbitrary and somewhat capricious act, unsupported by the data. In terms of informal associations and friendship patterns, the data supports the notion that the overlap of personal associations is considerable:

> It was discovered that the majority of Columbus respondents do not choose as close associates individuals whose social status is quite similar to their own. But neither do people usually associate, on an intimate level, with those whose social status is very much higher or very much lower

[17] See Vidich and Bensman, *Small Town in Mass Society* (New York: Doubleday & Company, Inc., 1960).

[18] See Maurice Stein, *The Eclipse of Community* (Princeton, N.J.: Princeton University Press, 1960).

[19] G. Lenski, "America's Social Classes: Statistical Strata or Social Groups?" *American Journal of Sociology*, **58** (1952), 134–44; and W. Kenkel, "Social Stratification in Columbus, Ohio," in J. Cuber and W. Kenkel, *Social Stratification* (New York: Appleton-Century & Appleton-Century Crofts, 1954), Chap. 7.

than their own. Each person, in a sense, marks off on the status continuum *his own* loosely defined "range of acceptance" and chooses his friends within this range.[20]

How and why individuals differ in the range of acceptance within which they choose their personal associates remains an interesting area for investigation.[21]

If we accept this continuum notion, then some other factors are also easier to accept. For example, Warner characterized each of his classes as having a definite *value* structure, with very little overlap. Kahl has aptly put the descriptions thus: the upper class: graceful living, the upper-middle class: career, the lower-middle class: respectability, the working class: get by, the lower class: apathy.[22] If we accept the notion that these values are arranged on a continuum, that the overlap is considerable and of importance, then the value descriptions just given make a little more sense. Novelists have long seen the advantages of a plot in which one person's values deviate sharply from the values of those who surround him. For example, in *An American Tragedy,* Dreiser's "hero," Clyde Griffiths moves from a job as a Chicago bellhop to membership in an old-line Eastern family, living the "American Dream" of social mobility, but with bitter irony. Certainly, many social critics have recently pointed out that apathy, considered a province of the lower class, has spread *throughout* the continuum of social status. Therefore, we should be as concerned for the "mix" and diffusion of these value dimensions through-out the status continuum as we are for the dividing lines (if any). We will return to this point later.

This discussion also suggests that the status *perceptions* of individuals, rather than of groups, needs much more attention. To whom does the individual refer for his standards? How does he go about using these reference groups, and to what ends? Hyman has put the matter well:

> The variables of status are mediated through an individual who acts selec-tively in his choice of reference groups, who strives selectively for status, whose personal values affect the composition of status and the emotional composition of a given status, whose conceptualization of a reference group may be different from its actual character, who is not affected by

[20] Kenkel, *op. cit.,* pp. 151–52.

[21] The ability of people to accept others from differing backgrounds and status levels has been insightfully studied by M. Rokeach, *The Open and Closed Mind* (New York: Basic Books, Inc., Publishers, 1960). A well-written account of research which is significant for all educators.

[22] J. Kahl, *The American Class Structure* (New York: Holt, Rinehart & Winston, Inc., 1957), 184–220. [*Excellent* notes, and probably the best summary volume on social stratification. See also B. Barber, *Social Stratification* (New York: Harcourt, Brace & World, Inc., 1957), for a good summary from the functionalist point of view.]

all aspects of the culture nor by all references in the environment. This essentially personal aspect of status cannot be ignored. We cannot deal with these variables independent of their meaning to individuals.[23]

The continuum model is certainly a reasonable one, and unquestionably eliminates much of the arbitrary and unwarranted categorization typical of the early community studies. On the other hand, it leaves us with *no* categories, *no* ways of making useful distinctions. More needs to be discovered about how individuals perceive status, and how these perceptions vary on the status continuum.

individual class consciousness

The major study of this phenomenon is by Richard Centers, entitled *The Psychology of Social Classes*.[24] Centers was particularly interested in the relationship between the occupation of a person and his attitudes, particularly in the political and economic realm. He found, as might be expected, that the higher the occupational status of the respondent, the more conservative his attitudes would be. However, this attitude change as one progressed up the occupational status ladder formed a continuum again, not a discrete series of closed categories. Centers was also interested in whether or not people could place themselves in a social class. For this purpose, he used the categories which a study in *Fortune* magazine had indicated were the most widely used—upper, middle, working, and lower, even though in the *Fortune* study it was made clear that about 28 per cent of the sample said they could not answer the question, and almost half used terms other than upper, middle, working, and lower.[25] Centers' interviewers therefore asked the following question, "If you were asked to use one of these four names for your social class, which would you say you belonged in: the middle class, lower class, working class, or upper class?" As might be expected, his original sample of 1,100 Americans avoided the upper and lower designations like the plague, 43 per cent calling themselves middle class and 51 per cent working class, leaving the tiny remainder for the top and bottom.

[23] H. Hyman, "The Psychology of Status," *Archives of Psychology*, 269 (1942), 80. See also the fine treatment of reference group theory in R. Merton and A. Kitt, "Contributions to the Theory of Reference Group Behavior," in P. Lazarsfeld and R. Merton, eds., *Continuities in Social Research* (New York: Free Press of Glencoe, Inc., 1950).

[24] (Princeton, N.J.: Princeton University Press, 1949). See also J. Haer, "A Comparative Study of the Classification Techniques of Warner and Centers," *American Sociological Review*, 20 (1955), 689–92. Using Warner's ISC in three cities, he found great differences in status perceptions.

[25] *Fortune*, Feb. 1940, esp. p. 14.

As one goes through the occupational status of respondents in Centers' study, one is struck by the fact that those whose work does not involve manual labor (large and small business entrepreneurs, professionals, clerical workers) overwhelmingly thought of themselves as middle class, while those whose work is with their hands (skilled and semiskilled manual, unskilled) considered themselves as members of the working class. Centers' research thus seems to support the "collar" view, that the white collar person has a "consciousness of kind" when compared with a blue collar person. There is considerable evidence, which will be presented in the chapter on mobility, that the "collar" line is a very difficult one to cross; that if a father is a manual worker, the chances are *very* good that his sons will also be manual workers.

Even this distinction is very blurred, in Centers' research, since every occupational category was represented in the "working class," and one also wonders if the doctor and the shoe saleman had the same thing in mind when each called himself a member of the "middle class." Thus the semantic problem of the meaning of class *for the respondent* remains unanswered. There will probably be as many answers to that problem as the number of respondents.

the concept of status consistency

It should be clear that we are driving for an interpretation of stratification which will be based on the "world view" of each individual we are studying. One way of doing this is by making the *individual*, not the group, the center of our statistical universe, then developing techniques for measuring his status in terms of major dimensions of human activity, such as religious, political, economic, etc., and comparing his rankings on each dimension to get some idea of how consistently his status rankings follow him through his most significant activities. The comparison of people with fairly consistent status evaluations with those exhibiting very inconsistent patterns has been done by Lenski,[26] as well as by many others now using this approach. Generally, four indexes are used for each person: occupation, income, education, and ethnic background. Although much more needs to be done, it is clear that those with consistent status ranks on the four criteria will have different political beliefs and patterns of social interaction, when compared to those whose consistency (or crystallization) is low. A striking example of this is the high rate of suicide among those

[26] "Status Crystallization: A Non-Vertical Dimension of Social Status," *American Sociological Review*, **19** (1954), 405–13; and also his "Social Participation and Status Crystallization," *American Sociological Review*, **21** (1956), 458–64.

who are moving *down* through the occupational status hierarchy, who are losing occupational status rapidly while maintaining "position" in some other areas.[27] Those with high status inconsistency perceive life as being more stressful than those whose status ratings are consistent.[28] As we said in Chapter 2, role consistency is one good index of mental health and stability.

With this approach, we are moving much closer to a formulation of how the individual sees *himself* and *others* in status terms. One general finding of importance is that people do not seem to operate on a basis of their average on the four status ranks—they do not total them and divide by four. (If that were the case, those moving downward through occupation could save their self-esteem by the other three categories, with the result that suicide rates for this group might not be so high.) *Each* of these areas—occupation, income, education, and ethnic origin—is a separate and important component of the person's status judgment.

Much more needs to be done, particularly in finding out what other major dimensions of status are used by people in their status judgments of themselves and others. For example, if the millions of dollars spent by manufacturers on advertising are successful, we would expect that automobiles would be a significant dimension of status. It may well be for some people (particularly at the time of purchase), but there is much evidence from the consumer organizations that after the "glow" has worn off, the auto is judged largely by factors of economy: mileage, maintenance, etc.

There are *developmental* patterns of status judgments that remain virtually unexplored. For example, on the occupational dimension, several studies have indicated that in the fourth grade, children think of fireman and policeman as being high-status occupations, but by the sixth or eighth grade, their perceptions have shifted and they consider the professions (medicine, law, education) as being of highest status.[29] What brings about these changes? What other status changes come about as the child grows to maturity, and from age 21 to death? How do men and women

[27] W. Breed, "Occupational Mobility and Suicide among White Males," *American Sociological Review*, 28 (1963), 179–88.

[28] E. F. Jackson, "Status Consistency and Symptoms of Stress," *American Sociological Review*, 27 (1962), 469–80. See also R. Hodge, "Status Consistency of Occupational Groups," *American Sociological Review*, 27 (1962), 336–43; and W. Landecker, "Class Crystallization and Class Consciousness, *American Sociological Review*, 28 (1963), 219–29. Also of interest in this regard are B. Segal and R. Thomsen, "Status Orientation and Ethnic Sentiment among Undergraduates," *American Journal of Sociology*, 71 (1963), 60–67; and E. Lauman, "Subjective Social Distance and Urban Occupational Strata," *American Journal of Sociology*, 71 (1965), 26–36.

[29] E. Weinstein, "Children's Concept of Occupational Stratification," *Sociology and Social Research*, 42 (1958), 278–84.

differ in their perceptions of status, particularly as they get older? These are exciting areas for future research. One thing is clear: there will probably be no *single* developmental sequence of status perceptions.

occupational and social class

Even with all of the foregoing taken into account, the most widely used index of social class is occupation. There are good reasons for this fact, in that information on occupation is relatively easy to get, easily quantifiable, easily broken into status divisions (professional, managerial, clerical, skilled manual, etc.), and correlates with other indexes of class very well.[30]

To a large degree, this is due to the fact that in an achievement-oriented society like our own, occupation is the *defining* characteristic— it determines how much money we can make, and, therefore, what type of house we can live in, and the neighborhood we can afford. (Educational level is a good predictor of occupational potential or level, but everyone knows that there is many a slip between the educational cup and the occupational lip.)

It also seems that there is a rather high amount of agreement on the status of various occupations within American society, based mainly on the research of North and Hatt for the National Opinion Research Center.[31] One can, however, question whether or not in *today's* occupational world the same consensus exists. Even in the North and Hatt data, compiled in 1946, there was evidence that lack of familiarity with the skills required by the occupation made evaluation difficult. For example, only 3 per cent of their sample was able to say what a nuclear physicist does, 55 per cent said they didn't know, and the rest gave answers which included, "Assistant to a physic. His job would be on the body." "I think he gives the anaesthetic." "I think nuclear is some kind of new plastic." "He's a spy." [32] Certainly since 1946 the number of jobs in scientific and technological fields with long names and totally unfamiliar activities has shown a drastic increase, making it virtually impossible for the layman to know what the person in that occupation *does* (the major dimension for Parsons, on which status is awarded). Every bit of evidence suggests

[30] E.g., A. Hollinghead and F. Redlich, *Social Class and Mental Illness* (New York: John Wiley & Sons, Inc., 1958), p. 394; R. Centers, *op. cit.*, p. 369. Even the most cursory glance through the stratification literature will reveal the extensive use of occupation as a single index, yet the title usually suggests that "social class" and not occupation was being measured.

[31] North and Hatt, "Jobs and Occupations: A Popular Evaluation," reprinted in Bendix and Lipset, *op. cit.*, pp. 411–26. The reader might wish to pursue the "situs" dimension of occupational stratification—see P. Hatt, "Occupation and Social Stratification," *American Journal of Sociology*, **55** (1950), 533–43.

[32] North and Hatt, *op. cit.*, p. 417.

that more of this complexity and vagueness of occupational titles and functions will occur in the future.

The *symbolic* inferential judgments of status, which used to correlate with occupation, no longer hold, at least to the same degree. It is difficult today to tell much about a person's occupation from the clothes he wears on the street or the golf course (or the fact that he is on the golf course at all). According to two informal reports, Cadillacs are owned in large part by the very rich and by the very poor. The workweek of the manual worker has been steadily reduced by vigorous union activities, so that professionals and administrators are often working *twice* as many hours a week as manual workers. (This means that if their salaries are twice that of manual workers, their per-hour rate is about the same.) The man on the golf course, teeing up the ball at 9:00 on a Saturday morning, is more likely to have the occupation of drill press operator than hospital administrator.

It is quite likely that in the next few years some major changes will develop in the perception of occupational status. As people become acclimated to more leisure and feel less guilty and more sophisticated in the use of it, comfort and security as occupational status-givers may begin to take over where the Protestant Ethic (service to mankind, work is good in itself) left off. The fact that several companies are developing training programs to allow workers to adjust to longer vacations may not be such a misguided notion. There are already notable shifts in the proportion of workers in each occupational category, with very great growth rates in some areas and declines in others: [33]

changes in the class structure of the U.S. *

	1947	1956	1947–56 (% change)
TOTAL EMPLOYED	57,843	64,928	+12.2
WHITE COLLAR OCCUPATIONS			
Professional, technical	3,795	6,096	+60.6
Managers, proprietors, officials	5,795	6,552	+13.1
Clerical	7,200	8,838	+22.8
Sales	3,395	4,111	+21.1
BLUE COLLAR			
Craftsmen, foremen	7,754	8,693	+12.1
Operatives, semiskilled	12,274	12,816	+ 4.4
Laborers (farm & mine)	3,526	3,670	+ 4.1

[33] Reprinted in Daniel Bell, *The End of Ideology* (New York: Free Press of Glencoe, Inc., 1960), p. 386.

MIXED OCCUPATIONS			
Service workers	4,256	5,485	+28.9
Private—household	1,731	2,124	+22.7
FARM OCCUPATIONS			
Laborers and foremen	3,125	2,889	− 7.6
Farmers, farm managers	4,995	3,655	−26.8

* *Expressed in thousands.*

A reading of *Blue-Collar World*,[34] an excellent recent collection of articles edited by Shostak and Gomberg, which deals with changing perceptions of occupational groups, particularly those "from the middle down," should indicate that many of our notions of the *kinds* of people inhabiting various occupational levels, the lives they lead and their views of the good life, need drastic revision.

class and caste

The distinction between class and caste is one with a long history in sociology. In human societies the caste system has endured for three thousand years and more, and still exists today. A caste is distinguished by hereditary membership; that is, one is in it for life, and outside of transmigration of soul in the Indian system, there is no chance of upward mobility from one caste to another. Castes are completely exclusive and totally define the social interaction of the members. Thus, intermarriage within a caste is virtually complete, bringing hereditary factors into play. As the system evolved in India, each caste performed a special function—the priests or Brahmins were the teachers; the warriors; the artisans; and the Sudras at the bottom did all the menial labor. (The system, it might be added has many parallels to Plato's organization of the Republic.) One never even ate with a member of another caste. (It should be said, however, that in the realities of Indian village life, the fourfold caste system never worked well, and thousands of minutely different castes have evolved.) At any rate, social mobility *within* the caste was possible and often encouraged, so that there were many honorific titles and functions to which the warrior or artisan could aspire. But the artisan *remained* an artisan.

Many have argued that the American Negro is involved in a system not of class, but of caste.[35] This was certainly truer twenty years ago

34 (Englewood Cliffs, N.J.: Prentice-Hall, Inc., 1964.)

35 On this issue see O. Cox, "Race and Caste: A Distinction," *American Journal of Sociology*, **50** (1945), 360–68; also A. Davis and B. Gardner, *Deep South* (Chicago: University of Chicago Press, 1941). For a stimulating account of caste, clan, and club, in India, China, and America, respectively, see F. L. Hsu, *Caste, Clan, and Club* (Princeton, N.J.: D. Van Nostrand Co., Inc., 1963).

than it is today. Yet, the American Negro, even today, is caught more than any other group in the curious dilemma, pointed out magnificently by Myrdal, of our *dream* of offering everything to everyone, and the *reality* of giving almost nothing to certain groups, particularly the Negro.[36] Although federal legislation dealing with the question is becoming voluminous and social action programs are gaining ground, there are good reasons for looking at the question carefully. First, "the poor," however defined, are unquestionably drawn in large numbers from the Negro ranks. (There may be more poor whites in actual numbers, but a far greater percentage of the Negro than white population is poor. For example, the Department of Labor states that in 1965 Negroes represented 20.6 per cent of the nation's unemployed, but only 10 per cent of the U.S. population.) Second, there is evidence that poverty involves from 16 to 25 per cent of the population, and this figure is not getting smaller, nor are the economic inequities between the poor and the rest of society getting any smaller. World War II did produce better economic conditions for the low-income groups in our society, but since 1944, the "gap" between the poor and the rest of the population has remained virtually unchanged,[37] and may actually be widening. Harrington has pointed out that the fifty million people he calls poor in America are increasingly invisible:

> Now the American city has been transformed. The poor still inhabit the miserable housing in the central area, but they are increasingly isolated from contact with, or sight of, anybody else. . . . In short, the development of the American city has removed poverty from the living, emotional experience of millions upon millions of middle-class Americans. Living out in the suburbs, it is easy to assume that ours is, indeed, an affluent society.[38]

One way to get at the caste-class distinction is to look at the occupational status and distribution of Negroes in the work force compared to whites. In 1960, of all employed Negroes, 4 per cent fell in the category of professional, technical, and kindred workers, while 11.3 per cent of the white work force was in that category; 2.7 per cent of Negroes were in the managers, officials, and proprietors class, in which 14.6 per cent of the white work force was; 20 per cent of the white force was highly skilled manual, with only 9 per cent of Negro workers in that category; semiskilled and common labor took 48 per cent of the Negro workers, but only 25.3 per cent of the white work force.

[36] *An American Dilemma* (New York: Harper & Row, Publishers, 1944).
[37] S. M. Miller, "The 'New' Working Class," in *Blue-Collar World.*
[38] M. Harrington, *The Other America* (New York: The Macmillan Company, 1962), p. 4.

occupational status *

	Negro	White
Professionals	4%	11.3%
Managers and proprietors	2.7%	14.6%
Highly skilled	9%	20.0%
Semiskilled and common	48%	25.3%

* *Department of Labor Statistics for year 1960.*

The astonishing thing about these figures is that they represent a vast *improvement* for the Negro compared to Department of Labor statistics for the past two decades.[39] However, Thomas Pettigrew of Harvard estimates that at the rate of employment gains from 1950 to 1960, Negroes would not reach a proportional representation among clerical workers until 1992, among skilled workers until 2005, among professionals until 2017, and among business managers and proprietors until 2730 A.D.[40]

The next question we have to ask is whether or not "class" (as seen in terms of occupation) overrides race. Is the Negro doctor seen first as a Negro and *then* as a doctor, or vice versa? Clearly there are many different personal responses to this situation, ranging from seriously ill white persons who have refused treatment by a competent Negro doctor and paid the price of death, to the Negro medical specialist whose highly developed skills may give him an all-white clientele.[41] If we add the other castelike tendency in our society, that of sex, and prepare Hughes' box analysis of all possible combinations of doctor and patient on these two castelike characteristics of race and sex, it is clear that the white male doctor has the largest accessibility to patients: [42]

	Physician			
Patient	*White male*	*White female*	*Negro male*	*Negro female*
White male				
White female				
Negro male				
Negro female				

39 *Ibid.*, pp. 73–74.

40 Quoted in C. Vann Woodward, "After Watts, Where Is the Negro Revolution Heading?" *The New York Times Magazine*, Aug. 29, 1965, p. 81.

41 See the excellent article by E. Hughes, "Dilemmas and Contradictions of Status," *American Journal of Sociology*, **50** (1945), 353–59.

42 *Ibid.*, p. 355.

Certainly, the Negro is not involved in a caste system in which *no* occupational choice is offered and intermarriage with members of other castes is *impossible* (Negro-white marriages and unmarried "miscegenation" are facts of American life and have been so for quite some time). However, both "Negro" and "female" categories have biological visibility from which the occupant cannot escape, and their access to certain areas of the occupational status hierarchy are limited. In other occupational areas, however, the Negro has virtually unlimited access, particularly in sports and entertainment. (In fact, the white jazz musician may find the going *more* difficult than an equally talented Negro.) [43]

As we have indicated, there are reasons for thinking that access to the educational and occupational status structures will increase for the American Negro, as it has for the American woman. (For both, gaining the right to vote and access to education seem to have been the crucial victories.) There seems, for example, to be good reason to believe that the stereotype of the Negro as being *innately* inferior to the white in mental ability is beginning to break down. As one example, a study conducted by the National Opinion Research Center in December 1963 showed that 30 per cent of white Southerners accepted school integration, as compared to only 2 per cent in 1942 and 14 per cent in 1956. In 1963, 75 per cent of white Northerners accepted school integration as a principle, compared to 40 per cent for that group in 1942 and 61 per cent in 1956. Acceptance of residential integration among southern whites rose from 12 per cent in 1942 to 51 per cent in 1963; among northern whites, it rose from 42 per cent (1942) to 70 per cent (1963). Perhaps most significantly of all, belief that Negroes possess intelligence equal to whites if given equal opportunities to develop it rose among southern whites from 20 per cent (1942) to 60 per cent (1963); among northern whites the rise was from 50 per cent (1942) to 80 per cent (1963).[44] (This same fight was, early in the century, carried on in relation to women, and many famous educators of the time gave long and serious speeches to the point that the brains of young women were not designed for further education, so that to place them in colleges and universities would be to drive them to madness, suicide or worse.)

One additional factor which may help to bring about wider access to the occupational status structure for the Negro is the enormous amount

[43] On this point, see the excellent study by Margaret Butcher on the Negro contribution to American art and literature; *The Negro in American Culture* (New York: New American Library of World Literature, Inc., 1957).

[44] Cited in A. Rose, "The Negro Problem in the Context of Social Change," *Annals of the American Academy of Political and Social Science*, 357 (1965), 16.

of sociological material being published on the Negro's plight.[45] As the inequities forced upon him are made clear (and accurate) to the general public, the invisibility of the Negro poor, which allows the rest of us the luxury of thinking of America as a *totally* affluent society, tends to disappear.

One often encounters a kind of positive prejudice in certain groups— particularly the somewhat liberal "Some of my best friends are..." variety. In order to protect their image as forward-looking institutions, many businesses (as well as colleges and universities) are engaged in a pell-mell rush to engage the top-notch, well-educated Negroes who come from good backgrounds. (More than one admissions officer has told this author that he is out to buy bright Negroes in just the same way that the football coach goes out to buy a quarterback.) There is little question that American society at present has more high-status occupational positions for Negroes than can be filled by the current "pool" of highly educated Negroes.

In conclusion, it would seem that the American Negro is not in a caste situation in contemporary America, although his freedom of latitude in voluntary associations, in educational attainment, and in occupational status may be limited in comparison with other groups of our society. But the *possibility* of totally eliminating the Negro's disadvantage exists today, and that possibility could never exist in a caste system. Certainly, we have come a long way from the time when these words rang out:

> God has not been preparing the ... Teutonic peoples for a thousand years for nothing but vain and idle self-admiration. No! He has made us the master organizers of the world to establish system where chaos reigns. ... He has made us adept in government that we may administer government among savages and senile peoples.[46]

That statement was made, not by a supporter of Hitler, but by a member of the United States Senate in 1899.

We must also keep in mind the fact that, as revolutions gain ground (and the Negro is in a revolution), the oppressed group's tolerance of unjust situations *decreases*, and inequities they used to consider as minor

---

[45] A few excellent sources are W. Mendelson, *Discrimination* (a summary of the report of the U.S. Civil Rights Commission) (Englewood Cliffs, N.J.: Prentice-Hall, Inc., 1962); "The Negro Protest," a special issue of *Annals of the American Academy of Political and Social Science*, **357** (1965); M. Grossack, *Mental Health and Segregation* (New York: Springer Publishing Co., Inc., 1963); R. Gunzberg, *One Hundred Years of Lynchings* (New York: Lancer Books, 1962), and several articles in *Blue-Collar World*.

[46] Cited in R. Hofstader, *Social Darwinism in American Thought* (Boston: Beacon Press, 1955), p. 180.

become of major importance. From this we would predict that as the Negro gains social and economic status, and begins to construct his reference groups with *whites* as well as with other Negroes, the possibilities for violence, frustration, and destruction will also increase. This is one of the great ironies of social progress, and a major task for those trying to control this social revolution.

education and social stratification

Since this author last wrote on this topic,[47] several interesting developments have occurred. These developments can be characterized under the general rubric of extending equality of opportunity through extending the number of years of schooling. Universal opportunity for education beyond the high school seems to be a major commitment of the Educational Policies Commission of the National Education Association, as well as of many other important educational groups. The battle, previously fought around the issue of universal access to high school, seems to have moved to the college level. The *expectation* of college as a normal part of "growing up" has certainly filtered from the upper classes and the Ivy League down through the middle and into the lower segments of our society. As an example, our high schools are now sending about 50 per cent of their graduates on to further education each year, but the expectation of college among parents of high-school students involves over 80 per cent. The consequences of universal *aspiration* for college from parents in a system in which there are not enough places in colleges for *all* their children may not be pleasant.

higher education—
"the higher the better"

The title phrase describes one of the most pervasive aspects of American education, from kindergarten to graduate school. Although the "tree" model of stratification we mentioned earlier might be more appropriate, we think of education, as social stratification, from "high" to "low." The semantics of "high" school and "higher" education, of "elementary" school, or the "lower" grades, gives us away. There is some agreement among those concerned with education that the most significant learning experiences occur in the early or "inner"" (not "low") grades, and that, as we will see in Chapter 8, the

[47] *Education in Social and Cultural Perspectives* (Englewood Cliffs, N.J.: Prentice-Hall, Inc., 1962), Chap. 2.

chance of making an educational impact on the student usually decreases as the student gets older. Nevertheless, the status hierarchy based on the age of the students is probably the single most important aspect of educational social stratification.

To a large extent, these gradations conform to our definition of social class—the students in grade three have a "consciousness of kind" that makes them different from those in grade two, while the college freshman is set apart from the college sophomore in much the same way. In each "grade," students have roughly the same age, and a somewhat similar heritage of experience acquired in moving up the educational ladder. Differential behavior can also be seen—in the second grade a boy may assume that girls are objects at whom rocks should be thrown, while the tenth-grade boy may have acquired some idea about other female virtues besides those of a moving target.

The reasons for this status system are undoubtedly complex, yet one reason stands out as important and relatively simple. Ours is a society of *specialists,* and it is true that the educational ladder leads to increasing specialization for teacher and student. The smaller the area one is held responsible for knowing, the greater the status. The "generalist" is not often highly regarded. In this connection, it is interesting to observe that the only two intervals in the educational sequence in which it is admitted that "elementary" things are discussed are the first several grades in grade school and the furthest reaches of the graduate school. (Set theory, which used to be the province of graduate school math programs, is now encamped in "new math" programs in the early years of elementary school.)

Generally, it would be admitted that the larger the number of students going on to the next level, the higher the status. Thus, we find high-school principals and school superintendents quoting the percentage of graduates who go on to college, while college officials are fond of referring to the increasing percentage of their graduates who go on to graduate school. (This principle does not hold at the elementary-school level, as promotion is virtually automatic, at least into junior high and high school.)

Because of these factors, teachers' status can generally be ascertained by (1) the educational level of their students, and (2) the possibility of their students' progressing further. For example, the neophyte high-school teacher is not generally given "college preparatory" students on the first assignment, and the newly recruited college teacher will probably find himself facing freshmen most of the time. Both teachers will be hampered by this fact, as neither the new high-school nor college teacher has been well trained for this virtually inevitable first assignment—their work in their field has generally involved "specialty" courses in the discipline. With years of experience, the teacher acquires bargaining power and status, and with it the right to teach students who are more interested in his specialty and who will go "higher" up the educational and occupational ladder (and who are easier to work with because of this interest). One latent function of this system of allotting students is that of a teacher's occupational initiation rite of passage—by giving the most difficult (least interested) students to the new teacher, one can assume a maximum of confidence about the teacher's future in the profession if he survives the first several years. Relatively high attrition rates from elementary, high-school and undergraduate teaching ranks might indicate that many are driven from the profession by this practice as well. Although the system does resemble an initiation rite in many respects, there is no symbolic award to those who survive—no rite of passage (unless one could consider the award of a merit raise, tenure, or permanent certification in that light).

Another interesting aspect of the desire for "higher" education is that, as progress to a new level becomes universal, new kinds of educational institutions come into being to "bridge the gap." When elementary school was no longer terminal for most, and passage into high school became the normal state of affairs, the junior high school came into existence to prepare the majority (who now were going on) for high school. Similarly, as college becomes a normal or expected experience for millions, the junior or community colleges have evolved to serve some similar ends. These colleges are for the most part a very new sight on the educational horizon. A reasonable guess would be that these very new institutions, financed through community, state, and federal money, have taken care of most of those whose desire for college is newly acquired. By 1970, about 50 per cent of all college students will be enrolled in two-year, junior or community colleges. In this, such schools are performing an invaluable service. However, the inexorable push of "the higher the better" can be seen here as well, as many of these two-year institutions, whether or not they admit it publicly, desire to become four-year institutions. (In much the same vein, four-year colleges are instituting graduate programs to acquire some of the status of a university, and university graduate schools are being privately compared by the number of postdoctoral fellowships they can provide.)

Outside of the graduate school, no other educational level seems to be able to admit that it is *terminal* for most of its students without risking the loss of status. For a teacher to admit that most of his students have reached the end of the educational line means that the teacher has also. Also, the responsibility of "having the last crack" at students is a heavy one, and most teachers and administrators would rather be able to pass the student along to another colleague who can share the blame. In this sense, the preference for students who will go furthest ("highest") in the educational system is a mirror of the social structure of American society, as amount of education has ceased being a *symbol* of high occupational and economic status and has become the defining *criterion* of it. Because of this "halo effect," the teachers who work with the future leaders of our society increase their status. Thus, the elementary teacher who gets the "top reading group," the high-school teacher who gets the "advanced placement" or "honors" students, and the college teacher who teaches "senior seminars" and graduate courses are all achieving status as teachers, due in part to the predicted academic, occupational, and economic potential of their students.

One of the most damaging effects of this pattern is the tremendous negative force to being in the middle or bottom of this student "social class" system. To be told that their child is only of "normal" intelligence is more than many parents can bear. As the aspiration for more and more education spreads into wider circles, we can expect more and more frustration and alienation among those students who are not in the upper half of the ability distribution. The flight to the suburbs is generally taken by those who have in some sense "made it"—formerly suburbs were almost entirely a middle-class or white-collar phenomenon, but today there are many suburbs peopled by manual workers, or members of the "common man" group.[48] These are people who are increasingly sensitive to status differences, and increasingly aware that education holds the key to "crossing the collar line" for their children, into the higher echelons of white-collar, nonmanual occupations. These aspirations are often unrealistic in terms of the children's ability and incentive, and in the future we can look for "social dynamite" in the suburbs as well as in the slums.

education and economic status

One of the most astonishing books to appear in recent years was *Education and Income*, by Patricia Sexton. Without getting overly involved in the confusing issues of social class membership, the book presents, more clearly than ever before, the bias of our educational system in favor of those students whose parents have money. This bias extends into virtually every aspect of life and is particularly visible in the school's estimation of intelligence, on the basis of which students are placed in "ability" groupings and their educational

---

[48] *Blue-Collar World.*

futures determined. Sexton compares IQ score with family income, with the following results:

Major Income Group	IQ Score Index
I ($3,000–4,999)	2.79
II ($5,000–6,999)	3.31
III ($7,000–8,999)	4.55
IV ($9,000 and above)	5.09

Furthermore, when the broad income categories were broken down into 26 smaller income categories, a great majority of the 26 "fine" income categories also showed consistent increase in IQ with increase in income, even when the amount of the income increase was only two or three hundred dollars! [49]

This socioeconomic bias in the educational system is not a new phenomenon; Allison Davis was reporting definite evidence of it in 1951.[50] The exciting thing is that, since 1960, serious and concerted efforts have been and are being made to overcome this bias. Many large city school systems, notably New York, have stopped placing students on the basis of single tests of mental ability. Test makers have accomplished much in the development of tests that use situations and experiences with which almost all children are familiar. Elementary texts no longer show only well-scrubbed suburban children playing neat (nonviolent) games in front of a clean, white house with acres of grass, without also showing urban situations—the excitement of the street, the mixture of races and religions, etc. Pilot projects have indicated conclusively that a large number of children who had previously been marked as "reject" by the schools have astonishing possibilities when given a chance. Colleges are experimenting with more flexibility in admissions policies, and are generally finding that high motivation can override lack of intellectual and cultural background. We are entering an era in which the "garbage factor" of American society (to which the schools and colleges have contributed) may well be considerably reduced, allowing a new source of talent and energy to become manifest in our society.

When this occurs in large numbers (as seems likely), there are bound to be serious repercussions in all parts of the educational system. For example, when research findings indicated that public school boys tend to do better in college (although private school boys *enter* college with a slight advantage), admissions policies, which had favored the "upper class" private school graduate, were usually altered to allow more of the

[49] *Education and Income* (New York: The Viking Press, Inc., 1961), p. 39.
[50] *Social-Class Influences upon Learning* (Cambridge: Harvard University Press, 1951).

public school graduates. This development naturally caused some anxiety among the elite preparatory schools, whose reputation was built largely on the ability to get a student into an elite college. Certainly, further readjustments will occur at the elementary, junior high, high-school and college levels as more flexible evaluations are made of student capabilities and achievements.

education, social class, and values

American educational institutions have, at least from the time of Cotton Mather on, put emphasis on deportment as well as scholarship. Teachers infer students' values from their behavior, often in a rather unrealistic way. The desired behaviors of a student signify obedience and compliance, working hard on abstract problems in absolute quiet, avoiding profanity, being neat and cleat, shunning physical aggression but being willing to compete wholeheartedly on intellectual tasks (to the glory of the teacher's and school's reputation). All of these desired behaviors (and the values which they signify) necessitate a very extensive set of internal controls, a superego which will allow the student to direct himself in these areas.

Among many groups in American society, particularly those with a very authoritarian family structure, the possibilities for development of these internal controls are limited indeed. These groups tend to concentrate near the bottom of the occupational and economic scales, and tend to involve ethnic groups who still "bring up the children in the old ways." These patterns of behavior emphasize the present at the expense of the future, immediate gratification of needs rather than postponement, the use of physical violence, especially as part of the "male" image, interest in things rather than ideas, and a generally fatalistic and negative view of their place in the world. Impulse gratification and expression are far more important than impulse repression and control.

It is clear that there is a conflict between the behaviors which the school considers desirable and the behaviors which typify the lower echelons of our society. Many students have been judged by the school as "evil" because they have been taught to express themselves physically. Being judged by a desired standard of behavior which is in conflict with those behaviors acceptable in his out-of-school environment, the student is often led to choose between the two—a choice in which the school values do not always win.

It is in this sense that the educational system is biased in favor of the "middle class"—the desired behaviors and values are those which people in the center of occupational and economic hierarchies tend to possess. (But anyone who has taught in a school in a "middle-class" suburb knows that there are many students who manifest "lower-class" values and behavior, if allowed, and many students in slum schools who possess "middle class" behavior patterns.)

An important and difficult decision that has yet to be made concerns whether students who possess behavior patterns which deviate from the normal or "middle-class" patterns should be taught to conform to these predominant school behaviors, or whether the standards of acceptable school behavior should be made broader and more flexible to allow the "lower-class" behaviors to continue in the school situation. The former seems at first more acceptable, but how feasible it is no one knows. The "conversion" of students with deviant behavior patterns is little understood, and certainly few teachers are trained in how to go about it. Much remains to be done in determining how (if at all) these students can be given a set of internal controls that will allow them to function effectively in a school setting and that can perhaps be "turned off" to allow the student to survive on the city street. There is an astonishing lack of educational research on the central problem of establishing order in the classroom.

The problem of deviant behavior is no longer a problem for the high schools alone. Colleges which are now experimenting with "high-risk" students may be welcoming to their campuses students in whose early lives petty theft, murder, alcoholism, narcotics, and totally uninhibited sex were everyday happenings. Whether or not colleges are up to dealing productively with students from this type of environment has yet to be established.

The job of all educational institutions in enforcing and reinforcing the "middle-class" standards of behavior and values is made increasingly difficult by many aspects of our culture which stress the immediate *gratification* of impulse rather than its repression. One has only to watch a commercial or two on television to observe the basic theme of "have it and experience it today—tomorrow may be too late." The installment plan gives economic validity to the idea of experiencing things immediately. In a consumer-oriented society we find ourselves playing vital social roles by using things up—this is partially how we define ourselves and others, in terms of how "well" (and how quickly) we consume. Thus, the people in commercials always seem to be up to their ears in gratifying their impulses. In a world of immediate impulse gratification, today becomes more important than tomorrow, and physical expression of one's feelings a natural corollary to "live for the moment." The television set acts as a cultural relay, sending out a message much more in line with the "deviant" ways of the slum street than with the "dominant" values and behaviors represented in educational institutions. The impact of the mass media on children has been clearly documented, as has the fact that for many families who are blocked from any occupational advancement, *compensatory consumption* (the buying of goods as compensation for lack of social mobility) is becoming a normal way of life.[51]

Some tensions are bound to result from this discrepancy between the educationally oriented values of thrift, impulse control, postponement of enjoyments, and emphasis on the future; and the consumer-oriented values of immediate gratification of impulses, giving-in rather than self-control, and emphasis on today rather than tomorrow. Whether or not these tensions can be resolved productively remains to be seen. It is a little too easy to say that the former are "right" and the latter "wrong," because the values and roles of consumership are with us to stay and will probably have *more* influence in the future, whether we like it or not. As this value discrepancy comes into sharper focus, the extent to which educational influences can "do battle" with other cultural elements, instead of passively reflecting them, may also be made clear.

conclusions

In general, the developments that have occurred in American society since the "social class" research of the community studies of the 1930's and 1940's give grounds for cautious optimism. There is still a system of inequality in America, but increasingly, judgments are made after people have been given a *chance*. One of the major problems which will have to be dealt with is that of runaway aspirations: the youth whose desires (culturally and parentally induced) are far in excess of his capacities. Many have argued that the delinquent has not *rejected* society—he steals the Cadillac precisely because the culture "tells" him that Cadillacs are good but gives him no socially acceptable way of acquiring one. To the extent that any culture creates astronomical aspirations and desires in the young, and then provides no *sanctioned* way of fulfilling these aspirations and desires, that culture will have the crime rate that it deserves.

One of the gravest problems facing American education involves the compensation for inequities produced by our system of social stratification. Many colleges are now engaged in compensatory admissions—lowering standards of admissions for those from underprivileged back-

---

[51] See D. Kaplovitz, "The Problems of Blue-Collar Consumers," in *Blue-Collar World*, pp. 110–20; and A. Gomberg, "The Working-Class Child of Four and Television," *Blue-Collar World*, pp. 429–36.

grounds. The next problem is compensatory *graduation,* on the theory that we cannot expect the same two- or four-year development from an underprivileged student as we would from a culturally advantaged one. This will be, in the future, a terribly divisive issue with faculties in high schools, colleges, and universities, and ultimately, in graduate schools. Most faculty members share a belief in Horatio Alger, egalitarianism and mobility, that everything should be done in education to allow the bright but underprivileged student to "get ahead." But at the same time, faculty are known to have convictions about academic standards—a degree from *their* institution means reaching definite levels of accomplishment. It is quite clear that we cannot have both clear, impartial standards of academic performance and a waiving of those standards to compensate for inequities produced by our system of social stratification. Some agonizing decisions on this issue will have to be made.

5: social mobility and "success"—who stole the protestant ethic?

In the last chapter, we concentrated on systems of social stratification that tend to form the stable, constant "backbone" of any society. These systems can change, as we have seen, but slowly. In this chapter, we will look into social change from the perspective of the individual member of the society. In the next chapter, we will look into patterns of community change. For want of a better analogy, if one considers a tire on a parked car, in the last chapter we looked at the tire standing still, in this chapter we will look at the molecules of air within the tire that exert pressure on the tire by their constant motion, and in the next chapter we will look at the tire in motion.

Individuals are constantly involved in changes of many kinds. The most obvious is that of growth, maturation, and aging, which Shakespeare refers to as the seven ages of man. Our awareness of this process of change is seldom continuous—we tend to wake up with a jolt one morning to discover that we are beginning to be bald, or gray, or whatever. Although there are some psychosomatic overtones, we are talking basically about physiological, or organic, change. There are some things a person can do to speed up or slow down these processes, but not by much—they will continue anyway.

Along with these physical changes will come changes in the perceptual field, or "life space," of the individual. The infant's universe will be his mother, then his house, his town, his state, his country, the world, the solar system, galaxy, and universe. (It now appears that we may dwell in one of a large number of universes, a concept difficult to grasp.) At the same time, we are developing a more complex value system, and more and more sophisticated patterns of personal interaction. Our "image," in the sense of what we comprehend or "see," is constantly changing.[1]

In the section on social stratification, it was pointed out that unless people were conscious or aware of differences in status, these differences could not be said to exist as social phenomena. A statistical class is not a social class unless the people involved "see" or comprehend it as such. In the same way, when we discuss a person moving through a system of stratification, *social* motion or mobility does not take place unless people are aware of it and perceive it. It must be part of the awareness context of the individuals involved. As we shall see, much of the research on social mobility does not take into account changes in the *individual's* perception of his place in the stratification system or systems. It is in the world of literature that we often find accurate, sophisticated accounts of interpersonal perceptions of social mobility.

the mythology of social mobility in America

The American Dream has, throughout most of our history, meant the "rags-to-riches" story typified by Horatio Alger, in which, in *one* generation, an individual could move from "nothing" to "everything." It is not strange that such a mythology developed in America—after all, as a nation, we have come very fast from nothing to everything; for the most part, we have not had a landed gentry or upper class controlling politics; our lives have been fluid with much traveling around; our focus has been the individual's performance, rather than facts of his birth; and also, a few men (highly visible) have "made it" in one generation. One Carnegie or Rockefeller can convince us that the myth is "true," even though it masks the fact that millions more have tried and failed. The successes consume us; we manage not to "see" the failures.

[1] For an excellent explication of this point, see Kenneth Boulding, *The Image* (Ann Arbor: University of Michigan Press, 1956).

For a clearer look at this myth, we could look at a representative work by a very bad poet who, nevertheless, is probably the most influential poet America has produced. During the twenties and thirties, it was the poetry of Edgar Guest that kept the myth alive: [2]

MERIT AND THE THRONG

A thousand men filed in by day
To work and later draw their pay;
A thousand men with hopes and dreams,
Ambitions, visions, plans and schemes.
And in the line a youth who said:
"What chance have I to get ahead?
In such a throng, can any tell
Whether or not I labor well?"

Yet merit is so rare a trait
That once it enters by the gate,
Although 'tis mingled with the throng,
The news of it is passed along.
A workman sees a willing boy,
And talks about his find with joy;
A foreman hears the word, and seeks
The lad of whom another speaks.

So up the line the news is passed
And to the chief it comes at last.
A willing ear to praise he lends,
Then for that eager boy he sends,
And gives him little tasks to do
To learn if all that's said be true.
Among the throng the lad is one
He keeps a watchful eye upon.

Oh, youngster, walking with the throng,
Although to-day the road seems long,
Remember that it lies with you
To say what kind of work you'll do.
If you are only passing fair
The chief will never know you're there,
But if you've merit, have no doubt,
The chief will quickly find it out.

One thing that immediately strikes the reader is that it is in the area of *work* that status is concentrated. If one works harder than anyone else and is nice to "The Chief" (a father figure quite unlike most chiefs known

[2] From *The Favorite Verse of Edgar Guest* (New York: Pocket Books, Inc., 1950).

to this author), life's rewards will come without fail. (It should be noted that in Guest's poetry and in the Horatio Alger stories, the *exact nature of these rewards* is never spelled out, as in the case of the poem above.[3] One is not to work for the rewards; one works hard because it is good to do so.) This faith that work has its own reward borders on religion.

In fact, it is the Protestant tradition that provides the first clue to this secular religion of mobility. For John Calvin, in particular, man was born in depravity and sin; the only thing he could do was to perform good works, not because God would necessarily reward him for it, but because the doing of good works was the only thing a man *could* do.[4] This activist tradition carries over in sayings like "The Devil finds work for idle hands to do," and legislation such as the "Old Deluder" laws of 1624 and 1647, in which it was determined that everyone should be able to read, so that Satan, the Old Deluder, would not find them idle and susceptible to his blandishments.

This Protestant tradition of asceticism and self-denial and doing good works was skillfully related to the spirit of capitalism by Max Weber.[5] Thus, the "good" capitalist never takes his profit; he plows it back into the firm, he looks to the future rather than today, he believes that work is good in itself because that is about all he has. If we now look back at the Guest poem "Merit and the Throng," we can see much of the flavor of Protestantism—"The Chief" is a fair and just God, "merit" (good works) may, if the youth is one of the "elect," get him into God's good graces, but he must not think about it in terms of getting rewards, for that is evil, etc. It is for the same reasons that the Alger stories are so vague on the question of rewards for working hard—earthly pleasures are evil and contaminating, and what else is there to buy with money? Therefore, to save money is proof that one has worked hard; to spend money is evil because of what money can buy. Later in this chapter we will return to this theme to try to ascertain whether or not the Protestant Ethic is still a viable notion for our affluent, luxury-filled, and pleasure-seeking society, and what the role of education might be in this area.

[3] Wohl, "The 'Rags to Riches' Story: An Episode of Secular Idealism," in Bendix and Lipset, *Class, Status, and Power* (New York: Free Press of Glencoe, Inc., 1953), pp. 388–95.

[4] Especially in *Institutes of the Christian Religion*, Book II, Chap. 2, "Man's Present State."

[5] See his essays, *From Max Weber* (New York: Oxford University Press, 1958); *The Protestant Ethic and the Spirit of Capitalism* (New York: Charles Scribner's Sons, 1958); and for an excellent account of the man, see R. Bendix, *Max Weber: An Intellectual Portrait* (Garden City, N.Y.: Doubleday & Company, Inc., 1962).

vertical and horizontal mobility

One of the earliest theoretical distinctions in the field was that between vertical mobility, which entailed a change in the person's status in his eyes and/or in the eyes of his reference groups; and horizontal mobility, which includes geographical movement in which no change of status is seen by the individual or by others.[6] It should be pointed out, however, that these categories do overlap: the bank teller in a small town who moves to become a bank teller in a big town may be viewed by his former friends as having "moved up," while his new friends may think of him as "coming in at the bottom of the ladder" even though his occupation remains unchanged. Many times, a geographical move can entail definite status connotations, and vice versa. To say that a ball-player who was playing for the New York Yankees and is now playing for the Oshkosh Jets has only experienced a geographical move is to make the understatement of the year. Conversely, an advertising man who is promoted, no matter where in the United States he happens to be, will tend to come to New York, the center of the industry. It could also be said that in many businesses, the frequency, distance, and style of travel (geographical mobility) is a very good index of status in the firm. Promotions tend to result in heavier travel schedules. Particularly in a travel-conscious society such as our own, it is inevitable that status connotations will develop around travel objects such as briefcases, suitcases, etc. High status seems to imply "traveling light," perhaps for functional reasons. If you see a man getting on an airplane staggering under the weight of a huge briefcase jammed with papers, you infer that he is a clerk or lower-level management type. On the other hand, if he gets on with a knife-thin attaché case, you can infer that he only carries a few very important papers. He is obviously a decision maker.

It should be clear from this that the vertical-horizontal distinction is not a clear one, nor is it terribly helpful in setting up empirical studies of social mobility. Status, after all, is related to what people *do*, and one of the things people do is to move around the globe. The vertical and horizontal dimensions of mobility interact.

the measurement of social mobility

The problems here are similar to social class measurement, in that we must interpret from statistical data what is really in people's minds. The central index for mobil-

6 Originally used by P. Sorokin, *Social Mobility* (New York: Harper & Row, Publishers, 1927).

ity studies remains that of occupation, as the Protestant-oriented mobility myth previously mentioned ("*Work* for the Night is Coming") would indicate. In general, mobility studies follow the pattern of comparing the occupational status of sons with that of their fathers. Mobility of a population is judged by comparing these figures with an abstract norm: "perfect" mobility would occur in a society in which father's occupation would have *no* effect on son's occupation; sons would disperse through the occupational structure in a random fashion. Opposed to this would be "zero" mobility, in which sons of bankers *always* became bankers.

By comparing the dispersion of sons through the occupational status structure with a "perfect" or random dispersion, one can make some, rough judgments about the relative rate of mobility. Because the occupational status structures of industrialized Western nations seem to be very similar, mobility rates in one country can be compared with those in another.[7]

Although this method of measuring intergenerational occupational mobility is unquestionably the most widely used one, there are certain weaknesses that must be pointed out. First, the studies make the assumption that the comparison of father's and son's occupation is of *social* significance to fathers and sons—that sons *do* actually evaluate themselves in terms of comparing their occupation to that of their father, and vice versa. It may well be that many if not most sons compare themselves with their peers, and not their fathers, in assessing their own status. Another related problem is that in order to compare the two occupational levels simultaneously, the father will be at or past his prime, while the son will just be starting out. This makes the comparison difficult. The difficulty is compounded by the fact that the occupational structure in which the son begins today is markedly different from that in which his father started to work twenty or more years ago. Also, it should be obvious that this type of study completely excludes women from consideration. Also left out are the informal mobility structures that tend to be present in almost every occupation: the machinist who is also the star pitcher on the company baseball team has accomplished, to a certain

[7] The best single volume is R. Bendix and S. Lipset, *Social Mobility in Industrial Society* (Los Angeles: University of California Press, 1960). For a good methodological critique, see S. Yasada, "A Methodological Inquiry into Social Mobility," *American Sociological Review*, 29 (1964), 16–23. Other good sources are M. Mack *el al.*, *Social Mobility: Thirty Years of Research and Theory* (Syracuse: Syracuse University Press, 1957); V. Glass, ed., *Social Mobility in Britain* (London: Routledge & Kegan Paul, Ltd., 1954); E. Gross, *Work and Society* (New York: Crowell-Collier & Macmillan, Inc., 1958); and N. Rogoff, *Recent Trends in Occupational Mobility* (New York: Free Press of Glencoe, Inc., 1953). One of the ground-breaking efforts is NORC, "Jobs and Occupations: A Popular Analysis," *Opinion News*, 9 (1947), 3–13.

degree, *occupational* mobility (even though his occupation has not changed, his status within his occupational group has).

Even with these difficulties in mind, however, studies of occupational mobility indicate that certain generalizations about the subject can be made with some confidence. First (and of great importance to education), there is general agreement that "crossing the collar line" from manual or blue-collar work to nonmanual or white-collar work is the most difficult mobility jump to make. Far more often than one would expect, sons of manual workers become manual workers themselves.[8] Also, the occupational life span of any single worker who begins in manual work will tend heavily toward a succession of manual jobs, with the same consistency for people who start in white-collar jobs.[9]

Another important consequence of these studies (and one which tends to shatter the mobility myth) is the conclusion that mobility rates in the United States are not significantly different from those in other Western industrialized societies,[10] particularly in relation to the chances of a boy whose father has a blue-collar job becoming, himself, a holder of a white-collar job. Those few who do move into prestige positions in business and government from humble origins, however, get a tremendous amount of publicity in America. (In many European countries, for example, a successful person from lower-class backgrounds will be very reluctant to talk about his origins, while in America he would brag about it.)

Many people have argued that as industrialization progresses, the class structure will solidify, thereby causing the amount of occupational mobility to decrease. (This argument is particularly held by those like Warner who believe that classes in America are rigid and fairly closed.) The evidence on this point, although somewhat ambiguous, indicates that no major changes in mobility rates have occurred in the last several decades. Mobility rates seem to a large degree dependent on the occupational structure in which they operate.[11] There is, however, clear evidence that the number of white-collar jobs has increased recently, as well as those manual but highly paid jobs like electronics repair and car body repair. Thus, even though the expanding number of white-collar jobs has run about parallel with population increases, the decline in unskilled

---

[8] Most of the above, plus Lipset and Bendix, "Social Mobility and Occupational Career Patterns, *American Journal of Sociology*, **57** (1952), 494–504; and Peter Blau, "Occupational Bias and Mobility," *American Sociological Review*, **22** (1957), 392–99.

[9] Bendix and Lipset, *op. cit.*, pp. 165–69.

[10] *Ibid.*, pp. 72–73.

[11] *Ibid.*; Rogoff, *op. cit.*; W. Form and J. Geschwender, "Social Reference Basis for Job Satisfaction," *American Sociological Review*, **7** (1962), 228–37; also Jackson and Crockett, "Occupational Mobility in the United States," *American Sociological Review*, **29** (1964), 5–15.

manual jobs will ultimately force a kind of occupational mobility to take place by default.

A small caveat concerning these studies should perhaps be mentioned here. In all of them, *any* move from manual to nonmanual is used as an example of upward mobility, and any move from white to blue collar is seen as downward mobility. To what extent is this interpretation justified? Certainly, any examination of job wage levels will indicate that a skilled manual worker can earn more per hour, often with greater job security, than a clerical white-collar person. He may have more liberal vacation schedules, better medical care provisions, and vastly superior retirement funds. He probably works a shorter workweek and gets compensated heavily for any extra time he puts in. The gap between lifetime earnings in all manual occupations and all nonmanual occupations is still in favor of the latter, but the gap is closing fast, and in many cases there is significant overlap. (It should also be mentioned that the figures for white-collar jobs have always been pushed up by professional workers, allowing us to neglect the fact that there are many nonmanual workers who are very poorly paid indeed; also manual worker averages are very much depressed by the unskilled or "common" labor category.)

changing patterns of occupational mobility

In the early days of industrialization and even before, skill hierarchies were developed vertically; that is, one went from apprentice upward, learning skills en route. Promotion was based on skill. When one reached a certain advanced level, he might become a foreman and supervise the work of others. It must be said that this vertical pattern of promotion was largely responsible for the "rags-to-riches" mythology, even though *very* few foremen ever got off the production floor and into an office.

As industrialization proceeded, however, manufacturing operations were broken down into smaller and smaller units, each requiring fewer and fewer skills. Worker mobility made it important that new workers be trained quickly so that production time would not be lost. Management could not be too dependent on the guildlike system of skill acquisition; it took too long and was too costly. It was also discovered that the skills which made a man a good machinist did not necessarily make him a good foreman. As a consequence, job patterns tended to lose their vertical dimensions and become horizontal: [12]

[12] Diagram from W. L. Warner, *American Life: Dream and Reality* (Chicago: University of Chicago Press, 1953), p. 134.

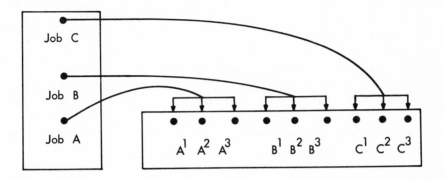

The "fellowship" of the manual workers, their control over their craft, has been largely destroyed by the development of sophisticated machine technology. Instead of learning from one's fellow workers, one goes to special training centers, either inside or outside the manufacturing establishment, to learn a smaller and smaller segment of an increasingly complex production system.

Production today has come to mean the largest possible output of *identical* goods—every item off a production line should be as much like the rest of the production run as possible. There are, of course, enormous advantages to this system, in terms of quality control, reliability of the product, etc., but it also must be said that certain things are given up in the process, such as the worker's knowledge of all aspects of his craft, and his striving for perfection in the finished product. All along the line today, tolerances for error in each manufacturing process permit the making of a product which is "good enough." But it is hard to believe that an auto worker could ever become very involved in the whole car, because he only puts one nut on one bolt.

As a group, manual workers seem to be very much aware that the realities of their specific jobs do not include many chances for advancement. As a result, there has been a pronounced shift in concern from individual to group mobility, brought about partially by very active unionization. If the company provides no upward pathways for a turret-lathe operator, then the individual will work to see that *all* turret-lathe operators advance in salary, not just himself. Also, when advancement is structured out of the picture, workers tend to think more about security, so that the man with the highest occupational status is the one who will be laid off last. Group mobility has as its general objective the betterment of every worker who does a particular job while he is still doing that job, while individual mobility meant the movement of an individual through the job structure by *changing* jobs. It is the difference between a stairway, which must be climbed by each individual under his own power, and an elevator, which takes everyone in it up without any particular effort on his part.

One obvious consequence of the shift from individual to group mobility is that the individual's ego-involvement with his job is bound to decrease. If *all* turret-lathe operators get the raise in salary, then the individual's own performance does not count for much. If a worker is punished for producing too much (or too little and of higher quality than necessary), then it is clear that his job is not providing him with the kind of achievement pattern that will be relevant to his notions of self. Without being overly romantic about it, the guild system and craft unions did provide a graded hierarchy of skill (and mobility and status without leaving the job) that could occupy a worker throughout his working career—status was awarded on the basis of skills that all could see and evaluate.

There are many reasons for thinking that manual workers are now resigned to this new role. For one thing, a new pattern of consumption has been developing which seems to be giving the worker the symbols of occupational advancement without any actual change in his occupational status—aptly termed compensatory consumption. For another, suburban life, which used to be a white-collar phenomenon, is now spreading to all aspects of the occupational structure.[13]

Perhaps it is time that we began to rethink our entire notion of occupational mobility. The studies we have referred to all indicate the bias of the sociologists doing them (a bias *perhaps* shared by the people they studied) in thinking that occupational mobility means changing jobs to acquire a better one. We are suggesting that in the minds of most manual workers, especially in heavily unionized occupations, social mobility has now come to mean more salary and benefits in the *same* job. The change from individual to group perceptions of occupational mobility spells the end of the widespread belief in the Horatio Alger myth. This is clearly an intermediate step in occupational ego-involvement as we move toward an automated, cybernetic society, in which vocation as such will have little indeed to do with the worker's sense of self-identity. As we shall see in the final chapter, the problem of the future may well be

[13] E.g., A. Blum, "Social Structure, Social Class and Participation in Primary Relationships," in Shostak and Gomberg, *Blue Collar World* (Englewood Cliffs, N.J.: Prentice-Hall, Inc., 1964). W. Spenrad "Blue Collar Workers as City and Suburban Residents," in *Blue Collar World;* W. Whyte, "Classlessness in Suburbia," Chap. 23 of *The Organization Man* (Garden City, N.Y.: Doubleday & Company, Inc., 1957); W. H. Form , "Status Stratification in the Planned Community," in W. Dobriner, ed., *The Suburban Community* (New York: G. P. Putnam's Sons, 1958).

to *reduce* the worker's involvement with work, so that he develops other nonoccupational activities in which status can be sought.

One important point of clarification should be entered here. The previous analysis would indicate that there is less occupational mobility today than in former times. In order to clarify the issue, we should differentiate between *inter*generational mobility (occupations of sons compared to occupations of fathers) and *intra*generational mobility (job movement of any one individual throughout his work career). The studies referred to indicate that in terms of intergenerational mobility, there has not been a major shift in rate. However, in terms of intragenerational mobility, our analysis would suggest that, although a man can move around the country at will, changing *employers* many times, he will not be able to change occupations very often. For both inter- and intragenerational mobility, the collar barrier of manual to nonmanual is still very difficult to cross.[14]

Ironically enough, one of the reasons intragenerational mobility may well decrease in the future has to do with education. We have already pointed out that the previous pattern of vertical ascent "up the line" of positions to the top of the factory has been replaced by a horizontal pattern, in which one gets "plugged in" at a given level in a variety of firms. (The horizontal pattern is much more suited to a fluid, urbanized society, in which people move from city to city and plant to plant, while the older vertical ascent structure was suited to a local, stable society, in which workers would stay long enough to make the hierarchy work.) The horizontal pattern has necessitated a rather elaborate set of educational prerequisites for virtually every job. Thus, education, which used to be a *symbol* of high occupational status, has become the major *criterion* on the basis of which persons are allocated in the job structure. The poetry of Edgar Guest aside, no matter how hard a person tries today, he cannot move from a "level five" job to a "level four" job without passing an examination or producing course credits. (The consistent use of the term "job levels" gives some indication of how the horizontal dimension of occupations has come into its own. If you are a "level five" person, you can move all over the country doing "level five" jobs, but before being plugged into a different level, an educational credential is increasingly necessary.)

nonoccupational mobility

Before moving on, it should be pointed out that there are in this country many ways of increasing one's social status without changing jobs. As we move into an economy in which

[14] Bendix and Lipset, *op. cit.*, Chap. 6.

the average worker spends more time and energy on leisure than on work (in fact, the whole distinction between work and leisure is being blurred),[15] new systems of social status will undoubtedly arise around these "nonwork" activities. Already, the mass media, particularly the "specialty" magazines, are busily informing the amateur about gardening, photography, stamp collecting, sports, music, cooking, etc. These magazines are surprisingly educational in function and quite didactic in tone. They not only convey the information about the activity, but do so in an atmosphere of euphoria, suggesting that the activity needs to be "sold" as one would a new car.

The comparative evaluation of visible, understandable skills is a healthy thing which seems to be deeply rooted in the human germ plasm. Unquestionably the new skills of leisure will come to be important sources of social status, and a meaningful context for the "getting ahead" motif. However, in order to increase one's status along these lines, one must have a group of people (a reference group) who can award the status and raise the ante if the performance improves. This can produce a problem in a highly fluid society like our own.

In the view of the author, leisure activities will begin to evolve through the same kind of cycle that occupational activities have: just as the worker gets plugged into a new job at his "proper" level in a new town or, more likely, city, social patterns will develop that will allow him to plug into his leisure activities in exactly the same way. The number of informal social organizations centered around a leisure activity is increasing rapidly, and should continue in a flexible pattern, allowing the perpetual newcomer to be quickly assimilated, then quickly "plugged out" when he moves away. In some contexts, the family has become the leisure reference group (note the large increase in family pool tables, swimming pools, etc.), but the award of status is difficult with the problems of age and skill differences within the family, etc. This type of need is already being met by several services that will locate a house for the person who is moving, make sure the neighbors are compatible, and arrange for the family members to join the activity groups they desire.

Theoretically, there are an infinite number of paths to social mobility, because every human activity can be evaluated differentially, and therefore improved skill could yield improved social status. However, the realities are that we award relatively few activities with status; since occupation has been such a determining factor in people's economic life chances, it has tended to be an all-encompassing status award. We have suggested that in the future a larger number of activities will be assigned

[15] For a compendious treatment of the issue, see S. DeGrazia, *Of Time, Work, and Leisure* (New York: Twentieth Century Fund, 1962).

status, making them possible areas of social mobility. There are, of course, other avenues to mobility besides jobs and leisure activities, the most prevalent one being marriage. This is certainly a major source of *social* mobility for women, and quite frequently for men as well. Not only does marriage allow the woman to move initially into the husband's social milieu, but also, with sociability being an important criterion for further promotions, the marriage will to some degree establish the limits to the husband's mobility in the future.

We cannot emphasize strongly enough the trend among workers (particularly manual ones) to conceive of "getting ahead" in terms of security in the job rather than changing jobs, as Chinoy has indicated:

> But workers do not see security, thus concretely exemplified, as an alternative to advancement . . . the respondents could see no difference between them. "If you've got security, if you've got something you can fall back on, you're still getting ahead," said a twenty-eight-year-old truck driver with three children. "If you can put away a couple of hundred dollars so you can take care of an emergency, then you're getting ahead," declared a forty-year-old nonskilled maintenance worker with four children. "If you work during a layoff, like back in the Depression, that's my idea of working up." . . . And a thirty-nine-year-old oiler summed it up: "If you're secure, then you're getting ahead." [16]

For these workers, the context of social mobility had clearly changed from that of playing occupational musical chairs to improving their lot in their present job. To a large degree, active labor unions have heightened this feeling by successfully endeavoring to improve the worker's *present* job status. (In fact, extensive occupational mobility would hurt the unions, because their best source of staff workers would thus migrate to other occupations.)

The sympathy we once felt for the man who works with his hands needs to be re-examined. That man's interests are carefully tended by lobbyists in Washington and in state governments. In an expanding economy such as our own, the greatest risk of not keeping up in terms of wages and benefits falls to the unskilled, the migrant workers, and the white-collar clerical worker, whose interests are not represented in government. At least one study has indicated that the two occupational

[16] *Automobile Workers and the American Dream* (Garden City, N.Y.: Doubleday & Company, Inc., 1955), p. 125. There seems to be a tendency, both in our culture and others, for risk taking in occupation to be a function of the higher socioeconomic classes, while the search for security is characteristic of poor groups. See Mizruchi, *Success and Opportunity* (New York: Free Press of Glencoe, Inc., 1964), pp. 119 ff. An interesting question concerns whether or not people *must* pass through this "security" phase before moving to the "creative" and risky business of looking for stimulation in a job.

groups which are making much more money than would be expected from educational level are managers and skilled craftsmen. The clerical white-collar worker fares as badly as the blue-collar machine operator on this index.[17]

the decline of the Protestant Ethic

There seems to be ample evidence for the statement that the Protestant Ethic is a declining force in the dominant or "core" culture in America. This is empirically documented by Kluckhohn, both in (a) a rise in value placed upon "being" as opposed to "doing"; and (b) increased interest in the present time orientation and a decreased interest in the future.[18] Our presentation of the "securiority complex" of manual workers also tends to support it, as does the Riesman thesis of increased "other-direction" rather than "inner-direction" in our culture. Also supporting Kluckhohn's position is the fact that an expanding economy is based on expanding spending by citizens, and installment plans and charge accounts make it possible to enjoy things in the present, rather than aspiring to enjoy things in the future. The consumer role (which is increasing in importance as occupational roles decrease) is basically a present-oriented, hedonistic conception in American culture.

Anyone who works with college students has seen this shift away from work as a good in itself (if, indeed, college students have *ever* felt that way!). The model of the "cool" student is he who can achieve without obvious effort—he who can "beat the system." In the minds of many students, the good things of life are postulated as a birthright, a given, not something to be striven for:

> I'm not money-mad by any means, but I'd like enough to buy a house, and have transportation, and of course good clothes for the family. Plus entertainments: I'd like to be able to see the good plays and movies. And I suppose I'd want a trip every year: visit around in the big urban areas, you know, Berlin, Paris, Rome. I can't set any exact amount I'd like to make, so long as it's enough for the *necessities* of life.[19]

In a very overgeneralized way, we can say that the Protestant Ethic, as applied to work, has been practiced by many non-Protestants as well.

[17] R. Hodge, "The Status Consistency of Occupational Groups," *American Sociological Review*, 27 (1962), 336–43.

[18] "Shifts in Values during the Past Generation," in E. Morison, ed., *The American Style* (New York: Harper & Row, Publishers, 1958), p. 207.

[19] From Hodgkinson, *Education in Social and Cultural Perspectives* (Englewood Cliffs, N.J.: Prentice-Hall, Inc., 1962), p. 231.

During the years when America was assimilating wave after wave of immigrants, it was the *spirit* of the Protestant Ethic that allowed the Irish, the Poles, the Norwegians, the Swedes, etc., to expend the extra energy needed to create their place in our culture. These workers knew that if they worked to the maximum, they would be able to pass on a somewhat better life to their children. This pattern of a new group coming in at the bottom and working terribly hard to move upward into American society has been a major source of energy and innovation.

Then, as technology developed and the white-collar middle classes became larger, as the suburban movement took the worker's home away from his smoke-clogged factory (the automobile is again the great emancipator), and as new patterns for buying goods and services developed, the interest in work for its own sake deteriorated. It is probably reasonable to say that in the forties, the Protestant Ethic was practiced by more Jews than Protestants, even though in terms of income, the Jewish population was doing well, and *should* have been satisfied with their lot. Why weren't they satisfied?

family structure and the need for achievement

In order to come to grips with the important question raised above, we will have to return to our notion of the Protestant Ethic. McClelland was probably the first to raise the question: How does the Protestant Ethic maintain itself? (Weber, after all, simply established a relationship between Protestantism and economic development.) McClelland's thesis was that the family was the missing link: [20]

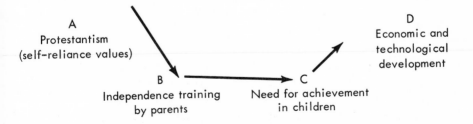

A
Protestantism
(self-reliance values)

B
Independence training
by parents

C
Need for achievement
in children

D
Economic and
technological
development

[20] "Some Social Consequences of Achievement Motivation," in *Nebraska Symposium on Motivation* (Lincoln: University of Nebraska Press, 1955). One of the most amazing tours de force in all of social science is McClelland's extension of the need achievement concept from individuals to nations. See his *The Achieving Society* (Princeton, N.J.: D. Van Nostrand Co., Inc., 1961).

It is unquestionably true that the family is the central agency in determining underlying patterns of motives in children, such as aspiration. But the issues are not as clear-cut as McClelland suggests. For example, independence training might be indicated by parents' allowing the child to go to the store for himself. If we saw two children going to the store, we might conclude that both came from homes in which independence training was considered important. However, in one home, the child may have been kicked out of the house because he was interfering with parents' activities, while in the other, he was carefully prepared by (overly?) conscientious parents for this little voyage toward manhood. Since McClelland's ground-breaking article, there has been much research which indicates that there is seldom a *specific* activity on the part of parents in response to a specific action of the child that will produce high need for achievement in the child. Also, we have indicated that the context of achievement has in many groups moved away from occupational musical chairs to "getting ahead" as security. Along with this, we have pointed out that sociability has become a major criterion for "success," both occupationally and in all of life.

Putting all of this together, we may make a few generalizations on the relation of family structure to aspiration. First, it would be hard to disagree with Swanson and Miller's thesis that family structure has shifted, as has the occupational structure: away from entrepreneurship and toward collective membership, or bureaucracy (further proof that the Protestant Ethic, which practiced entrepreneurship above all else, is declining in importance). As they put it:

> The child who is to be trained for the intricate human relations of the bureaucracy is not ready for adulthood, even after receiving an intensive basic course in responsibility training. He must learn the nuances of human relations and must be able to clarify them in his own thinking so that he can study his own relations to others and gain better control over himself and his associates. . . . The family is again the school for the job, only now it is the school for the job's human relations, not its technical skills.[21]

Another factor that now seems fairly clear is that the extreme permissiveness in raising children, which Warner and others took to be the defining characteristic of the "lower-class personality type," no longer exists; indeed, lower classes may today be less permissive than the middle classes.[22] (Here again, however, permissive *behavior* on the part of par-

[21] *The Changing American Parent* (New York: John Wiley & Sons, Inc., 1958), p. 202.
[22] See the excellent study of Donald McKinley, *Social Class and Family Life* (New York: Free Press of Glencoe, Inc., 1964).

ents is not always as easy to define as permissive *attitudes*.) As far as specifics of family interaction patterns are concerned, the only conclusive finding seems to be that severe authoritarian fathers seem to reduce the need for achievement in sons.[23]

However, a word needs to be said about the need for achievement studies. The desire to establish a standard of excellence for one's own performance does not exist "across the board" but only in certain specific areas of activity. The studies, which rely on respondent's projective stories to TAT pictures, must be rated and scored using the researcher's context of achievement motivation, not the subject's. (For example, to say that John Dillinger had no need for achievement because of an unenthusiastic response he made to a picture of a boy holding a violin means simply that J.D. did not aspire to being a concert violinist— the "standard" high score response.) It is the awareness context of the *achiever* that is sadly neglected. If one might speculate on this point without much empirical support, one might argue that the trend in contemporary America is toward seeing *sociability itself* as a skill and achievement, a goal toward which to strive for excellence, a need to be met by individual effort. Not only is sociability important for participation in the "fun subculture," it is a vital characteristic for occupational success as well.[24]

We also should point out that although people seem to agree rather well on ranking occupations as to status, there are a number of other variables at work, such as the amount of time spent in training for the job, the type of training, the actions performed on the job, the initial salary, the earnings over a job lifetime, the nonsalary benefits, the amount of control one has over the lives of others, etc. The impact of the family structure on each of these somewhat independent variables has yet to be considered.

In conclusion, then, we can say that although occupational mobility *rates* (occupation of father compared to son) have not changed in recent years, the occupational *structure* on which these rates depend has been altered drastically, particularly away from the small entrepreneur toward the large-scale industrial organization. Although the "collar line" seems

---

[23] E.g., *ibid.*; Bernard Rosen, "Socialization and Achievement Motivation in Brazil," *American Sociological Review*, **27** (1962), 612–24; F. Strodtbeck, "Family Interaction, Values, and Achievement," in McClelland *et al.*, *Talent and Society* (Princeton, N.J.: D. Van Nostrand Co., Inc., 1958), pp. 135–94.

[24] On this point, see W. Whyte, *The Organization Man*, especially the appendix called "How To Cheat on Personality Tests," in which criteria for "good" sociability are discussed. See also Seeley *et al.*, *Crestwood Heights* (New York: Basic Books, Inc., Publishers, 1956).

to be as difficult to cross as ever, there may be less reason to strive for white-collar work than formerly. (Not only does a skilled craftsman do well financially, but as we shall see in the last chapter, his chances of being replaced by a machine are less than that of many white-collar clerical workers.) In terms of access to suburban living, consumer goods, and leisure time, there are few significant differences between white- and blue-collar workers. Promotional patterns have shifted from locally oriented ones, in which a man working in a factory for forty years could expect to make some vertical moves in the status structure, to cosmopolitan-oriented industries, in which the job structure is horizontally oriented, with education serving as the major factor in moving to another horizontal layer.

Both the home and school have responded to this shift, emphasizing sociability as an achievement more than formerly. Among manual workers, there is no conflict between security and "getting ahead"; security *is* getting ahead. As one moves up the occupational status ladder, more people seem willing to take risks by job jumping. This may indicate that different personality variables are involved in occupations at different socioeconomic levels. (For example, the manual worker is looking for security in a job; the professional may be looking for challenge, service to others, self-fulfillment, stimulation, etc.; suggesting that different personality dimensions are at work in feelings about occupations.)

The Protestant Ethic, as applied to the sphere of work, is not so much dead as it is obsolete. It was a marvelous motivational structure in an economy based on scarcity and individualistic competition but does not seem appropriate to the development of mass, bureaucratic, industrial complexes. However, this should not be interpreted to mean that the motivational patterns implicit in the Protestant Ethic are of no value in our lives *outside* of the occupational sphere. Social mobility, after all, refers to a change in social status as perceived by the individual and the groups to which he refers. If reference groups outside of the occupational area increase in importance, it may well be that some aspects of the Protestant Ethic are still very relevant to our lives, if not to our jobs.

social mobility and education

We cannot overemphasize the vital role that formal education has come to play in establishing the place of a person in the occupational structure. In fact, this instrumental role of education (a means to a vocational end, rather than an end in itself) has created a major motivational problem for educators at all levels. For many students, the acquisition of skills, ideas, and values is not as important as being able to say that they have "passed through" a certain series of educational levels. (This is behind the statement made by one college sophomore that "College is important for two reasons—getting in and getting out.")

Only one of the many difficulties with this development is that students who are chiefly interested in "passing through" educational experiences will have few scruples about playing the rules of the game. If the material to be learned has no intrinsic value or interest to the student but simply represents one stage of "passing through" to a good job, then why *not* cheat? Every time a cheating scandal hits one of the military service academies (which happens with considerable regularity), there is grave concern for the Future of Youth that lasts for several weeks, then recedes back into indifference. The service academies are, unfortunately, good examples, since the content of courses is often deliberately presented as something that "just has to be learned" and will have little or no future utility.[25] Cheating is particularly shocking at service academies, because candidates are selected not only for academic promise but for "character" and "leadership" as well.

But the cheating problem is virtually universal among American schools and colleges, and widespread in professional schools such as law and medicine as well, even though it receives almost no attention in educational publications. For example, the *Reader's Guide* lists no articles under Cheating from March 1963 to February 1964, three up to February 1965, relating to the Air Force Academy cheating scandal, then a brief flurry during 1965, almost all relating to the *one* incident. Only one of these articles was in a professional education magazine.

There is only one major study of cheating in recent years, and that tends to support the thesis we are developing here, that the more a student sees his academic work as a means to a vocational end, the easier it will be for him to cheat, and the more often he will cheat. The following chart indicates the percentage of students who admit cheating in college according to their major field of concentration: [26]

25 The Air Force cheating scandal of 1965 was covered in news media but not in educational journals. For a good picture of some of the factors at work in service academies, see David Boroff, "The Air Force Academy: A Slight Gain in Altitude," *Harper's,* **226** (February, 1963), 86–88.

26 William J. Bowers, *Student Dishonesty and Its Control in College* (New York: Bureau of Applied Social Research, Columbia University, 1964), p. 106. Also important is Rose Goldsen, *What College Students Think* (Princeton, N.J.: D. Van Nostrand Co., Inc., 1960).

Major Field	Per Cent Cheating
Business and Commerce	66
Engineering	58
Education	52
Social Science	52
Fine and applied arts	50
Physical science	47
History and area studies	43
Humanities	39
Language	37

Similarly, high-school students whose major orientation is social and not academic cheat far more often: 42 per cent of the academically oriented high-school students admitted cheating, while 68 per cent of the socially oriented students cheated. To point out the severity of the cheating problem, of 5,369 college students used in this study, only 1,703, or 32 per cent, went through both high school and college *without* cheating.[27] This research suggests that we should reappraise our notions of cheating as a minority activity.

As support for our thesis that vocationalism increases the propensity to cheat, there is some evidence that in medical schools material which is not directly relevant to the student subculture's view of what a general practitioner's job entails will simply not be done, at least not in the quantity requested by the instructor. It is also clear that the idealism which the neophyte student brings to the medical school is quickly eliminated, replaced by a rather cynical, expediential code of doing the minimum required to "get through." [28]

It is this narrow vocationalism, seeing education only as a means to occupational mobility and not as an intrinsic good, that is behind many of the gloomy prophecies over the early demise of the liberal arts colleges (and, indeed, of the liberal arts themselves!). With some notable exceptions such as M.I.T., arts and humanities courses seem to be giving ground to more specialized courses in the student's major. The desire for specialized training has reached down through the high school as well, through the various advanced placement programs. Even here, unfortunately, the vocational emphasis can be found. (A few weeks before this was written, the author heard two ninth-grade students discussing two advanced placement courses they could take in high school on the

[27] Bowers, *op. cit.*, p. 128.
[28] See H. Becker and B. Geer, "Student Culture in Medical School," *Harvard Educational Review,* **28** (1958), 70–80.

merits of whether or not they would help in being admitted to *graduate* school.)

It is unquestionably true that the formal education enterprise has vastly increased in status in the last ten years. Teachers in schools and colleges are better paid than in the past, and this trend will continue in the future, partially through the constantly perpetuated doctrine of the "imminent teacher shortage." [29] Money is available for experimental projects in large quantities. It is our contention, however, that this renewed status for education has very little to do with educating, and very much to do with somewhat misleading statements made to students as to how much their earnings will increase if they just stay in school. For example, the income difference between the high-school drop-out and the high-school graduate is minimal compared to the difference between the high-school graduate and the four-year college graduate. Thus, we may be deluding the student when we convince him to stay through high school on the grounds that this will have a major effect on his earning power.[30]

A related myth concerns our concept of the high-school, and to some extent college, drop-out as a total failure. One study, reported in 1963, indicates that between 10 and 25 per cent of high-school drop-outs go on to further education and training at a later date, plus a sizable number who get extensive on-the-job training.[31] Similarly, although only about 25 per cent of college students graduate from their original college "on time" four years later, a vast number come back to some college and graduate. (In fact, any college official can verify the fact that many college students *should* drop out for a while, and that they do markedly better work upon their return.) To mask all drop-outs as personal, occupational, and educational failures is to miss the wide range of interests and potential within the drop-out group. A typology of different kinds of drop-outs is very much needed.[32] For instance, how many drop-outs (a voluntary term) are actually "push-outs," forced to leave by school authorities? How many leave because the course content is not meaningful or interesting? How many leave because they lose faith that the degree will have a major impact on their lives? How many leave because they must support their families?

[29] The "teacher shortage" certainly does not exist across the board—at the high-school level, there are more teachers being graduated in English and social studies than there are jobs available. At the college level, see the excellent article by Allan Cartter, "A New Look at the Supply of College Teachers," *Educational Record,* **46** (Summer, 1965), 267–77.

[30] S. M. Miller, "The Outlook of Working-Class Youth," in *Blue Collar World,* p. 125.

[31] *Ibid.*

[32] On this score, see S. Miller and I. Harrison, "Types of Drop-Outs: The Unemployables," in *Blue Collar World,* pp. 469–84.

education and the Protestant Ethic

The preceding discussion points up some crucial problems for educators at all levels in the future. In a culture characterized by a rather hedonistic, leisure-pleasure ethic on the part of adults, we continually say to youth that if they stay in school for only sixteen years (and in Crestwood Heights these are some of the "best" years of life), study hard (even though the material is intrinsically uninteresting and not related to future occupational goals), compete with other students in a very pressure-filled environment, taking tests "that will decide their future" (yet retaining at all times the façade of fun and sociability, while sacrificing the immediate enjoyment of youth in all its dimensions), *then* the good things of life may be theirs. One wonders if John Calvin himself could have withstood the temptations and survived such a regimen. As the core culture becomes more affluent and less ascetic, and as we extend the number of years of schooling we expect most youth to attain, we are creating an increasingly schizophrenic situation, as adult society becomes present-oriented while we insist that youth live in terms of the distant future, long past the time when, in other cultures, their biological maturity would be an indicator of the acquisition of adulthood. (To make matters worse, there is recent evidence that due to improved diet, biological maturity in terms of the onset of menstruation is occurring in girls at an increasingly early age, making the number of years of biological maturity but social immaturity even longer.)

The work ethic was unquestionably a good device for educational motivation in a time of scarcity, such as that surrounding much of Edgar Guest's poetry. It provided inducement for the very able to move upward economically, on rare occasions. But it also provided the notion that those who did not move up were failures. The crucial question is whether the schools can do anything for those who do not move up occupationally. Miller has put it well:

> The emphasis on educational and occupational mobility obscures the like-lihood that a variety of low-paying, low-skill jobs will remain in the economy. What will happen to people in these jobs? Do we not have to improve the conditions of these low-level jobs as well as to encourage people to get better paid, more productive positions? In our emphasis on mobility, we seem frequently to forget those left behind.[33]

Should education do anything to enrich the lives of those who do not wish to engage in occupational competition? If so, what and how? Be-

[33] Miller, "The Outlook of Working-Class Youth," p. 133.

cause of the commitment to reward those who prepare to "get ahead" occupationally, is the school being hypocritical in working hard with those who don't?

In a way, this dilemma in education is simply a reflection of a larger problem in American culture: the relation of prestige and esteem. We like to think that what is really important is the quality of performance a man turns in on whatever he does (esteem), but in actuality we seem to reward occupational position (prestige) far more. Here is the real paradox in our culture that Orwell put so well in *Animal Farm*: all men are equal, but some are more equal than others. Can we really believe both? It is certainly difficult for a teacher to operate as if *both* were true.

Perhaps it is time to try to bring esteem back into the status system, particularly when prestige no longer confers the economic rewards that would be commensurate with the extra effort in the occupational sphere. Perhaps the best way to force the issue is to describe the uppermost goal (in prestige terms) of many a business—the "top executive":

> We have, in sum, a man who is so completely involved in his work that he cannot distinguish between work and the rest of his life—and is happy that he cannot. Surrounded as he is by a society ever more preoccupied with leisure, he remains an anomaly. Not only does he work harder, his life is in a few respects more ascetic than the businessman of half a century ago. His existence is hardly uncomfortable yet . . . his style of living is not signally different from that of the men in middle management. And the fact doesn't concern him overmuch; the aspects of luxury that he talks about most frequently concern things that are organic to his work—good steak dinners, comfortable hotels, good planes and the like. . . . His house will never be a monument, an end in itself. It is purely functional, a place to salve the wounds and store up energy for what's ahead. And that, he knows full well, is battle.[34]

For such a man, should we feel only admiration and envy? Or perhaps a shred of pity as well? Is this the only view of the "good life" that teachers should convey to their students?

Perhaps the key involves the restructuring of the status system to include more nonoccupational criteria. We are clearly moving into an era in which few men will be *allowed* to fail—Medicare is here, and proposals are being brought to the federal government for a guaranteed income per family to be supplied by federal funds if necessary, and two years of free, compulsory college education for every child. In this type of world, a man does not just stand or fall on his own efforts. This is probably the hardest thing for Americans to get used to, yet it is clearly the direction in which we are moving. In such a world, perhaps the school

[34] W. Whyte, *Organization Man*, pp. 164–65.

should begin to provide some nonoccupational systems of esteem that will provide the student with some standards and incentives for that increasing part of his time and energy not directly related to his job. Certainly the football field is one place it is done successfully; yet for the spectator, there is little that he can use in his later life.

We are suggesting here that the reference group for esteem be changed to a new context—that of the individual himself. If the individual internalizes standards that will give him *self*-esteem when he performs some meaningful activity at a high level, then it matters not how many times he moves around geographically. Each individual should develop some activity, totally unrelated to his occupational life, which he can participate in, and out of which he will develop criteria for further improving his own performance. It is here that the arts and humanities *must* develop in schools and colleges, to provide students with meaningful activity and standards of excellence that will be useful all their lives. Also, it is here that the Protestant Ethic, no longer as relevant for the world of work, is still vital, if we are to strive for excellence in anything. Sustained, intensive effort is still necessary to produce anything in the arts and humanities, as on the football field. It seems to be a universal characteristic that we come to love the things for which we've suffered or worked hard, if the choice to suffer was a *voluntary* one. (This explains why the assembly line worker does not come to love his work.)

We are suggesting, then, that a return to a new kind of inner direction is possible and necessary. In earlier eras, the inner-directed man was that way by default—if he wished to support his family and survive, he *had* to work hard. With a twenty-hour workweek just around the corner for many workers, that position is a thing of the past. The kind of inner direction that is possible today is a more genuine one, based on choice, not default. In a way it is a new question to the human race: *Outside* of what I do for a living, what else is worth working hard for? Dedicating myself to? Giving up other things for? Its newness is partially what makes the question upsetting, but even more disturbing are the underlying questions: Who am I? What do I really believe in and stand for? The Protestant Ethic, calling as it did for a blind dedication to one's vocation and to a fixed set of notions about what was worthwhile, did not require a man to work through these problems for himself; he merely took the pledge of allegiance. This is clearly easier than working out the problems of meaning and existence for oneself.

One of the reasons that high-school and college students often seem vague and confused is that there is a great deal for them to be confused about. A welfare economy, a society in which a vast majority will not be *allowed* to dedicate themselves totally to their vocation, forces the individual to be more introspective. Whatever order there will be in his life will be largely created by him. Winston White has put the matter nicely:

> The impact of the current change on the individual has spread through the society virtually within a lifetime [Shift from developing economic resources to developing human personalities]. Unlike previous changes, it must be confronted by the individual not by the family, the church, a class, or an economic or political interest. It is one that the individual must confront by making choices without dependence on ascriptive guidance. He is, indeed, forced to be free.[35]

The reader may well ask at this point: What does this have to do with formal education, as it is currently being practiced? The answer is clear and obvious—practically nothing. Courses are seldom if ever designed to help (or to make) the student decide something about himself. Such a course is hard to comprehend—what would be its content? The answer is again clear: virtually any discipline *can* be taught in such a way that the students' lives will be changed or enriched, not through the acquisition of facts but through the inculcation of intellectual skills (and the slum youth has *plenty* of intellectual skills; they just don't happen to be ones we like) and the growth of the ability to make value discriminations, which must occur before value choices can be made.

The emphasis on sociability and fun, which has been the response of many educational institutions to this problem, does not meet it head on, except as training for affable, meaningless lives. One of the reasons why teachers have difficulty conceiving of the problem we are presenting here is that we ourselves were weaned on the Protestant Ethic, subscribed to the proper codes, and seldom worked out for ourselves why we wished to teach. One of the reasons the statement made by the college student a few pages back galls us so much is the possibility that he is *right*. We think his view of the good life is superficial, but it is nevertheless possible.

Of all the institutions in American culture, it is the educational institutions that have the greatest responsibility for developing some non-occupational sources of personal identification and esteem. Never before in history has a culture developed which makes a majority of the people choose freely how they will spend their time and energy. In that this choice is continual, education must be continual. In the past, education ceased when the person went to work—education was preparation for vocation, so once vocation started, education could stop. The trends in

[35] Winston White, *Beyond Conformity* (New York: Free Press of Glencoe, Inc., 1961), pp. 163–64.

adult education make clear that education and occupation are not dichotomous, that work is just one phase of life, while education concerns all.

We are suggesting here that Riesman's analogy of the inner-directed man as possessing an internal gyroscope to keep him "on course" is not quite accurate—the person who manifested the Protestant Ethic had the gyroscope implanted in him by the family and culture. The sort of inner-direction we are talking about occurs when the individual builds his *own* gyroscope to steer his own course. This does not mean that anarchy, suicide waves, or Big Brother are about to overtake us. We like to feel that that would be the consequences of "welfare" programs, and therefore most Americans believe that the suicide rates in countries with strong centralized governments like Sweden are very high. In fact, the reverse is true. In 1963, rates were much higher in Hungary, Austria, West Germany, Finland, and Denmark, while Switzerland, Taiwan, Japan, Australia, and France had rates about equal to Sweden's. (West Berlin, that center of the free enterprise spirit, had a suicide rate more than twice that of Sweden in 1963.) [36]

As we move toward more centralized governmental structures, as we become even more of an urban nation, the direct, highly visible participation in government typified by the town meeting will become a thing of the past. There will be a tendency to become lost in the mass, *if* we use the mass as our reference point. On the other hand, if our reference point is in our *selves*, we can find new types of personal freedom and new avenues of personal fulfillment, released from the burden of scratching for our daily bread. But the adjustments that will have to be made are severe. Never has education had a more important role to play, and never has it been less prepared to play it. The research on cheating, mentioned previously, indicates clearly enough what the consequences are when the educative content has no intrinsic meaning to the student's life as he sees it. This emphatically does not mean that we must pander to every student whim. It does mean that in teaching we try to provide "handles" either in skills or values, which the student can grasp, and which will have some impact on his notions of his present and future self. Above all, "success" must be presented to students as a concept relevant to *many* areas of human activity, not just reserved for those who wish to compete for high-prestige occupational positions.

[36] Gunnar Myrdal, "The Swedish Way to Happiness," *The New York Times Magazine,* Jan. 30, 1966, p. 17.

6: the quest for
community

As soon as we begin speaking of communities in American culture, we come again to the problem mentioned in the introduction: what shall be our focus? We could use a virtually limitless array of perspectives, from the family to the apartment house, the city block, the farm, the town, the county, the city, the state, region, nation, etc. Some sociologists have chosen the city (Robert Park, for example), others have written about the whole society as a community (Durkheim), while others have used a street-corner gang as a community model (Whyte).

The fact that writers *can* work on the nature of community at so many different levels indicates a very important thing about the nature of community in our time: *overlapping jurisdiction*. This overlap involves political, economic, ecological, religious, personal, emotional, and many other aspects of man's behavior. Because of this overlap of jurisdiction, no person can really say that he lives in only one community. There are, of course, many advantages to this arrangement, particularly for a culture in which people move around a great deal. But there are some clear disadvantages also. Because the individual splits his allegiances among so many communities, he truly belongs to none of them. Likewise, none of the various communities with which he associates can be of much assistance to him in getting on with the problems that beset him.

In most primitive societies, by contrast, there was a single community, in which the individual knew with little ambiguity what the rules of the game were. The Noble Savage was by no means always noble; he felt the same feelings of greed, lust, guilt, aggression, and fear that we "civilized" folk feel, but with one important difference:

> The important thing is that in primitive societies there are customary methods of dealing with these common human problems of emotional adjustment by which they are externalized, publicly accepted, and given treatment in terms of ritual beliefs; society takes over the burden which, with us, falls entirely on the individual. . . . This is easy in primitive societies where the boundary between the inner world of the self and the outer world of the community marks their line of fusion rather than separation.[1]

Clearly, this kind of primitive community allowed individual emotional problems to be made visible, acceptable, and treatable—it is probably fair to say that this *therapeutic* function of the primitive community is not too distant from the function of the psychiatrist in our culture.[2] If Weber is correct in his assertion that the world is steadily becoming demystified, it is also true that by the loss of ritual, myth, and symbolism that touch our daily lives, we have lost one of the most effective methods for handling personal and emotional problems by the community.

The overlapping jurisdiction of communities in our time and culture is also responsible for the lack of clearly defined selfhood, which is variously referred to as anomie, *angst,* marginality, etc. The question "Who am I?" is one which in many cultures with a single sense of community would simply never arise; therefore, the title of this chapter—the quest for community is in our time the quest for personal identity, a quest which would not be necessary except for the fact that different levels of community tell us different and conflicting things about ourselves. This diversity, however, does fall into a relatively small number of kinds of communities for analytical purposes.

---

[1] From Meyer Fortes, *The Institutions of Primitive Society,* quoted in M. Stein, *The Eclipse of Community* (New York: Harper & Row, Publishers, 1964), p. 243.
[2] On this point, see Maxwell Jones, *The Therapeutic Community* (New York: Basic Books, Inc., Publishers, 1953).

urbanization and cities

One of the central facts of our time involves the increasing urbanization of populations, both in this country and throughout the world. There are many reasons for this trend, but certainly one of the principal reasons is the rapid improvement of farming technology, allowing fewer people to grow much more food. This technology operates to benefit the large farm and to drive the small farmer out of business and into the city. Because the city dweller is totally dependent on the "outside" for food (as well as for many other things), city population growth is dependent upon growth in agricultural efficiency.

The exact size at which a town becomes a city is very difficult to determine, and a wide variety of figures are put forward as the cut-off line. For sociological purposes, however, we can define the city not by number of inhabitants, not by a given set of ecological, geographic, or economic factors, but as a way of living, "a state of mind, a body of customs and traditions, and of the organized attitudes and sentiments that inhere in these customs and are transmitted with these traditions." [3] The city is, therefore, a cultural pattern. Throughout most of history, the city has been the place where "civilized" and "urbane" men have dwelt. "High culture" has been a city product. (Before getting too ecstatic over the glories of cities, however, we should say that "slum culture" also resides there.)

Looking at the matter psychologically, we can say that the city dweller has a very high dependence on others, whether he is consciously and continuously aware of it or not. The self-sufficiency of the farm family (if, indeed, it ever existed) is definitely not for him. His contacts with others tend to be secondary (indirect, little face-to-face, or physical contact, rational), rather than primary (direct, face-to-face, emotional).

One of the factors that has always characterized city life is diversity —of personality types, income levels, nationalities, occupations, styles of life, kinds of entertainment, types of dwellings, variety of food, etc. This diversity is not random—the city dweller soon learns that there are patterns in the way these variables interact. The most noticeable of these are restricted *living* areas (slums, high-rise apartment districts) and re-

---

[3] From the classic essay on the subject by Robert Park, "The City; Investigations of Human Behavior in the Urban Environment," reprinted in P. Hatt and A. Reiss, *Reader in Urban Sociology* (New York: Free Press of Glencoe, Inc., 1951), p. 2. The following analysis draws heavily on Park's formulation.

stricted *function* areas (downtown shopping areas, manufacturing zones, etc.). Earlier thought in sociology assumed that these restrictions always occurred in a pattern of circular waves radiating out from the center—thus the so-called "concentric zone" theory.[4] It now appears that the pattern in each city is to a large extent unique, although it comes as a response to a common set of factors and pressures. For example, the central business areas may expand outward into areas previously used for slum housing in one city, while in another the expansion of the business district will move into an area committed heavily to manufacturing. Thus, the *response* to the expansion of the business district will be dependent upon the unique constellation of factors at work in each city, even though the pressure for change is brought about by a factor common to both.

Although it is generally agreed that cities are in a state of constant flux, it should be said that most of the analytical efforts dealing with cities have used concepts that are in their nature static. One of the few exceptions to this is Maruice Stein's analysis of the *processes* whereby all cities change, assuming that the response to these processes will be to some extent unique.[5] For Stein, the basic process is that of urbanization, or as Park would see it, the interrelationships of variables within the city in response to pressures of growth. Just as the eruption of a volcano can be attributed to changes in underground pressures, so the rapid growth of suburbs can be seen as a response to many pressures—economic, ecological, status, political—within the central city. Along with this major process, Stein cites industralization and bureaucratization as the other major processes delineating directions of city development.

The advantage of Stein's theoretical formulation is a central one: it allows *any* level of analysis—from street corners to city blocks to suburbs —to be fitted into a model of the development of a given city as a whole, based on the interaction of the parts. It also allows for interpretations taking into account change through time. (Chicago in the thirties is not Chicago in the sixties, but the working out of Stein's three processes there today can be related to the impact of these processes on Chicago as it was in the thirties.) Stein's view is that one consequence of these processes in all urban areas is a trend toward increased interdependence and decreased local autonomy (this is, of course, in agreement with our

4 For a good summary of the "concentric zone," "multiple nuclei," and "sector" theories of city organization, see C. Harris and E. Ullman, "The Nature of Cities," in Hatt and Reiss, *op. cit.*, 222–32; also K. Lynch "The Pattern of the Metropolis," in an excellent book edited by C. Elias, *Metropolis: Values in Conflict* (Belmont, Calif.: Wadsworth Publishing Co., 1964).

5 "Toward a Theory of American Communities," in Stein, *op. cit.*

opening statement on overlapping jurisdictions). We might go further and say that this increased interdependence has been a major force in the depersonalization of much of city life—we are increasingly dependent upon people we do not know. As we become more dependent on experts, there is also a greater tendency for standardization to arise (Detroit now tells us all about cars, Hollywood about movies, and Washington about politics and government). Virtually every product is now sold to a national market by advertising in national mass media, and most production and distribution facilities are geared to that level. It might be hypothesized that with the decrease of local and regional differences (radio and television announcers now sound remarkably alike anywhere in the United States), an increase in nationalism would logically result, because that would be the real paramenter of our feeling of community. There is no disciplined study to support or reject this view, but certainly the context of many, if not most, organizations has moved to the national level, even if judged by such a simple criterion as the rapidly increasing number of national conventions that take place annually. This should not be interpreted to mean, however, that individual feelings of patriotism and loyalty to the nation have increased as involvement with local institutions has decreased; in fact, the reverse may be true.

Another important factor, seldom mentioned, is that as cities have increased in size and complexity, the average urbanite knows less and less about the city he lives in. (For example, there are people who have lived in New York City all their lives who do not know that a day at the beach is only a subway ride away.) We tend to run in our own little ruts, unaware of the myriad services and activities the city has to offer. It is this lack of awareness of and participation in the totality of the community in which one lives which is largely responsible for the expressions of rootlessness and anomie found almost as a party line in contemporary literature. (Cities may indeed be depersonalizing, but judging from suicide figures on some small towns and rurally dominated states, those seem to be rather good at it also.)

In the view of this author, many of the writers who feel that the city is totally destructive of individual personality and integrity should go back and reread Sinclair Lewis's *Main Street*. The truth of the matter resides elsewhere:

> Is the modern metropolis, then, a freeing agent that enhances creative options and opportunities for self-expression? Or does it destroy personal identity and lead to inferior, mass tastes? These are not simply competing perspectives. Paradoxical as it may seem, the metropolis is a crucible for

both freedom and bondage, for creation *and* destruction of self and society.[6]

In the writing on urbanization, three major foci have been used, and we will deal briefly with each of them in turn: the slum, the suburb, and the megalopolis.

the slum and delinquency

It should be clear at the outset that poverty *per se* is not a defining characteristic of slums alone. Many if not most towns have fairly extensive areas of extreme poverty, and even the lush, beautiful rural countryside of Appalachia masks some of the most severe poverty in the United States. Thus, we cannot determine a slum simply by a per capita or family income level. A slum is also a sub*culture,* with a set of norms and values that can be perpetuated through time. Never have the subcultural aspects of slum life been given such a clear treatment as in William Whyte's brilliant treatment of an Italian slum district in Boston, *Street Corner Society.*

The author, one of the first to use participant observer techniques, spent an extensive period of time acclimating himself to the "gang" he was studying. Though most studies of slum life emphasize disorganization, confusion, and despair, Whyte found a great deal of cohesion and solidity. It must be said, however, that this study was done in the depression, when a group of twenty- to thirty-year-olds could spend most of their time together, since there was little work to be found. Also, the district was almost exclusively Italian, adding considerably to the possibilities for cohesion. Although there were significant differences, there were also astonishing similarities to the conventional "middle-class" value pattern, particularly in relation to loyalty, service, and honesty. Even the gang's codes regarding sex expressed this: the uninitiated girl was to be protected in an almost chivalric way.[7]

A vast majority of the writings on juvenile deliquency indicate that it is *formed* by conditions of deprivation in slums. Because gangs were found in slums, it was assumed that the slums had produced the gangs. The basic force that organized the gangs was thought to be frustration and resentment against adult society, which promised so many things and then prevented any possibility of attaining them, at least through legiti-

---

[6] Robert Lee, *The Church and the Exploding Metropolis* (Richmond, Va.: John Knox Press, 1965), p. 12. See also the very readable book by Harvey Cox, *The Secular City* (New York: The Macmillan Company, 1965).

[7] See W. F. Whyte, *Street Corner Society,* 2nd ed. (Chicago: University of Chicago Press, 1955).

mate channels. Thus, the gang was a way of "getting back" at adult society.[8]

The fact of the matter is that gangs have always been a part of growing up, at least for the American male—for example, the nostalgic accounts of small-town gangs mentioned in Thomas Bailey Aldrich's *Story of a Bad Boy* are revealing. If the same *behavior* had been manifested in a slum area, we would classify the boys as delinquents without much hesitation. Thus, illegal behavior produced by gangs is definitely not a phenomenon of slum life, in any exclusive sense. (In fact, when we think of the possibilities for violence which the slum environment provides, we would have to conclude that there is remarkably little.)

As an example, let us consider another gang, this time the "Dukes":

> While the Dukes manifested the familiar pattern of poor academic and work performance, on the one hand, the street-corner violence and petty theft on the other, the members did not appear especially deprived either by objective or subjective criteria. A more plausible explanation seems to be that their academic failures, their disinterest in conventional occupational roles, and their emergence as a delinquent gang were all attributable to the same underlying factor: a failure to develop commitments to adult roles and values.[9]

Hamilton Park, the residence of the Dukes, is a better-than-average living area in a large Midwestern city, and most of the Dukes came from reasonably good homes. They were clearly not being blocked by the social structure; indeed, those members who wanted to achieve occupationally and educationally had little difficulty. The fact was that most of the Dukes didn't *want* to. They much preferred their total involvement in the "youth culture," particularly, as we would have surmised, in the virtues of "fun." They had no interest in acquiring the responsibilities of adulthood. They were not poor—when they needed money for a purpose, such as a car, they would work until they had enough money, then quit. From this example of the Dukes, we could argue that the more the adolescent is surrounded by comfort and fun, the greater will be the tendency to remain uncommitted to adult values until later in life; ergo, the greater the tendency to remain in a juvenile gang. This might mean

---

[8] E.g., A. Cohen, *Delinquent Boys* (New York: Free Press of Glencoe, Inc., 1955), and R. Cloward and L. Ohlin, *Delinquency and Opportunity* (New York: Free Press of Glencoe, Inc., 1960). The first specific reference to this approach is probably R. Merton, "Manifest and Latent Function," in *Social Theory and Social Structure* (New York: Free Press of Glencoe, Inc., 1949), pp. 72–81.

[9] L. Karacki and J. Toby, "The Uncommitted Adolescent: Candidate for Gang Socialization," in Shostak and Gomberg, *Blue Collar World* (Englewood Cliffs, N.J.: Prentice-Hall, Inc., 1964), pp. 165–76. See also a brilliant study by Kenneth Keniston, *The Uncommitted: Alienated Youth in American Society* (New York: Harcourt, Brace & World, Inc., 1965).

that we could expect delinquent gangs in *any* socioeconomic area, including the very wealthy ones. Certainly the slums can no longer be accused of being the only breeding ground of delinquent behavior. Better crime reporting has already indicated that middle-class areas of large cities and suburbs are also good breeders of delinquent gangs, as well as crimes committed by adults.

Besides crime, slums are well known for their ability to produce mental illness in residents, and because of inadequate treatment facilities, to transmit this tendency to future generations. Recent research also indicates a tendency for slums to contain an unusually large number of downwardly mobile persons (speaking occupationally), who also seem to have a predisposition toward mental illness.[10] The precise causes for this increase of mental illness in slum areas are, of course, varied, but among them certainly are unstable marital relationships, poor-quality housing (although often amazingly expensive), rapid movement of people in and out of the slum, high unemployment rates, and high rates of disease.

The slums that Park (and to a large degree, Whyte) wrote about could be characterized by the term "ethnic slum." These were slums in which people knew each other—they shared a common heritage of race, religion, and national origin. They knew that the best, or hardest-working, members would get out of the slum; there was a significant level of aspiration. The recent changes have been well documented by Harrington:

> Where the ethnic slum once stood, in the "old" slum neighborhood, there is a new type of slum. Its citizens are the internal migrants, the Negroes, the poor whites from the farms, the Puerto Ricans. They join the failures from the old ethnic culture and form an entirely different kind of neighborhood. For many of them, the crucial problem is color, and this makes the ghetto walls higher than they have ever been . . . above all, these people do not participate in the culture of aspiration that was the vitality of the ethnic slum.[11]

To the degree that a given slum area now contains more than one race or nationality, we could call them "integrated," but certainly this has little to do with equality. The enclave or ethnic slum was confining, but people did not move in and out with the rapidity which characterizes today's slum areas, so that some genuine human communication was possible. Slum dwellers today probably have less in common than was true

---

[10] L. Srole *et al., Mental Health in the Metropolis* (Vol. I of the Mid-Town Manhattan Study) (New York: McGraw-Hill Book Company, 1962), p. 250. See also A. B. Hollingshead and F. Redlich, *Social Class and Mental Illness* (New York: John Wiley & Sons, Inc., 1958).

[11] M. Harrington, *The Other America* (New York: The Macmillan Company, 1962), p. 143.

of slum residents at the turn of the century, making the possibilities for cooperative action to improve conditions much more difficult.

The culture of slums today also contains tremendous quantities of noise and the continuous possibility of violence and danger. Without the support that the "ethnic slum" culture could offer, feelings of ineffectuality lead to an exaggerated lust for power, expressed often through weapons and episodes of sadistic violence.[12] It must be said that even new housing projects will not in themselves eliminate the *subculture* of poverty in slum areas. To expect the newly arrived tenant of a new housing project to shed his slum culture values and attitudes at the door and behave like a neat, clean, orderly "middle-class type" who will take immaculate care of his new apartment is to forget all that is known about cultural conditioning. The literature on slum clearance is voluminous, but there is virtually nothing written on the clearance of slum *culture*. This will involve a conversion of values, a notoriously difficult task.

suburbs

Suburban development has come into being so rapidly and comprehensively that most of us think the term has been with us forever. Actually, it is a rather new concept, for a good reason. There can be no suburb without some sort of rapid transportation, because the suburb is dependent on the "central city" and must have access to it on short notice. The suburb is therefore not a "city in the country," in that it is not an autonomous entity. In the past, a fairly clear line could be made between rural and urban areas. Through the astonishing growth of suburbs, that line is now extremely difficult to draw.

As an example of this evolution, consider the case of Harlem, an internationally known Negro slum area. Surprisingly enough, Harlem was a very prosperous white suburb of New York from about 1870 to 1904–1905, when the building boom in that area collapsed. Ads for houses and apartments in that era emphasized the virtues of "country living." The growth of Harlem as a suburb was premised on the extension of three elevated trains over 129th Street, providing rapid transport to the "Central City" of New York. Without this rapid transport, it is unlikely that suburban developers would have been interested in the area. With

12 For an unusually perceptive account of the life of a "new" delinquent, as well as an analysis of the misconceptions we have about "curing" him, see Anthony Burgess, *A Clockwork Orange* (New York: W. W. Norton & Company, Inc., 1963). Here is a "hood" whose delight in beating old ladies with tire chains is aroused by hearing, of all things, Beethoven's Ninth Symphony! On housing project delinquency, see Harrison Salisbury, *The Shook-up Generation* (Greenwich, Conn.: Fawcett Publications, Inc., 1958).

the cessation of new building in 1905, Harlem progressed very rapidly from an all-white suburb to an all-Negro slum.[13]

Although a good typology of types of suburbs has yet to be developed, there are certainly a few studies that do indicate in a clear way what major differences can be encountered. Each will be discussed briefly, with the hope that the reader will investigate some of the sources. To a degree, each represents an "ideal type," or central tendency, of suburban patterns.

the exurb

Spectorsky's justly famous description of exurbanite life was one of the most popular of community analyses, clearly written and perceptive. The exurbs Spectorsky studied were indeed "far out," at least in terms of geography. The populations studied were for the most part highly paid workers in the communications fields, who also had some artistic pretensions (the ad man who wishes to write the Great American Novel). The exurbs are hard to see, from the ground or air, largely due to the attempt to retain the rural and bucolic flavor of earlier times in Bucks, Westchester, Rockland, and Fairfield counties. The exurbanite is a "back-to-the-soil" man who, after working with symbols all day, wishes to come home and work with his hands. His house is usually a very expensive remodeled farmhouse with a barn-"studio." Even with a sizable salary, the exurbanite lives much beyond his income. He generally tries to farm some of his land, with a tractor which he knows nothing about and which the indigenous types charge inflated prices for fixing when it breaks down. His week ends are full of hustle and bustle, and the Thoreauvian contemplation of Nature, which drew him to exurban life initially, never comes. His wife runs a transportation agency, with down-to-the-minute schedules to get the children to each activity on time. Family life tends to be matriarchal by default—even in the families in which the artist father does not need to go into New York every day, he remains stuck in his barn-studio.

The value system of exurbia is a strange mixture of arty Bohemianism and money-grubbing conservatism. One can draw an interesting parallel between the dream of the blue-collar assembly-line worker of owning his own small store (freedom from the "rat race," independence, calling his own shots), and the exurbanite's dream of writing a Great Novel or doing serious painting (which also would free *him* from the "rat race," give him independence to call his own shots). Yet, both are trapped in

---

[13] The story of Harlem is a fascinating one. See Gilbert Osofsky, *Harlem: The Making of a Ghetto* (New York: Harper & Row, Publishers, 1966).

the present; neither can make the break. An interesting comparative study could be done comparing the reaction of the blue-collar worker and the exurbanite to the realization that the secret dream is not going to come about. Spectorsky sums up the matter rather well: "In the average exurbanite's personal equation there is one constant: his insecurity; one steadily growing value: his obligations; one steadily diminishing factor: time."[14]

Levittown

As the exurb typifies the highly individualistic suburb, so Levittown represents another "ideal type," the mass community of virtually identical homes, constructed by Abraham Levitt and Sons. In 1947, plans for a development of 2,000 units, renting to veterans for sixty dollars a month, were announced. In 1951, 17,447 homes had been completed. The Levitt house was a mass-produced, "standardized" house, complete with built-in appliances.

The Levittown family is a young family, with an average age for adults of 35 in 1957. Young children abound in virtually every family. Without question, the Levitt idea provided about the only way whereby middle-income families ($5–8,000) could own their own home. About three hours a day, the Levittown male is occupied with getting to work and home again. Although one would suspect that the residents would be as standardized as the houses, a strong (but debatable) case can be made for a high degree of diversity, in occupation, income, ethnicity, religion, etc.[15]

Friendship patterns tend, according to some observers, to proceed on clique lines rather than "straight down the block." Entertaining is informal, with a great deal of outdoor barbecuing in summer weather. The population shifts quite frequently, since these are young men "on the make." This creates a severe problem for the school system, as does the fact that the average Levittown family has more than two young children with no intention of stopping there. A vast majority of Levittowners moved to the suburbs to get a better education for their children, yet they knew virtually nothing about the school systems in the community they moved into. Although they express great interest in education, 40 per cent of eligible voters actually voting is a high score.

Levittown was originally restricted racially, the first contracts read-

[14] A. C. Spectorsky, *The Exurbanites* (New York: Street & Smith Publications, Inc., 1955), p. 269.
[15] Harold Wattell, "Levittown: A Suburban Community," in W. Dobriner, ed., *The Suburban Community* (New York: G. P. Putnam's Sons, 1958), pp. 287–313.

ing: "No dwelling shall be used or occupied by members of other than the Caucasian race, but the employment and maintenance of other than Caucasian domestic servants shall be permitted." Second contracts eliminated this clause, but in 1958 there were only three Negro families living in Levittown.[16]

Park Forest

This is a suburb like Levittown socioeconomically, but as different as night and day in other respects. The major difference is the regimen of Enforced Sociability in Park Forest. The kaffee-klatch for wives is a constant, compulsory thing; the educational system operates on a curriculum of teaching and testing for sociability. Even the ads for Park Forest make the point:

A cup of coffee—symbol of Park Forest!
Coffeepots bubble all day long in Park Forest.
This sign of friendliness tells you how much neighbors enjoy each other's company—feel glad they can share their daily joys—yes, and troubles too.

Come out to Park Forest where small-town friendships grow—and you still live so close to a big city.[17]

The trouble with these ads (and with Park Forest) is that they emphasize belongingness, security, and permanence. However, 30 per cent of the population moves every year, so that no one wants to put down deep, emotion-laden roots in Park Forest, which will have to be painfully torn up when they move on. On the other hand, all residents want to belong, and Park Forest is as close to a home as they can see in the future. "The trick," as one veteran puts it, "is to pretend to yourself that you're here for keeps and to join. If you don't, you'll keep putting off doing anything year after year, and you'll just make yourself feel more temporary than you actually are." [18]

There is some differentiation in Park Forest—the houses are not furnished identically, there is variety in food and leisure activities, but this variation occurs within very fixed limits. If someone steps over the bounds, by reading Kafka instead of *Sports Illustrated*, or listening to Bach rather than Lawrence Welk, the error is usually made very clear to him. Riesman has spoken of this as marginal differentiation: variation

---

[16] *Ibid.*, p. 303.
[17] W. Whyte, *The Organization Man* (Garden City, N.Y.: Doubleday & Company, Inc., 1957), pp. 314–15.
[18] *Ibid.*, p. 303.

is permitted, but only along carefully controlled lines. Riesman's notion of other-directed people also applies beautifully to the Park Foresters —they can be friends with anybody and everybody, and are. If your neighbor moves out, another will come in, and you will be friendly with him in precisely the same way, just as you are with everybody else. Neighbors are, and apparently must be, seen as interchangeable parts.

Crestwood Heights

This is the first example of a suburb studied as meticulously as the community study projects of the "Chicago School" in earlier decades. It differs from Levittown and Park Forest in that it is a well-to-do suburb for people at their peak earning potential—it is a terminal community, not one from which one aspires to move up to something better. Here, as in exurbia, houses are independent entities, and one does not find the compulsive sociability of Park Forest. The "training ground" period is definitely over—the word "Heights" tells the story. From this suburb, there is only one way to go—down. The residents are of high economic levels but, unlike the artistically oriented denizens of Exurbia, these are independent professionals, businessmen, and senior executives; this is the end of the occupational mobility line.[19] Educational levels of both husbands and wives are very high.

Perhaps because of the authors' own interpretation, there seems to be an amazingly high degree of concern with notions of mental health and "normality" in Crestwood Heights. Experts in these fields are in constant demand, both in the school system and outside. Mothers (perhaps *because* of their intelligence and ability) are aware of the ambiguities and contradictions in the child training literature, yet are committed to the idea of bringing up their children in the "right" way. One solution to this problem for the mother is to turn the child over, at an increasingly early age, to social science-oriented specialists. Yet the mother is as interested in new "fashions" in child development theories as she is in new fashions in interior decoration or clothes.

One mode of analysis of this community must emphasize the difficulty sons will have in competing with such successful fathers—upward mobility for most sons would be a logical impossibility. The parents often try to shield their children from the grubbier side of life, knowing that when the time comes, their children will have to fight as they themselves did. This is certainly one of the major anxiety producers in Crestwood Heights parents.

[19] J. Seeley *et al.*, *Crestwood Heights* (New York: Basic Books, Inc., Publishers, 1956).

Also clear in this suburb is a theme we have expressed before: the tendency for social experiences (dating, wearing cosmetics, school dances, nursery school) to be moved down to earlier and earlier ages, both to free the busy mother and to get the child into the hands of "experts." The reason for this is obvious: the business or professional world in which the father operates is one of professional competence—Crestwood fathers are themselves, as a group, "experts," and this mentality tends to diffuse into every aspect of their lives, even the raising and educating of their children.

Partially because of this respect for competence, regardless of other factors, Crestwood Heights has a large Jewish population (in fact, a majority). It would seem that of all the groups which have been subject to minority persecution, the Jewish people have indeed excelled in terms of getting into the most fashionable suburbs, due partially to their reverence for education, the *use* of learning to further their own needs, and their overrepresentation at the highest economic and occupational levels. There is some evidence that this is true throughout all of American suburbia; in fact, one could say that the "higher the class" of the suburb, the greater will be the proportion of Jewish representation.[20] Another reason for this, however, is that religion plays a very small part in the lives of the people who live in Crestwood Heights, so that discrimination along religious lines would not be very likely. (Race is, however, a different story.)

The single most important impression one gets from the study of Crestwood Heights is the incredible worship of youthfulness. We have mentioned earlier that for the exurbanites, as well, there is a feeling that time (which is seen as a commodity) is running out. Yet, this is a more mature community than Park Forest or Levittown, made up of very successful people who are no longer "on the make," who ought to be able to grow older gracefully while enjoying life. This does not seem to be the case. The golden age seems to be the twenties to the middle thirties, and the further they get away from those years, the more disturbed they become. The onset of menopause can be traumatic for both husband and wife—it is a signal, among other things, that retirement is near, that the children will be moving away soon, if they haven't already done so, and that a smaller house in a less desirable community will be their future, when they can no longer afford the "Heights."

One gets the feeling that one of the major reasons for the constant pushing of children into activities for which they are not biologically or socially ready comes from the parents' own reverence for youth—the

[20] For an excellent study of this problem, using suburbs like Newton, Mass., and St. Louis Park, Minn., see A. Gordon, *Jews in Suburbia* (Boston: Beacon Press, 1959).

desire (perhaps fulfilling some of their own dreams) to pack these "wonderful years" of their children's lives with joyful social experiences, experiences for which they, the parents, had little time even at more appropriate age levels. Realizing that they themselves were not completely "normal" children, they desire nothing more than that their children will be completely "normal," supremely well adjusted (adjusted to what is a different problem), and *devoutly happy*. Perhaps this is a natural consequence, as we saw in the last chapter, of the kind of risk taking and drive that characterizes those in professional and executive roles—their needs for security may be magnified, and expressed through their children. It is somehow tragic to think that their own training for the battles of life (obviously successful training, as here they are in Crestwood Heights) is being completely reversed in their children.

megalopolis

A short while ago, the author got into his car (about 100 miles north of New York City) and drove to Warrenton, Virginia, about fifty miles southwest of Washington, D.C. The highway was under the jurisdiction of about twelve different authorities, yet there was not a single traffic light on the whole stretch. Over 35 million people lived along the way. Here we have the ultimate in support of Stein's thesis about urbanization—increased interdependence and decreased local autonomy.

This trip covered most of what has come to be known as Megalopolis —a region of about six hundred miles, stretching from Portland, Maine, through Norfolk, Virginia. It includes Boston, New York, Philadelphia, Baltimore, and Washington. Well over forty million people live in the area. The area is not a randomly selected piece of geography—it is an *entity*, in almost every sense of the term. There is no rural-urban split in this area, and the overlapping jurisdictions mentioned earlier are the rule, not the exception. In megalopolis (roughly translated as "supercity") we do not find large cities with neatly arranged satellite suburbs —around New York, one cannot say whether a given community "belongs" to New York, Philadelphia, Trenton, Newark, or New Brunswick. Indeed, Newark and Trenton *themselves* are now, in many ways, "suburbs" of New York, although Trenton is also closely tied to Philadelphia. In many respects, megalopolis is more like a nation than a city, as Jean Gottman has pointed out.[21] Most of the nation's business is transacted there, and

21 Gottman, *Megalopolis* (New York: Twentieth Century Fund, 1961), p. 9. An excellent paperback summary is now available: W. von Eckardt, *The Challenge of Megalopolis* (New York: The Macmillan Company, 1964).

it is, in a real sense, the hub of the nation, although improperly placed for such an analogy.

It now apears that this megalopolis is only one of many. Similar areas are forming between Pittsburgh and Cleveland; Detroit and Cincinnati; Chicago, Milwaukee, and St. Louis; Los Angeles and San Diego; San Francisco and Sacramento; Tacoma, Seattle, and Portland. In these seven or eight centers, transportation and communication facilities are highly coordinated within the megalopolitan area. Although the emergence of our conscious recognition of megalopolis as a fact of life is new, it is clearly based on developments that have been in the making for at least a hundred years: rapid, inexpensive systems of transport and communication, an expanding population and economy with increasing per capita income, rapid growth in white-collar industries (communications media, etc.), and increases in the number of white-collar jobs in manufacturing concerns, as well as increased farm productivity, allowing vast quantities of land to be freed for other uses,[22] particularly the sprawling out of activities formerly occurring within city limits.

Speaking sociologically, we cannot call megalopolis a community in any sense. There is too much diversity, too much competition, too little recognition of common concerns. (After all, the major megalopolis in the eastern seaboard consists of ten states, 117 counties, and the District of Columbia. Whether human beings can ever learn to perceive so large an entity as a community is problematic.) But the major internal problems of our time—water supply, air pollution, lack of space—are megalopolitan problems. (There are at least twenty overlapping jurisdictional areas that will have to cooperate with each other before New York City's water shortage can be dealt with.) Increasingly, our economics, politics, transportation, and communication will occur at a level of complexity (megalopolitan) and size which we cannot comprehend *socially.* How could anyone say, with a feeling of pride and loyalty, that he lives in Megalopolis One? It is this level of organization that Huxley was criticizing in *Brave New World,* and Orwell in *1984.*

It may well be that in the future, the need for coordination at the megalopolitan level will produce a vast change in our system of politics and government. The present organization of governance, based largely on the notion of small-town, agrarian America, makes little sense in megalopolis—problems will increasingly exist at a level greater than the jurisdictions of city, county, or state, and some new form of government will inevitably come into being which can deal with megalopolitan problems, the only alternative being that the federal government might

[22] See especially Chap. 11 of Gottman's book, "The White-Collar Revolution," pp. 565–630.

assume virtually full control at the regional, or megalopolitan, level. Planning, even at the city level, is still a revolutionary notion, suspect in many quarters; yet we are saying that "The city . . . is increasingly interdependent with the rest of the complex living and working environment we have called Megalopolis." [23] City planning is not large enough in scope for this task.

education and the quest
for community

This seems a logical point to summarize the material thus far presented, with particular emphasis on ramifications affecting education. First, it appears that the suburb is the wave of the future. Already more than one American of every four lives in a suburb, and the proportion, particularly of young people, is rising. The suburb feeds off the central city in most instances but represents a net loss economically to the city which supports it. A suburb has been described as a city trying to have its cake and eat it too.

Suburban parents tend to be extremely concerned with youth, both the loss of their own and what their children are doing with theirs. The school is increasingly *the* instrument for socializing the child. Not only are there "experts" at it in the school system, but the mother is therefore relieved of both the burden of caring constantly for a young child and the burden of total responsibility for things in her children she doesn't like. Many people have pointed out that the school today is serving almost the exact function of the church in earlier times.

The suburb reflects the carrying through of business perspectives into the community. The schedules kept by suburbanites are remarkably tight —life is ordered around the minutes, not the hours or days, even on weekends. Suburbs tend to be matriarchies by default. The further away the community from the central city, the less time, effort, and sheer physical presence can the father give to his family. Compulsive sociability is often the rule, particularly in suburbs that cater to young, upwardly mobile families. In this context, the role of the school is that of a training ground for smooth personal interactions. According to Whyte, when Park Foresters were asked what they wanted the school to emphasize, their answer was overwhelmingly "to teach students how to be citizens and how to get along with other people." [24] It is conceivable that this tendency to "keep busy" on a constant schedule, both in school and out, is a last vestige of the Protestant Ethic—no longer applicable to occupational

[23] W. von Eckardt, *op. cit.*, p. 125.
[24] Whyte, *The Organization Man*, p. 434.

endeavors, it nevertheless is still telling us that we should cram every hour with activity, that idleness is evil, and contemplation a "waste of time." The suburb is also the last vestige of the "small-town" virtues; the ideology is very egalitarian—every suburbanite feels that there are no social classes or stratification in *his* town. Several studies have indicated that this is not the case,[25] yet suburbanites persist in the twin beliefs of egalitarianism and self-sufficiency.

It is also clear that, since a majority of our working population is now in white-collar work, we can expect more and more people to yield to the urge to move out to suburbia. The other side of the coin concerns those who are left in the central city, unable to escape constantly deteriorating slums. If Harrington is correct, there is, in America, approximately one slum dweller for every suburbanite, yet we very seldom see the slum dweller, partially due to the "blinders" which the suburban culture puts on its citizens. Civilizations in the past have existed for the most part on the efforts of a poverty-stricken *majority* of the population. In our time, poverty is a minority-group position. The suburbanite, devoted to his house, his family, his leisure, his schools, is seldom if ever aware that he is creating and perpetuating vast inequities in the economic life of the city. He is dependent on the city for work, transport, amusement, yet he pays no taxes to the city, and even his purchasing power, which had previously helped the city, has been drawn off by the suburban shopping centers. Suburbs tend to attract those bright, upwardly mobile people who particularly want better schools for their children (a major reason for suburban residence), leaving a large cadre of malcontents in slum schools to be dealt with somehow. (Suburbs tend to attract bright, upwardly mobile *teachers* also, leaving for the slums the less-than-good and the truly dedicated.) Most of the nation's finest schools are suburban schools, but their excellence is often bought at the heavy price of inferior education in the very central cities that make those suburbs possible.

It would probably be safe to say that the vast majority of teachers produced by teacher training institutions are prepared for careers in suburban schools. Student teachers tend to be placed in suburbia far more often than one would expect by chance. Because salaries are generally higher in suburban schools, because children and parents are more interested in education (albeit for the wrong reasons in many cases), suburbia is a goal for many teachers. Even more important, our criteria for "good teaching" tend to give the suburban teacher a large initial ad-

[25] E.g., W. H. Form, "Status Stratification in a Planned Community," in Dobriner, *op. cit.,* pp. 209–24. See also A. Vidich and J. Bensman, *Small Town in Mass Society* (Garden City, N.Y.: Doubleday & Company, Inc., 1958); and W. Whyte, *The Organization Man,* Chap. 23, "Classlessness in Suburbia," pp. 330–44.

vantage. Acquisition of large chunks of subject matter, manifesting the "proper" values, and getting into a good college are all easier in the relatively homogenized suburbs that have little poverty and no "hard-core ethnics" whose cultural background makes them impossible to teach. How do we define good teaching, when the teaching tasks are those of getting the students to eat regular meals, take a bath once in a while, and keep quiet and stop fighting, at least in school? It is easy to scoff at this argument and say that such things are unimportant, but anyone who has spent even an hour in a room of thirty pupils who have *not* learned these behaviors will testify to their importance. But how do we train teachers for this sort of task? If the schools don't do it, who will?

Around a city, there may be ten or more suburban areas, each with an absolutely autonomous school board in complete control. With a few notable exceptions (Cleveland and Washington are two), there is little coordination at the governing level of a city and its suburbs, yet most of the problems of urban educational systems are caused, at least in part, by the suburbs that surround them. No one is complaining about the excellence of most suburban schools, but should this excellence be purchased with money which belongs to the cities?

Moving out to an even larger perspective, we can see that megalopolis is also performing some of the functions of the suburb in relation to the city. For example, the eastern megalopolis works as a "brain drain," drawing off much of the top talent from other sections of the country. (It should be noted, however, that this trend is apparently decreasing, due partially to the development of other megalopoli that can compete effectively with the original one. In college teaching, for example, there seems to be a trend to go either to the East or the West Coast.) The original megalopolis contains a very high percentage of well-educated adults (living in suburbs) *and* a high percentage of very poorly educated people (living in slums).[26] It is too early to specify what sort of educational coordination is needed at the megalopolitan level, but certainly something that can restore some of the pressing imbalances within the megalopolis is desperately needed.

It should be clear to the reader that the definition of "community" in suburbia is indeed a superficial one. We might expect, therefore, that some sort of wave of dissatisfaction might sweep over a community in which one had no privacy, no right to read certain kinds of books or listen to certain kinds of music ("good" books and "good" music), and in whose schools one's children would be evaluated in terms of how nice they were to everybody. In a way, the saddest thing about suburbs is

[26] W. von Eckardt, *op. cit.*, pp. 90–91.

that such thoughts seldom arouse suburbanites. As Stein puts it, "The social system of Park Forest with its enforced sociability and its marginal differentiation hardly causes concern to most persons participating in it. William H. Whyte's book *The Organization Man* probably held few surprises for the well-trained organization men who read it; indeed, some of them must have wondered what all the shouting was about." [27] Suburban schools do little to allow students to question suburbia and its values, and nothing to make them see other possible kinds of community organization which might not exploit cities. We are still a long way from *Communitas*,[28] and the next generation will have to plan communities more effectively than we have done. However, there is at present little or no desire to improve suburbia, and little awareness of the *reciprocal* relationship of city and suburb, currently working against the interests of the central city.

The question of teachers for slum schools remains a controversial one. Should they be recruited from the "middle classes" or from the slums themselves? This raises the larger question: should the values of the teacher and students be compatible? There are advantages, of course, to having as a slum teacher someone who has come from that area and "made it." At the moment there is not enough evidence to answer this question, but it is a crucial one, especially for teacher training institutions that will be recruiting and training the teachers who will be dealing with the problem. As the racial balance within the central city continues to move toward a Negro majority in terms of students (as is currently the case in a large number of cities), should the teaching staff also be moving toward a Negro majority?

At the moment, it seems reasonable to assume that slums, both in terms of buildings and human culture, will be with us for quite some time. Present efforts at slum *clearance* tend to remove slum housing and replace it with middle-income housing which slum residents cannot afford—therefore, forcing them to move into another slum area somewhere else. The really difficult problem is the elimination of the slum *culture* or way of life. The school is at present the only institution that can deal with this most pressing of problems, yet it is doing little. The slum culture does not come out of the blue; it is inherent in tenements, open sewage, lack of privacy, ever-present crime and violence, and the futility of unemployment. Even busing slum children out to good suburban schools is no solution to the promulgation of slum *values*, which are to some

[27] Stein, *op. cit.*, p. 294.
[28] See Percival and Paul Goodman, *Communitas* (Chicago: University of Chicago Press, 1947), for a brilliant account of the problems and possibilities of community planning.

extent inherent in the environment to which the slum child must return each night. Any solution to the problem of education in the slums will have to follow some drastic economic changes, including a drastically increased program of clean, subsidized low-income housing projects that take into account the *entire* environment into which the buildings will go, as well as an awareness of the reciprocity of slum and suburb, each being partially a cause of the other.

Lest the reader feel that suburban schools are utopian, several of their problems might be stated before we conclude. First, few suburbs were properly planned for *before* the migration took place, leaving them with few if any zoning restrictions to make sure that residential areas stay residential. (The author is aware of many cases in which heavy industry moved right into the middle of very desirable housing areas in suburbs, totally ignoring protests of the residents.) Once any industry has moved into a residential area, it can no longer be blanket-zoned, and spot zoning has to be done to try to prevent further deterioration. Without enforceable zoning and acreage restrictions, builders can erect houses on tiny plots of land, increasing the population density far past that which was originally planned for. (A typical suburban problem exists when houses are so close together that one man's septic tank is only a few feet from the next man's well.)

These community problems reflect themselves in the schools, where double sessions are quite common, due to drastically increased population density. Long-range planning for school development is difficult indeed under these circumstances. Although salaries are higher than in the city, it is difficult to attract unmarried women (a prime source of elementary-school teachers) to the suburbs, due to the fact that suburbs are composed almost entirely of married families. There may not be an eligible male for twenty miles.

Another frequent problem in suburban schools arises when parents get so interested in school problems that they try to run things, putting teachers, administrators (and even students) in a difficult position. There are many communities in which parents have master's degrees about as frequently as the teachers, making it difficult for parents to give, and for teachers to receive, deference. Parents' overly zealous concern for their children's success leads both parents and children into undue grade consciousness at ridiculously early levels, often the first three grades of school. As we have seen, cheating in school and college is produced by seeing education as a means and not an end—a lesson the suburban child often learns from his parents.

Another problem that suburban teachers face but don't talk much about is the fact that outside of Levittown and the few other totally "planned" communities, most suburbs have an "old guard," the bucolic types, usually practicing subsistence farming, who were there long before the urban exodus. Often, they control the local politics and work against building more schools, hiring more teachers, etc. Their children are often just as "culturally deprived" as the slum child, and they may get worse treatment in suburbia, where they are a minority, than they would in a slum school. In most suburban schools, the overwhelming majority of students plan to go on to college (often not because of any inner drive to do so, but because they never considered doing anything else). This means that the commercial and vocational curriculums, enrolling a small minority of students and operating at a great cost per student in equipment, will tend to get short shrift. Because of their being such a minority, this student group may be branded as "failures" in a more damaging way than in the slums, where at least they are one of a respectable number, living in a community that has some respect for manual work, which is looked at with scorn in some white-collar suburbs. In this way, suburban schools make clear that the egalitarian myth in suburbia is a myth, that a person's ultimate vocation is still a pervasive factor even in the suburb's evaluation of him.

Finally, it should be said that the search for community in America is not yet over. New forms of community will undoubtedly arise, particularly as more and more industry leaves the central city, and as various versions of megalopolis complete their internal coordination and begin to interlock with others. Exactly what form these new communities will take is difficult to say, with one exception: the small town—independent, insular, and rural—is a thing of the past. The suburb is not a replacement for it. Whatever forms of community we develop, they will be interdependent and urban. One likely possibility is that the only form of community we have left in relatively unchanged form is the family. It may well be that the quest for personal identity, which has in the past been the quest for community, will focus increasingly on the family and on the school. Whether either the family structure or public education are ready for this increasingly important task is a question open to debate.

7: creativity as
a social phenomenon

Nueva, a young female chimpanzee, was tested three days after her arrival. She had not yet made the acquaintance of the other animals but remained isolated in a cage. A little stick was introduced into her cage; she scrapes the ground with it, pushes the banana skins together in a heap, and then carelessly drops the stick at a distance of about three-quarters of a metre from the bars. Ten minutes later, fruit is placed outside the cage beyond her reach. She grasps at it, vainly of course, and then begins the characteristic complaint of the chimpanzee: she thrusts both lips—especially the lower—forward, for a couple of inches, gazes imploringly at the observer, utters whimpering sounds, and finally flings herself on the ground on her back— a gesture most eloquent of despair. . . . Thus, between lamentations and entreaties, some time passes until—about seven minutes after the fruit has been exhibited to her—she suddenly casts a look at the stick, ceases her moaning, seizes the stick, stretches it out of the cage, and succeeds, although somewhat clumsily, in drawing the bananas within arm's length. Moreover, Nueva at once puts the end of her stick behind and beyond her objective.

161

... One phenomenon is certain and I can vouch for its absolute certainty; the sudden and immediate appearance of a solution at the very moment of sudden awakening. Once being awakened very abruptly by an external noise, a solution long searched for appeared to me at once without the slightest instant of reflection on my part— the fact was remarkable enough to have struck me unforgettably —and in a quite different direction from any of those which I had previously tried to follow.

At last two days ago I succeeded, not by dint of painful effort but so to speak by the grace of God. As a sudden flash of light, the enigma was solved. . . . For my part I am unable to name the nature of the thread which connected what I previously knew with that which made my success possible.

When you have satisfied yourself that the theorem is true, you start proving it.[1]

These statements describe apes and humans in a common act: the act of *discovery*. It is an astounding process, one of the real wonders of our existence. Although these examples are from creative geniuses (and there are geniuses among apes as well as humans), the creative act, the "Aha!" or "Eureka!" response, is one that all of us have experienced, to a greater or lesser degree.

What is this process like? Perhaps the word dis-covery is our best clue, as it suggests that when we create, we simply remove, or uncover as by lifting a curtain or veil, to reveal something that was there all the time but which we had not perceived before. Aristotle describes the job of the sculptor as that of intuiting the "true" form that lies within his block of stone—once this is done, the actual sculpting is simply removing the excess stone from around the form. By uncovering, the sculptor reveals what was there all the time but was never seen. It can occur in a variety of contexts: a problem that must be solved, such as Archimedes' sudden awareness that the volume of his body raised the water level of his bathtub, so that to find the volume of a gold crown he was trying to measure he could simply "give the crown a bath" and see how much the water level rose. It is important to note here that Archimedes was not the first man to note that, when one gets into a bath tub, the water level rises. But he *was* the first man to discover (or uncover) the principle that the volume of the solid will be equal to the volume of the water displaced by the object. He did this by relating, or juxtaposing, two previously unrelated aspects of his experience.

[1] All of these from an excellent book by Arthur Koestler, *The Art of Creation* (New York: The Macmillan Company, 1964), pp. 101–18. See also on a general level, B. Ghiselin, *The Creative Process* (Berkeley: University of California Press, 1952.)

The creative act thus alters one's perceptual field, so that what Archimedes saw when he encountered solids and liquids was different after he made his discovery.[2] In similar fashion, the ape of Kohler's who discovered that branches could be taken off trees and used as tools would never be able to "see" a tree in the same way after he made his discovery. Before, it was a thing to climb in and get food from, etc.; after, it became all these things *plus* a tool collection. We should add, however, that we cannot call all alterations of the perceptual field of the individual creative. The child who learns that the sign 4 stands for a numerical quantity one more than 3, one less than 5, or that the things he puts on his feet are called shoes, has simply learned names for things.

Another interesting thing about the creative act is that it seldom happens to people who are deliberately trying to be "creative." Like Sartre's schoolboy who is trying so hard to act like a student that he hears and learns nothing, the Bohemian who "acts creative" is not going to be very successful. (As Bruner has observed, the road to banality is paved with creative intentions.)[3] The problem that the creative person is working on has "gripped" him; he has an *intrinsic* interest in it: it is not a means but an end in itself.

The solution, as seen in some of the remarks at the beginning of this chapter, is not arrived at on a straight road; it often comes with a shock as a jolting surprise. Often it occurs when one is not consciously involved with the problem at all, as in this description of his "vision" by the famous mathematician Poincaré:

> Just at this time I left Caen, where I was then living, to go on a geologic excursion under the auspices of the school of mines. The changes of travel made me forget my mathematical work. Having reached Coutances, we entered an omnibus to go some place or other. At the moment when I put my foot on the step the idea came to me, without anything in my former thoughts seeming to have paved the way for it, that the transformations I had used to define the Fuchsian functions were identical with those of non-Euclidean geometry. I did not verify the idea: I should not have had time, as, upon taking my seat in the omnibus, I went on with a conversation already commenced, but I felt a perfect certainty. On my return to Caen, for conscience' sake I verified the result at my leisure. . . . Most striking at first is this appearance of sudden illumination, a manifest sign of long, unconscious prior work. The role of this unconscious work in mathematical investigation appears to me uncontestable. . . .[4]

[2] One of the best theoretical models dealing with perception is Donald Snygg and A. W. Combs, *Individual Behavior: A Perceptual Approach to Behavior* (New York: Harper & Row, Publishers, 1959). See also Max Wertheimer, *Productive Thinking* (New York: Harper & Row, Publishers, 1945).

[3] In Howard Gruber *et al.*, eds., *Contemporary Approaches to Creative Thinking* (New York: Atherton Press, 1962).

[4] From Koestler, *op. cit.*, p. 115.

These are a few of the more spectacular aspects of the creative process, which can be seen in all of us in a somewhat less glamorous fashion. One does not need to produce something that is new to the consciousness of the whole human race—the small boy who comes to see a reciprocal relation between plant and animal life is being creative within his *own* frame of reference. But being told that it exists and "seeing" that it exists are two somewhat different things.

There are a tremendous number of definitions of creativity in current research, but perhaps the most inclusive comes from a British economist:

> Men imagine outcomes which come into their minds we know not whence; these outcomes can be new in the most absolute and radical sense, untraceable to the individual's past or present, sprung from nowhere. If these can steer his choice of act, the decision to perform that act can be properly called creative, opening on each occasion, perhaps we might almost say, an extra dimension to that abstract conceptual space in which things happen.[5]

From what we have said thus far, it should be clear that the creative processes (and the plural is used advisedly) are not easy targets for study by the social sciences. First, the phenomenon cannot be produced on demand; you cannot sit a person down and tell him to "be creative." Second, it does not depend on a fixed sequence of events and can happen anywhere, not just in geographical proximity to the problem. Third, the individuals themselves cannot describe what goes on. Because of this visionlike aspect of creative acts, there is at present no clear-cut theory of creative behavior, either the mechanics of it, or of why it appears so strikingly in some people and so little in others.

It is clear that the creative act can involve either a restructuring of elements already in the perceptual consciousness of the person, or the creation of entirely new elements that were not "seen" before. A machine can be (and has been) built to do the former, but certainly not the latter.[6] Thus, the process is defined by the product: when one produces a creative solution or relationship, we say (after the fact) that creativity has happened. But there are no *pre*creative clues which could

---

[5] G. L. S. Shackle, *Decision, Order, and Time in Human Affairs* (London: Cambridge University Press, 1961).

[6] A fascinating account of this development can be found in the paper by Herbert Simon *et al.*, in Gruber, *op. cit.*, pp. 63–119. Their computer program, called the Logic Theorist, works effectively on the recombination, or reductionist, process. But Simon considers *all* creativity to be simple problem solving, recombining elements to find THE answer. Some problems have many answers, all "correct," and some have many roads to each answer. It is delightful to hear that the first paper "written" by the Logic Theorist was rejected by the *Journal of Symbolic Logic*, although it is doubtful that the machine experienced the usual reactions to this situation.

be used experimentally to "cue" creative responses, other than that of try-ing to free the mind from its normal, stereotyped perceptions. If one assumes, therefore, that the creative response is made to some creativity-producing stimulus in a direct S-R relation, one would be in considerable difficulty.

Thus, it should not come as a shock to the reader to find that the major studies of creative behavior were done at least several decades ago by the Gestaltists: Kohler, Lewin, and Wertheimer. Many of the present behavioristically inclined students of psychology would rather work on problems more immediately susceptible to "scientific" verification. In most experimental situations, the opportunity for creative or unorthodox re-sponses is usually avoided. The T-maze, for example, is designed to give the experimental animal *only* a choice of turning left or right to get food, neither of which is a particularly creative option. Kohler, on the other hand, designed his experiments to discover whether or not his apes could find creative solutions to problems, and found the answer was often yes. The often unstated assumptions of the experimenter, therefore, will tend to make him select experimental situations that are compatible with these assumptions. As Lord Russell put it:

> One may say broadly that all animals that have been carefully observed have behaved so as to confirm the philosophy in which the observer be-lieved before his observations began. Nay, more, they have all displayed the national characteristics of the observer. Animals studied by Americans rush about frantically, with an incredible display of bustle and pep, and at last achieve the desired result by chance. Animals observed by Germans sit still and think and at last evolve the solution out of their inner con-sciousness.[7]

This fact does not, of course, mean that the social sciences are "unsci-entific," because experiments in the physical and natural sciences are also based on belief systems—unproven, or unprovable, assumptions. The ex-perimenter must deal with the world *as he sees it*. If the results are con-sistent and can be replicated, one can assume that a relationship does exist between the factors studied. One can*not*, however, assume that this is the *only* relationship possible. After all, the physicists have decided that light can be, according to the experiment, either a wave *or* a particle. (The fact that we experience disbelief at the notion of something being both wave and particle means that somewhere, beyond our present ability to conceptualize, there is a better notion of the nature of light which will resolve the apparent paradox.)

This, then, should explain why experimenting on creative activity is

[7] Quoted in H. Hodgkinson, *Education in Social and Cultural Perspectives* (Engle-wood Cliffs, N.J.: Prentice-Hall, Inc., 1962), p. 193.

extremely difficult—it is always after the fact. There is, however, a significant amount of work in the field of personality that can shed some indirect light on the problem.

All of this research has indicated that, for most people, clinging to a belief or attitude is often a psychological necessity, even if it does not square with the world of experience. For example, Festinger, in his investigations of various religious sects that prophesied the end of the world on a certain date, discovered that when the date came and went, and the world still went on, they did not give up their belief but clung to it all the more strongly, rationalizing by setting up an error in the calculation of the date, etc.[8] We have probably all been in the position of adhering to a belief or perception long after the facts are beating us over the head, because giving up the belief would be even more painful.

This tenacity is understandable, in that our personality is based on what we perceive, so that an alteration of our perceptions or beliefs is an alteration of our *selves*. According to Rokeach, who has done much significant research in the area, our beliefs are not isolated entities but exist in relatively consistent *systems*. The dual nature of belief systems has been well expressed by him:

> The beautiful thing about a belief system is that it seems to be constructed to serve both masters at once: to understand the world insofar as possible and to defend against it insofar as necessary. We do not agree with those who hold that people selectively distort their cognitive functioning so that they will see, remember, and think only what they want to. Instead, we hold to the view that people will do so only to the extent that they have to, and no more. For we are all motivated by the desire, which is sometimes strong and sometimes weak, to see reality as it actually is, even if it hurts.[9]

Since the development of Adorno's F-scale (the F stands for fascist), it is clear that for certain people (we can call them authoritarians), defense against the world is far more important than understanding it.[10]

---

[8] L. Festinger, *When Prophecy Fails* (Minneapolis: University of Minnesota Press, 1956).

[9] Milton Rokeach, *The Open and Closed Mind* (New York: Basic Books, Inc., Publishers, 1960), pp. 400–1. His research centers around the person, and not the environment or "field," while that of Snygg and Combs represents the other pole: "All behavior, without exception, is completely determined by, and pertinent to, the perceptual field of the behaving organism" (*op. cit.*, p. 20).

[10] T. W. Adorno, *et al.*, *The Authoritarian Personality* (New York: Harper & Row, Publishers, 1950). On this point, see also Eric Hoffer, *The True Believer* (New York: Harper & Row, Publishers, 1951); Leon Festinger, *A Theory of Cognitive Dissonance* (Stanford, Cal.: Stanford University Press, 1957); Erich Fromm, *Escape from Freedom* (New York: Farrar, Straus & Giroux, Inc., 1947). One of the most interesting studies of the maintenance of belief *systems* is the study by Norman Dain, *Concepts of Insanity in the United States, 1789–1865* (New Brunswick, N.J.: Rutgers University Press, 1964). Dain's thesis, simply stated, is that although

At the other end of the scale: "The reason Christ-like figures such as Gandhi and Schweitzer are idealized is that they have the capacity to love those who disagree with them no less than those who agree with them, and to love all to a far greater extent than most men are capable of." [11]

These patterns run in consistent directions within the varied experience of each individual. For example, as Rokeach and others have discovered, the white Southerner's rejection of the Negro is not an isolated phenomenon; the white Southerner consistently tends to reject *all* non-whites. His rejection of the Negro is overshadowed by an even greater rejection of *anyone* who disagrees with him. [12] Thus, prejudice against a particular ethnic group should not be seen in isolation but as one component in a fairly consistent *system* of beliefs.

Various experimenters have used various terms to suggest this dichotomy, from closed to open, from authoritarian to tolerant, from rigid to flexible, etc. Perhaps the best way to see the difference is to consider the person who erects huge barriers to keep the world out (and there are many reasons for doing so), compared to the person who has a great number of lines or "feelers" out to bring the world in. [13] As Rokeach and others have mentioned, this dichotomy is *not* to be equated with terms of liberal-conservative dimensions, since the closed-minded, rigid authoritarian can exist at either the right or the left of the political spectrum. The crucial dimension here is the personal stability necessary to entertain divergent views of others as being possible and perhaps even reasonable.

It should be pointed out here that we all possess this inability to alter our responses, referred to in an earlier chapter as "trained incapacity." The chickens who have learned a direct path to food will continue to try this path long after it has been blocked. Their previous training will blind them to the solution of an indirect route to the food. And so it is with all of us. Consider for a moment the "Denny Doodlebug" problem:

> The hero is a little creature named Joe Doodlebug. Joe . . . is a strange sort of bug. He can jump in only four directions: north, south, east, or

---

knowledge about mental illness increased greatly during this time period, and new techniques were developed to deal with mental *illness,* the general attitude of most people about the mentally ill *person* did not show change.

[11] Rokeach, *op. cit.,* p. 392.

[12] *Ibid.*

[13] For a complete summary of the testing and measurement devices which have been developed on this topic, see Chapter 20 of an excellent book by John Horrocks, *The Assessment of Behavior* (Columbus, Ohio: Charles Merrill Books, Inc., 1964). Particularly welcome is the interest, throughout the book, on the nature of *what is being measured,* including intelligence, abilities, and personality. Interestingly enough, it contains no chapter on creativity.

west—not diagonally. Once he starts in any direction he must jump four times in that direction before he can switch directions. He cannot crawl, fly, or walk—he can only jump; he can jump very large distances and very small distances. And he cannot turn around.

Joe's master . . . places some food, larger in diameter than Joe, three feet directly west of him. Joe stops dead in his tracks, facing north. After surveying the situation, Joe concludes that he will have to jump four times to get to the food. . . . Joe is dead right in his conclusion. He must take four jumps, no more, no less.[14]

Lest the reader get unduly disturbed, it should be mentioned that very few subjects can describe Joe's actions, even with help, in 30 to 45 minutes. The problem is an excellent example of our "trained incapacity," which blocks us from the creative solution. One has, first, to "unblock" at least three notions about Joe: first, he does not have to face his food in order to eat it—he can land on top of it; Joe does not have to be "pointed" in the direction he moves—he can move sideways or backward; at this given moment, Joe may be in the middle of a sequence of jumps, not necessarily at the end of one. Once we have unlearned these things, the creative integration of a solution is not too difficult.

As another example of the need to remove the blinders of habit before creativity can occur, consider the famous story of young Gauss, the mathematician. When he was very young his teacher asked the class to find the sum of $1 + 2 + 3 + 4 + 5 + 6 + 7 + 8 + 9 + 10$. Gauss had the answer before the others had begun to work. Instead of taking each number as it came in the left-to-right sequence, he saw that there were *nonsequential* relationships, that 1 and 10 were 11, 2 and 9, 3 and 8, etc., making 5 pairs of 11, for a total of 55. He saw the problem not this way:

$$1 + 2$$
$$+ 3$$
$$+ 4$$
$$+ 5 . . .$$

But in this way: [15]

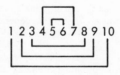

[14] Rokeach, *op. cit.*, p. 172. The solution is on p. 173.

[15] From Max Wertheimer, *Productive Thinking* (New York: Harper & Row, Publishers, 1945), pp. 89–93.

Thus, it was really the unblocking of the left-to-right "push" of the problem to take each number as it came that allowed Gauss to find a more original and interesting solution. Here is a good example of how language and print itself determine our view of a problem and hide alternative views. The word "plus" generally means "add this thing to the *next* thing," which is what most of us would do.

Most revolutionary creative acts are achieved in the face not only of existing dogma but of "common sense," or the "conventional wisdom." When Columbus took off for the East via the West, it must have appeared ludicrous to the masses, whose justification is still feasible: any idiot *can* see that the world is flat. Similarly, the notion that time and space are not independent entities but have a reciprocal relation with each other still seems absurd, long after Einstein's discovery. As Koestler puts it:

> Words are essential tools for formulating and communicating thoughts, and also for putting them into the storage of memory; but words can also become snares, decoys, or strait-jackets. A great number of the basic verbal concepts of science have turned out at various times to be both tools and traps: for instance, "time," "space," "mass," "force," "weight," "ether," "corpuscle," "wave," in the physical sciences; "purpose," "will," "sensation," "consciousness," "conditioning," in psychology; "limit," "continuity," "countability," "divisibility," in mathematics. For these were not simple verbal tags, as names attached to particular persons or objects are; they were artificial constructs which behind an innocent façade hid the traces of the particular kind of logic which went into their making. As Sidney Hook has put it: "When Aristotle drew up his table of categories which to him represented the grammar of existence, he was really projecting the grammar of the Greek language on the cosmos." [16]

The highly creative person who steers around the rocks of language and comes to a new view is often seen as a childlike figure, because his view seems so simple, so ludicrous and absurd to the rest of us. Indeed, Einstein has said that his preoccupation with time and space was simply the interest of most young children, which just happened to come to him in later life. We are often shocked by children's questions, because they penetrate the wall of verbal and perceptive categories we have erected to get through the day. What for example is a parent supposed to say to the question, "Why is the sun?" To the child in search of a key to the cosmos, we can only offer platitudes. But when an *adult* asserts that clocks go faster in different parts of the universe, or that the speed of an object's motion alters its size, we feel threatened and may take aggressive action.

[16] Koestler, *op. cit.,* p. 176.

The unusually creative person, from Christ to Socrates to Galileo, thus has a good chance of getting his head chopped off. He represents a major threat to the established values and "ways of looking at things" of his society. The relationship in the popular mind of creativity and insanity is probably less an accurate description of the creative person, and more of a protection against his strange and threatening ideas. The "mad scientist" as viewed in the mass media (particularly in the television cartoons for children) is simply one of the many examples of this defense mechanism, designed to keep at a safe distance that which we do not understand.

It seems reasonable to assume, in the absence of evidence to the contrary, that a newborn child has enormous creative potential. It is also reasonable to assume that much of this creative potential is drained off *in the process of socialization,* as the individual learns the "right" ways of perceiving things. There is a clear paradox here, because the acquisition of words and concepts is essential to any understanding of the world, yet these tools usually tend to become barriers to any further acquisition of tools.

Socialization, in this context, is a process which continues throughout life, although its customary usage is to describe the process whereby a child becomes an adult. (When an adult is introduced into a new group and changes his behavior to conform to the norms of that group, we can certainly say that he has been *socialized* to that particular group.) Although this continuous socialization process may provide new alternatives and ways of looking at things, it is unlikely that we can completely forget or unlearn the perceptions and actions we used with prior groups we have encountered. Thus, socialization is seen here as a *continuous* process in which we put blinders over the blinders we already have. The old man who has achieved certainty has really only acquired a total isolation from alternatives.

We could assume from the foregoing that conformity (or socialization) would have a negative effect on the creative ability of a person. Crutchfield, whose research confirms this position, says, "Conformity inhibits the person's ability to sense and grasp basic reality, and the loss of this contact with reality is fatal to creative thinking." [17] He makes a distinction between people who are mainly concerned with the consequences of the solution of a problem for themselves (status, promotion, money, etc.) and those who are "wrapped up" in the problem itself. For the first, the

[17] Crutchfield, "Conformity and Creative Thinking," in Gruber, *et al., op. cit.,* p. 120. See also Nathan Kogan and Michael Wallach, *Risk-Taking: A Study of Cognition and Personality* (New York: Holt, Rinehart & Winston, Inc., 1964).

problem and its solution is a means to an end; for the latter, it is an end in itself. This distinction between ego-involvement and task-involvement has been amply supported in research which has established that ego-involvement can impair cognitive functioning and reduce creativity.[18] As we said in the chapter dealing with actors and roles, the student who is totally engrossed in the machinery of being a student—nodding his head, looking intense, etc.—will never learn anything. Total consciousness of *self*-investigating-problem will inevitably deter total consciousness of the *problem*.

Thus, it seems reasonable to assume that conformity to the norms of a group, as well as hyperconsciousness of self, will deter the individual's ability to be "gripped" by a problem, and hence will diminish his creative potential. There is, however, one other personality dimension that has a deleterious effect on creativity, and that is the case of the person who denies *all* group judgments and norms, right or wrong. This person (Crutchfield calls him the Counterformist) [19] self-consciously rejects all norms, largely because they restrict his "individual initiative." Again, the person sets up defenses instead of feelers and, by self-consciously deviating from all group judgments, is as far from total immersion in the problem as the person who self-consciously conforms to all group demands. The self-styled Bohemian who rejects society as well as art will probably not paint very well. The truly creative person is simply *independent*— he can accept both society and himself.

It should also be said here that the personality dimensions which seem to encourage creativity may differ with the field of intellectual activity involved. We would expect, for example, that the characteristic of empathy, the ability to respond to the emotions and feelings of others, would be much more important for the painter, poet, or novelist than for the chemist or physicist. McClelland's research on creative physical scientists supports this point. He found that physical scientists as a group are unusually dedicated to their work, often to the exclusion of everything else; they avoid interpersonal contact whenever possible, and simply withdraw from situations in which intense emotions are involved. Significantly, they like music very much but are not interested in art or poetry, in which emotion probably plays a more obvious part.

They found it very difficult and frustrating to make up stories in response to the ambiguous pictures in the TAT and other projective tests. This suggests that the creative scientist is searching for a cool, rational certainty in science as some sort of retreat from the ambiguities and

18 Crutchfield, *op. cit.*, pp. 120–23.
19 *Ibid.*, pp. 137–39.

strong emotions of human existence.[20] We would expect that the highly creative person in the arts would be exactly the opposite, thriving on the complexities and ambiguities of human motivation and emotion, instead of avoiding them. However, this seemingly self-evident statement has not yet been verified.

Before we consider a sharp dichotomy between scientific and artistic creation, the argument should be made that these are really aspects of a continuum, different qualities being emphasized at different places, as suggested below: [21]

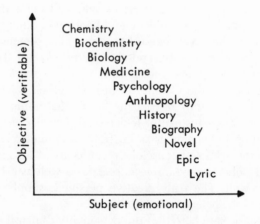

However, there seems to be, in *all* creative activity, a sense of *beauty*, which for the scientist may be represented by rational consistency, while for the poet it may be in the complex description of human emotion. As Koestler puts it:

> Beauty is a function of truth, truth a function of beauty. They can be separated by analysis, but in the lived experience of the creative act—and of its recreative echo in the beholder—they are inseparable as thought is inseparable from emotion. They signal, one in the language of the brain, the other of the bowels, the moment of the Eureka cry, when "the infinite is made to blend itself with the finite"—when eternity is looking through the window of time. Whether it is a medieval stained-glass window or Newton's equation of universal gravity is a matter of upbringing and chance; both are transparent to the unprejudiced eye.[22]

[20] David McClelland, "On the Psychodynamics of Creative Physical Scientists," in Gruber *et al.*, *op. cit.*

[21] From Koestler, *op. cit.*, p. 332.

[22] *Ibid.*, p. 331.

Another commonality in the creative experience is the ability to *play* with a number of possibilities at once. For the creative person, this juggling is fun and gives him pleasure, while for many people the idea of juggling alternatives for a long time without making a final, unequivocal decision is a threatening idea—they prefer finality, and as quickly as possible. This suspension of the impulse to make a quick decision and get it over with must require considerable personal stability on the part of the creative person. We might suspect that along with this playfulness would exist a good sense of humor, particularly in terms of the pun, basically an exercise in playing with the many alternatives and ambiguities of language.

This, then, is an overly brief summary of the available evidence on the creative process and creative people. We can now turn to a more direct consideration of the relationship of these factors to education.

creativity and education

To begin with, education in our society is *system*atic. From kindergarten to graduate school, bells ring. Assignments are given. Credits (the academic equivalent of money) are awarded. Math is on Tuesday and history is on Thursday. In a "rationally" ordered system such as this, the parts or components are interdependent —if teacher X goes past the time allotted, the student is deprived of some of the time of teacher Y. Classes basically function to bring forth, from the student, information that has been previously acquired.

We have seen that creative activity simply does not fit into this picture. Spontaneity, playfulness, the "Eureka!" reaction which seems to come from nowhere, the relative lack of self-consciousness and awareness of the creative process on the part of the individual, the ability to be independent from some group norms—these all suggest that creative performance cannot be produced *on demand*.

Some support for this position can be found in the research of Getzels and Jackson, who separated their sample of children into two groups— one group selected for high IQ scores; the other selected for very high creative potential, as measured by a number of tests.[23] Their findings, although not to be taken as certainties, are of significance at all educational levels. First, it appears that intelligence, as presently measured, is not an adequate measure for creative abilities—they are relatively independent variables. Second, the highly creative children (although they had lower IQ's) had about the same level of school performance as the high-IQ

[23] Jacob Getzels and Phillip Jackson, *Creativity and Intelligence* (New York: John Wiley & Sons, Inc., 1962).

group, even though the IQ is supposedly a measure of school performance! This cannot be explained away by saying that the creative children
"try harder," because measures of the need for achievement in the two
groups showed no major differences. The third major finding is perhaps
most significant for our discussion—with great consistency, their teachers
preferred the high-IQ students to the highly creative students, even
though the high creatives were doing *better* than their IQ would indicate,
while the high IQ's were performing only as expected. Teachers preferred
the "safer," more predictable responses of the high-IQ children. Here is
another example of the unfounded reverence many teachers have for
the IQ.

Although the Getzels and Jackson research was done on a high-school
population, the implications for higher education are obvious, particularly
in admissions. Certainly, two of the major criteria for getting into college
are the scores on the Scholastic Aptitude Examinations (very like the IQ
test), and teachers' recommendations. Granting equal high-school grades,
the odds on being admitted to college on these two criteria are with the
high-IQ student and against the highly creative one. (The interview is
the other major criterion, and it is difficult indeed to impress an admissions officer with how creative one is in the usual half-hour interview.)
Although both the highly creative and the high-IQ students understood
the norms for success in adult life in about the same way, the highly
creative student was much less willing to pledge his personal allegiance
to this view of "success," which could also cause raised eyebrows in admissions offices.

There is some evidence that, at the college level, teachers' prefer-
ences change from the straight-A student to those with creative abilities,[24]
but it is hard to believe that this is the norm for American education in
the sixties. Graduate admissions blanks generally reflect the same criteria used in undergraduate admissions—one simply substitutes the Graduate Record Exam for the Scholastic Aptitude Test. When classes get
larger, as they certainly will, the creative student will get even more lost
in the crowd. (And for that matter, how many high schools, colleges, or
graduate schools will take a chance on hiring an unusually creative
teacher, whose unorthodox views about politics, religion, sex, etc., might
be offensive to the members of the governing board?)

The fact is that American society has *always* considered the highly
creative person with grave suspicion, at least until the Russians were able
to orbit an object in space. This feat could be said to have inspired the
current interest in creativity, which is much more involved with scientific

[24] D. Brown, "Non-Intellective Factors and Faculty Nominations of Ideal Students" (Mellon Foundation, Vassar College, dittoed).

than artistic creation. As proof of this, consider the very rapid establishment of the National Science Foundation with a remarkably large budget, while a National Humanities Foundation has been a long time in coming. There are a large number of on-going studies dealing with the development of future scientists but few, if any, dealing with the development of future poets, musicians, and painters. American interest in creativity is not as an end in itself but as a means of accomplishing a technological end.

Before discussing more specific aspects of creativity and teaching and learning, let us return to the Getzels and Jackson research to ask one more question: Why is it that the high-IQ adolescents (who we can assume do have creative potential) did not develop it? What happened in their childhood to stunt this portion of their intellectual growth?

the paradox of socialization in America

Everyone who has had contact with young children has seen the characteristics of curiosity, wonder, joy in discovery, and open-mindedness about the world that virtually all children possess to a large degree. This interest and curiosity extends into the world of the arts, and to watch a group of children painting, making up a song, story, or poem can be a memorable experience. Yet, to watch this same activity among, for example, junior high-school students, suggests a different view of the human race. To be a boy and to express major interest in art or music is often to be considered feminine in this school culture. The same is true for the girl who expresses an abiding interest in science. In brief, these students have developed a concept of adult sex roles and are beginning to shape their lives toward this end.

The problem of identification is particularly difficult for boys in our society—girls have watched the specific activities of their mothers in house-cleaning, etc., while the father generally works outside the home, leaving few activities for the son to imitate and practice. To a large extent, the son is left to the mercy of the mass media for his ideas about how males in our society should behave. Anyone who has turned on a television set knows that the views of masculinity presented there (besides having little to do with reality) tend to suggest physical strength, not emotional sensitivity; "winning" by force, rather than sympathy and understanding; physical and sexual prowess, rather than intellectual and artistic skills.

One can also see, particularly in American advertising, the two major dimensions of child training practices in the home: one sees, on the one hand, the lone individual, often clad in cowboy garb, riding across the prairie directly into New York City (exactly how this is accomplished is never made clear). It is clear that he is an *independent* man, and a powerful one—captains of industry and pretty girls are obviously dependent on him, while he is obviously dependent on no one. One also sees ads in which the emphasis is on the happy, well-adjusted group, in which everyone gets along with everyone else, and in which social skills and fun are the only ends in life. (For some reason, the cowboy sells things to smoke, while the fun-group sells things to mask unpleasant smells such as perspiration and bad breath. This is probably a pretty good division of labor, since the cowboy, bringing with him as he does the smells of manure and other bucolic delights, might not be a very good "ideal type" model for the sale of deodorants.)

In America, the first model for the upwardly mobile middle classes was that of the independent individual who saw the world as being basically against him. The present was not as important as the future, which he could control by hard work and individual initiative. Group affiliations could be detrimental, holding the individual back as he tried to move up the success ladder. The object was to make others dependent on him. One had to be clever, hard working, and could not trust others too much. Individual success, not necessarily happiness, comfort, or fun, was the major goal. This we can speak of as the *entrepreneur* model.

Opposed to this is a more recent model, emphasizing the individual's relations to groups as being primary. Having fun is more important than hard work for its own sake, the present is more important than the future, and "success" is accomplished by group affiliation rather than individual striving. Fully in accord with the "installment plan" mentality, one should gratify his needs now and defer stress as far as possible into the future. The most important skills for the achievement of "success" (which here means happiness) are *social* skills, and the development of frictionless social relationships becomes an ideal to work for. One *should* become dependent on others. One's norms and standards come from the groups he is involved with; they are not generated internally through tradition or conscience. This model can be called the *bureaucratic* model.

These two models can be considered as goals or ends that parents have had in mind in their raising of children. The entrepreneur model was certainly strongest in the period between the two world wars, enforced as it was by the psychology of the period. Watson and others urged the dangers of not controlling the child, the importance of depressing needs rather than getting instant gratifications, the importance of parental dominance. During the forties, however, the pendulum swung hard to the other side. Under the influence of Freudian psychology and

Dewey (often misinterpreted in popularized versions) and perhaps as a reaction to the tensions and hardships of enduring the war, the tables were turned, and the repression of the child's needs and drives was seen as a major sin. Children were basically good, and if people would let them develop "naturally," they would become good adults. The child had to learn his own discipline; one should not punish children, because this established neuroses, complexes, etc. Reward, gratification, and pleasure were seen as the *only* ways of controlling the behavior of the child. (Many of the behaviorist psychologists of this period developed their models using *only* positive reinforcement.)

In the late fifties and sixties, the pendulum has returned to a middle position, allowing emphasis to be placed on *both* freedom and on control, thereby enabling the parent to be selective and situational about how he operates. (As an index of our return to relative sanity, several recent articles have been written accepting the need for punishing the child, not for what it does to the child but for reducing the frustrations of the parents!) There are, of course, experts who still urge that child training move toward increasing permissiveness, and other experts who advocate increasing control, but the main consensus is clearly between the two extremes.

In that both the entrepreneur and bureaucratic ideals can be found in our highly symbolic contemporary advertising, it is reasonable to assume also that these ideal types are in the minds of parents as they try to create adults out of their children. Because these two types tend to contradict each other, there is currently some honest confusion about what parents are doing and what they think they are accomplishing. This confusion is partly due to the fact that different classes have different rates of access to new psychological theories and child training advice. (For example, Dr. Spock's book reached the middle classes long before reaching the lower classes, thus creating a time lag.) [25]

There is, however, very little evidence linking creativity to family or child training. McClelland has found that creative scientists come from strict, Protestant homes, in which aggression is very carefully controlled. Their fathers were stern and "in charge." Thus, we could infer that the entrepreneur family pattern will tend to produce creative *scientists*, but whether or not it also produces creative artists is not known. The scientists developed a decided lack of interest in art and poetry, but others placed in entrepreneur family settings may respond with an artistic pattern of creation.

[25] See Urie Bronfenbrenner, "Socialization and Social Class Through Time and Space," in Maccoby, Newcomb, and Hartley, eds., *Readings in Social Psychology* (New York, Holt, Rinehart & Winston, Inc., 1958).

It would seem a reasonable hunch (but only a hunch) that the bureaucratic family pattern would tend to produce lower levels of creativity in virtually *every* area of endeavor because of its emphasis on happiness, reduction of all tensions, and importance of social relationships. The creative response is often tension-*promoting* and requires a dissociation from social demands of others. The creative processes often take one away from social life, and the bureaucratic ethos frowns on anything which does so. Bureaucratic families also tend to produce lower levels of aspiration than do entrepreneur families, and level of aspiration (which may mean either rapid rise up the success ladder or the desire for deep, complex, meaningful experiences and a rich life) may be related to creativity. At least, it is hard to conceive of a placid person with a low level of *intensity* as being very creative; and in that smooth, frictionless social relations tend toward the superficial, one could suggest that children raised in the bureaucratic family will encounter fewer intense experiences than the child who has been raised as some sort of entrepreneur.

However, in contemporary standards for "success," there is no question that the skills provided by the bureaucratic family structure are of major importance. To say that American society is becoming more other-directed is certainly nothing new. Various social skills are becoming *necessities* for certain jobs, and concern for how an applicant will get along with his fellows seems to be almost universal. The Horatio Alger myth *is* a myth, and is being recognized as such, in that group mobility is increasing faster than individual mobility, at least in the occupational sphere.

It should be clear by now that parents are in a cruel dilemma, since the goals of happiness, fun, ease, and comfort do not seem to be compatible with those of intensity, significance, and expanding awareness. One pays a price on either side. The creative scientist, working alone in his lab, is certainly missing many rich and productive social experiences, while the person whose thinking is always determined by the groups he is with, who has never felt awe, wonder, or intense, insatiable curiosity, has certainly missed at least as much. There is certainly no "recipe" which can be given to parents that will automatically produce children with high levels of creative performance, but the following may be of use to everyone interested in expanding the horizons of those under 75.

planning for creativity

The first problem (and perhaps the hardest) is to select those areas of life in which creative activity should be encouraged. There are many roles that do not call for highly creative performances. Imagine a highly creative airline pilot who is thinking up new engine designs while trying to land a passenger jet at a windy airport, or a creative sergeant. Nor do these roles call for the other extreme of social awareness (think of a surgeon whose main concern was over whether or not the nurses and interns were getting along happily, while he was performing an operation). What is needed here is a compulsive concern with the problem at hand: the pilot should be obsessed with landing the plane safely and nothing else. Thus, for many human tasks, the freedom and spontaneity of creative behavior is out of place. When the pilot gets his flight plans, that settles the matter.

But in the area of human learning, the amount of creative potential in the learner and the material is staggering. The number of roads into almost any problem is vast—and once "inside" the problem, the avenues toward solution are even greater. The learning potential of the grade-school child has undoubtedly been vastly underrated (who would have thought that the theory of sets, which used to be reserved for graduate students in mathematics, would have become one of the "foundations" for elementary-school arithmetic!), and the whole notion of sequences or hierarchies of knowledge, based on increasing levels of difficulty, is being re-examined, and in some cases (as in the example) the hierarchies have been reorganized and even reversed.

One thing which seems to stimulate creativity is a problem orientation—that is, the material is not simply a body of fact to be "covered" (indeed, this happens all too often) but a collection of possibilities, hunches, and bits of evidence to be *un*covered. As in the classic case of young Gauss mentioned earlier in this chapter, the student made a real problem out of a dull chore. Teachers can do the same. By asking for alternative solutions, by changing the sequence of events within the problem ("What would have happened if . . . ?"), by encouraging speculation, the same wonderfully creative situations Wertheimer describes for mathematics can exist in any subject area.

It is very important that the feminine connotation of creative activity be removed whenever possible. One way to do this is to discard the notions that only in art class are children supposed to be creative, and that art and music are to be considered as feminine (even though most major artists, composers, and musicians are men). There is no reason on earth why a young man cannot be interested in sports, music, and poetry at the same time. Outside of the purely skill courses, such as typing and shorthand, it is hard to think of *any* topic, from kindergarten to graduate school, that would not benefit from the student's use of his own imaginative powers.

Just as every subject can become more meaningful to teachers and students through a creative treatment, so every student can benefit from such teaching. With the present interest in the development of tests of creative ability, it is likely that we will develop standardized norms and pronounce one group of people THE creative group. This was done with the IQ (Terman considered anyone with an IQ over 140 a genius and limited his sample of geniuses to those people with IQ's over this range. He was amazed as he followed them through their lives that they were as well-adjusted to society as they were. We now know what Terman didn't: that creative genius and IQ are by no means the same thing). Every effort should be made to provide creative experiences for *all* young people, not just a select few.

There is a major problem here for all educators, as the culture is moving in the direction Weber suggested—toward an emphasis on the rational and an attempt to de-mystify the world. In the field of children's toys, for example, several manufacturers have produced the "ideal" toy that "leaves absolutely nothing to the child's imagination." Adult culture is moving in steadily on the children's years, bringing literalistic values along. The ambiguous toy (the teddy bear, the rag doll) which could be anything the child wanted it to be has been replaced with the doll who "*really* wets, *really* talks, *really* eats," etc. The years of pretend, of fantasy play, of dream and wish, have been reduced to the vanishing point. As Getzels and Jackson put it:

> The child's well-recognized early curiosity, his joy in new things, his drive to seek the unknown, to explore the mysterious, to seek excitement seems to undergo alteration with age. The "open" world to be savored and appreciated is turned into a world of objects seen from the perspective of how they can be used for some purpose, or avoided in order to prevent pain or social displeasure. The universe to be explored is turned into a cocoon in which to be imbedded.[26]

The same movement can be seen in the adult world as well. Several publishers are making money with encyclopedias of sex, which list all sexual topics in a handy reference guide, so that "nothing is left to chance or imagination." It is often suggested that the book be left on the bedside table "for easy reference when needed." Even in an area as personal and individual as this, we are told that we must take our cues from others, those experts who know the "correct" procedures. For every human activity of which the mind can conceive, there seems to be available a "Handy Reference Manual," supporting Riesman's thesis that increasingly people get their directions and standards from others, not from themselves.

We have already noted that the socialization process itself, by establishing socially sanctioned patterns of behavior, will limit the individual's

[26] Getzels and Jackson, *op. cit.*, p. 116.

capacity to conceive of alternatives. We all become, to some degree, creatures of habit, and for many human activities, such as shaving, brushing teeth, wearing glasses, etc., habituation is necessary and desirable. But the job of the educator is to keep his students' minds *open* in as many areas as possible, for as long a time as possible, even though this conflicts with many powerful (and well-endowed) forces in our culture that seem to profit from closed minds.

What is being suggested here is not the development of specialized courses in creative behavior (one college catalog lists a course called "Creativity 241—the development of the student's creative powers." There is no subject matter to the course, making it hard to see what the students will be creative *about*). Nor are we suggesting that a teacher set out a fifteen-minute period each day for creative play, etc. We are suggesting that the use of the students' imaginative and conjectural powers be made a central focus of *every educational activity*. To learn the techniques of disciplined speculation, the creation of hypotheses, the development of new ways into problems, to see the large number of alternative positions, to be able to see process as well as product—these are of great importance to every student of every age.

This sounds easy to do, but in fact it is very difficult. The major difficulty is the tendency of a great many teachers to conceive of their subject matter as a series of closed answers to closed questions. Thus, their job is to communicate the correct answers to the students as quickly as possible—anything else is seen as a waste of time. Attention is focused entirely on the answer, none on the question. The longer the teacher teaches a given topic, the greater his difficulty in remembering what it was like to approach the topic for the first time, as the student must see it. Highly successful teachers seem somehow to understand the perceptual fields of their students, although no one knows quite how they do it.

The adjective "creative" can therefore be applied to teaching as well as learning. The characteristic of openmindedness, the ability to entertain new notions of his own specialty as well as ideas of how it may relate to other fields, is vitally important to the *teacher* if he is to induce these same qualities in his students. Finally, it should be said that the first thing that comes into a student's head is not necessarily creative. Free-association techniques, or "brain-storming" may be helpful in freeing a person's mind from habitual patterns of thinking, but it is unlikely that a poem, a rigorous hypothesis or theory could be produced this way. A creative approach is not necessarily one devoid of logic or rigor. It is in the *relationship* of spontaneity and rigor, freedom and discipline, conjecture and analysis, that productive and creative activities can occur.

8: the impact
of the american college
on student values *

The context in which this chapter should be read has been well put in
two statements, the first by Nevitt Sanford, the second by Daniel Bell:

> Granting that the current scene may be one marked more by rigidity
> than by stability, the contrasts with other recent periods of our history are
> none the less marked. We are not now experiencing anything like the ex-
> citement, the mobility, the ferment of the jazz age, or the depression, or
> World War II. Correspondingly there is relative quietude on the intel-
> lectual and ideological fronts. In the early years of the century we had the
> movement toward greater freedom for women; in the twenties we had
> Freud and the revolution in morals; in the thirties we had the depression,
> social change, and the influence of socialist economic theory; in the forties
> the war, fervent democratic idealism, imaginative postwar plans. What
> are the big ideas of the fifties? The automatic anti-communism of recent
> years has not been exactly inspiring. Efforts to bring about a return to

* Some of this material was originally prepared for the Committee on Research and
Planning of the Commission on Higher Education, National Council of the Churches
of Christ, in 1964.

religion or to evolve a new religious outlook have been rather feeble—in some cases, perhaps even phony. One does not hear much intellectual discussion on the campus for the simple reason that there is not very much to discuss. Times will undoubtedly change, and new ideas will appear, but for the time being we are in cultural and intellectual doldrums. This I would posit as a major source of student lethargy.[1]

THE SCHOLAR AND THE INTELLECTUAL

The differences between the scholar and the intellectual, without being invidious, are important to understand. The scholar has a bounded field of knowledge, a tradition, and seeks to find his place in it, adding to the accumulated, tested knowledge of the past as to a mosaic. The scholar, qua scholar, is less involved with his "self." The intellectual begins with *his* experience, *his* individual perceptions of the world, *his* privileges and deprivations, and judges the world by these sensibilities. Since his own status is of high value, his judgments of the society reflect the treatment accorded him. In a business civilization, the intellectual felt that the wrong values were being honored, and rejected the society. Thus there was a "built-in" compulsion for the free-floating intellectual to become political. The ideologies, therefore, which emerged from the nineteenth century had the force of the intellectuals behind them. . . . But out of all this history, one simple fact emerges: for the radical intelligentsia, the old ideologies have lost their "truth" and their power to persuade.

The ideologies of the nineteenth century were universalistic, humanistic, and fashioned by intellectuals. The mass ideologies of Asia and Africa are parochial, instrumental, and created by political leaders. The driving forces of the old ideologies were social equality and, in the largest sense, freedom. The impulsions of the new ideologies are economic development and national power.

The young intellectual is unhappy because the "middle way" is for the middle-aged, not for him; it is without passion and is deadening. Ideology, which by its nature is an all-or-none affair, and temperamentally the thing he wants, is intellectually devitalized, and few issues can be formulated any more, intellectually, in ideological terms.

It is interesting to observe that Mr. Sanford could have described the student as lethargic, such a short time ago. Student activism, particularly in terms of civil rights, seems the order of the day, if one reads the magazines and newspapers. But the reporting has certainly not been representative—few have gone into the dormitories to talk to students who did *not* take part in the demonstrations. On most campuses, the activists are a minority, but they are certainly present in far greater numbers than was the case in the "Silent Generation" days of the early 1950's. The student leader of today is, to use Bell's dichotomy, more of an intellectual

[1] Quoted in M. Freedman, *Impact of College* (Washington: U.S. Office of Education, 1960), pp. 16–17. An excellent short summary of the area, through the research up to 1959. The Bell quote below is from his *The End of Ideology* (New York: Free Press of Glencoe, Inc., 1960), pp. 372–75.

than a scholar. The intellectual is, therefore, egocentric (today's student leaders are certainly that) and is interested in translating ideas into personally relevant forms. Thus, the world of space exploration, the unraveling of the DNA structure, even current investigations of the origin of the universe, leave him relatively unmoved, because they do not affect him directly—he cannot build an ideology out of them.

Even in existentialism, phenomenology, and contemporary arts and literature, no vision is provided of the future—they are seemingly used to explain our dehumanization, rather than to provide a transcendent vision toward which youth can devote its efforts. There is concern for assuring that all receive the rights guaranteed them under the Constitution and Bill of Rights, there is deep concern for economic and political inequality, and there is new sophistication in the establishment and use of organizational pressures against coercive authority, both on and off the campus. There is also new frankness in discussing openly such problems as sex and drugs. (It must be added, however, that such discussions and student demonstrations seem to take place far more often when there are reporters and photographers present. For example, the Berkeley "revolt" of September and October 1964 has produced a plethora of commentary material, including over one hundred books and magazine articles. The event apparently "caught fire" in the minds of adult pundits more than in the hearts of college students across the country. Dire predictions were made that within the academic year, lawlessness and rebellion would sweep the campuses of large, "liberal" universities. As of this writing, the event has not come to pass.) Students are, of course, protesting what they consider unjust decisions of administrative officers, but students have *always* done this. It was the deliberate attempt to topple or immobilize the institutional structure of the university which was predicted but has not come to pass.

But in the midst of the tidal wave of publicity that occurs every time a college student lifts a placard, there are questions that still remain: What are they *really* like? How (if at all) does the college experience change them? What sort of adults will they make? Can we shape their values in directions adults think desirable? Around these questions has grown a considerable field of inquiry, which will be briefly surveyed in the pages to follow.

history

Educational research in America has swung like a pendulum for a number of years. The period of 1900–1930 was a time of great interest in education as a center for research, and the work of Thorndike,

Watson, and others was based in part on the educational system in schools and colleges. This research was, however, largely mechanistic in nature and was not concerned with, or equipped to handle, the questions of *personality* change and impact. This lack of research on personality factors was due in large part to the paucity of theoretical models on which personality research could be based. (It must be remembered that Freudian theory was developed in large part to explain the behavior of seriously maladjusted and disturbed individuals, and has never been particularly helpful in research on the "normal" majority of the population.)

Since the thirties, a gradual increase in theoretical sophistication has been seen in relation to personality research. Murray's use of needs as the basis for personality,[2] White's conception of personality as constantly changing and adapting through time,[3] and Festinger's cognitive dissonance approach [4] are only a few of many important contributions. Out of Murray's schema have come the Thematic Apperception Tests, Mc-Clelland's need-achievement concept, and other projective devices that give us indirect as well as direct assessment of personality development.

The stage was now set for the action which began unfolding around 1950, and remains very much alive today: the heightened interest on the part of psychologists, social psychologists, and sociologists in the college student as a *person*, and in what happens to him as a consequence of the collegiate experience.[5] (In a sense, this interest may be due to the desire of the social scientist to eliminate as many extraneous factors as possible. The college student, living in a somewhat isolated and insular world, represents a small improvement over a random sample of the U.S. population, as well as a captive audience.)

Another major reason for the burgeoning of this type of personality research was the development of multivariate analysis, along with machines which could handle elaborate programs of factor analysis with ease.

---

2 H. A. Murray, *Explorations in Personality* (New York: Oxford University Press, Inc., 1938). A classic work in personality theory.

3 R. H. White, *Lives in Progress* (New York: Dryden Press, 1952). An eminently readable treatise on the development of personality.

4 L. Festinger, *A Theory of Cognitive Dissonance* (Stanford, Cal.: Stanford University Press, 1957). The argument that we tend to overvalue the things for which we have suffered provides psychological support for the Protestant Ethic.

5 As yet, no theoretical framework has been provided for the analysis of personality development in college. The empirical researchers, however, do not seem to be deterred by this fact.

academic changes in students

There are many studies which indicate that, in terms of the acquisition of facts (imparting of knowledge), our colleges do well enough. Seniors almost universally know more than freshmen *at the same institution.* However, it is interesting to report that the freshmen at some institutions know more than seniors at other institutions. The variability *between* institutions is incredibly vast. McConnell and Heist have reported that the mean ACE scores of freshmen in private liberal arts colleges in the North Central region varied from 94 to 123. In the South (excluding institutions open only to Negroes), the mean freshman score varies from 68 to 123. Just as much variation can be found *within* a freshman class, although the more selective institutions naturally have less variation.[6]

However, these studies and the measures derived from them, such as the SAT, MAT, and ACE, leave much to be desired as predictors of success (or survival) in college. They neglect completely the psychological and sociological variables that play a major role in student success and development. (Many would willingly sacrifice the SAT score for a GQ— Guts Quotient, which would predict the student's ability to stick to a task when the going gets rough.) The reason for the tremendous number of these studies is obvious. Every admissions office, every registrar's office, every high-school principal's office is inundated with student report cards and scores on multiple-choice tests of factual knowledge.

A corollary to Parkinson's law would be that educational research will be done in an area in direct proportion to the amount of data already available in the area. Thus, studies are carried through in large numbers, simply because, like the famous mountain, the data are there. *Qualitative* analysis of how good the data may be is something else again. The establishment of a correlation between two factors, such as high-school and college grades, simply means that two factors tend to appear simultaneously; it does not mean that one *causes* the other. One can correlate almost anything with something else (the tenacity of asphalt on city streets used to correlate nicely with the frequency of children's diseases, but we would not eliminate disease by changing all asphalt streets to concrete).

Another reason for the huge number of studies of the student's present, and future, acquisition of facts, is the relative ease with which a correla-

[6] "Do Students Make The College?" *College and University,* **35** (1959), 442–52.

tion can be established statistically. Quantitative indexes can be developed with the greatest of arithmetic ease.

The fact remains, however, that the use of these tests, such as the SAT and ACE, does not produce good results in all colleges. For example, the so-called experimental colleges, which place a good deal of emphasis on student initiative, independent study, and *verbal* seminar participation, find them not terribly helpful in predicting academic success.[7]

It is also not very encouraging to contemplate the fact that, according to the available evidence, the college graduate will have forgotten between 50 and 75 per cent of the factual material he learned in college by the time he has been out for two years. Clearly, if you will pardon the pun, we must look at the college as something other than a *fact*ory. What happens to the student as a person?

changes in the student as a person

First, the enormous complexity of this problem should be explained. In order to isolate which personality changes were produced by the college experience, and not by the maturation that all 17- to 21-year-olds undergo in American culture, we would have to have two *identical* groups, one going to college and the other not, then do a longitudinal study of each group, not only for the college years but perhaps over a ten-year span, because many of the college experiences may not produce effects for a number of years after graduation. Such a study would be almost impossible, since *all* parameters of personality development would have to be studied and intercorrelated with *all* "educational" experiences. However, even without this ideal study, there is much that is known and much more that can be speculated.

Although the colleges do fairly well at imparting factual knowledge (which most students promptly forget), they do not seem to be too suc-

---

[7] Reported to the author at a conference on the experimental college held at Goddard College in February 1963. Finally, there is now available a volume which summarizes in a competent fashion all the research on the prediction of academic success in college, broken down into four categories: intelligence and ability factors, personality characteristics, sociological determinants, and sociopsychological factors. See David E. Lavin, *The Prediction of Academic Performance* (New York: Russell Sage Foundation, 1965). For anyone who wishes an experimental overview to the problem of predicting academic success (with insights relevant to high-school predictions as well as college level), this volume is highly recommended. A good summary of the larger issues of operating colleges concerned with student development can be found in Dennis and Kauffman, eds., *The College and the Student* (Washington, D.C.: American Council on Education, 1966).

cessful at such variables as teaching "critical thinking." One major study has reported that those instructors who consciously strove to increase their students' ability to think critically were no more successful than those instructors who paid no conscious attention to teaching critical thinking at all.[8]

Another aspect of the problem concerns the entering student's level of personal maturity, or readiness to accept new experiences and assimilate them. Again, there is vast divergence *within* a freshman class, and also *across* freshman classes at different institutions. However, there are also at each college, characteristic patterns of behavior that tend, through time, to produce at least superficial uniformity. This centralizing effect is produced by what is known as the student subculture, a self-perpetuating set of folkways and mores which seems to be relatively free from the influence of faculty and administration (although few administrations have *tried* to influence the student culture as such).

The intensity of this student culture will vary from college to college, but its existence, in both high schools and colleges, is unquestioned.[9] Like all systems of folkways, it is transmitted and perpetuated by imitation and identification, and not through direct communication in which the senior tells the freshman what the rules of the game are. The freshman must find out, through trial and error and rather subtle modes of communication, what is taboo and what is not. (It may be that it is the *effort* of finding out the dimensions of the student subculture that makes the students so loyal to it. People seem to come to love the things for which they have suffered.)

It is the student culture, in at least one medical school, that effectively kills the almost militant and authoritarian idealism with which the entering student arrives.[10] It may be that student cultures in most colleges function to reduce, quickly, the euphoric and oceanic idealism of the neophyte. (It would be extremely interesting to discover if other countries, particularly the poorer ones that seem to be able to produce obviously idealistic *graduates*, have college student subcultures which differ greatly from those in America.) Thus, one of the major determinants of personal change during the college years will be the "goodness of fit"

[8] P. Dressel and L. Mayhew, eds., *General Education—Explorations in Evaluation* (Washington, D.C.: American Council on Education, 1954).

[9] First noticed by Willard Waller in *The Sociology of Teaching* (New York: John Wiley & Sons, Inc., 1932). The high-school subculture has been studied by J. Coleman, "The Adolescent Subculture and Academic Achievement," *American Journal of Sociology*, 65 (1960), 337–47. On the college level, see H. Becker and B. Geer, "The Fate of Idealism in Medical School," *American Sociological Review*, 23 (1958), 70–80.

[10] Becker and Geer, *op. cit.*

between the *expectations* the students brings to college, and the *perceptions* of college life, as mediated and interpreted through the student culture.

Another factor that should be discussed here is the phenomenon of self-selection. Those colleges which have a definite and concrete image, as seen by high-school graduates, may find that many students will not even bother to apply if they do not think they meet the qualifications. Thus, colleges like the "experimental" group, which have very definite views on education and very definite ways of implementing these views, can build up excellent freshman classes with relatively few applicants. The suggestion here is that many colleges become known as places in which impact on student personality does occur, and hence will attract a majority of those students who *want* to be "shook-up." The self-fulfilling prophecy leads us to assume that, if a student comes to college anticipating that his values will change in important directions, the change will occur more often than not.

There is a great deal of recent evidence to support the supposition that certain colleges (a distinct minority) have a peculiar potency in changing students' beliefs and attitudes, as well as other personality dimensions. These colleges share certain obvious characteristics—they are residential, they tend to be relatively small, and they are very heavily committed, both in money and energy, to *teaching* and intellectual considerations. However, *many* colleges fit this description but do not produce much student impact. Riesman has attributed this unusual potency to characteristics of the student body, rather than to the institution itself. Much recent evidence suggests that the successful colleges attract students who tend to be inner-directed, socially independent, receptive to learning, nonauthoritarian, theoretical, unconventional, and creative.[11] As Heist has said, "The merit of certain institutions lies less in what they do to students than it does in the students to whom they do it." [12]

The student cultures in these "potent" colleges probably differ from those colleges which do not have impact value for their students; comparative studies are being done. However, an interesting study at Vassar (and, thanks to the Mellon Foundation, the Vassar student is probably the most-studied person in America) provides another clue. When members of the faculty at Vassar were asked to nominate "the ideal student,"

11 P. Heist *et al.,* "Personality and Scholarship," *Science,* 133 (1961), 362–67.

12 *Ibid.* There are two studies now in progress which attempt to assess differences in impact of various types of institutions. One is sponsored by the Council for the Advancement of Small Colleges, directed by Arthur Chickering; the other, by the Center for the Study of Higher Education at Berkeley, directed by James Trent, Paul Heist, and others.

many of them chose, not the straight-A students, which one might have expected, but those students who manifest the attributes we have just mentioned: creative, independent but aware of the needs of others, non-authoritarian, theoretical, low on ethnocentrism.[13]

We can easily infer from this that the faculty member is a crucial factor in the college's impact, particularly the *faculty as a whole*. If most of the faculty share these values, are dedicated in time and energy to teaching, and are willing to experiment with new ways of looking at problems both in and out of the classroom, then impact of the *college* (not just classroom) experience, is likely. Recent research on creativity has made it clear that the creative student (who tends to have his own ways of approaching problems) is not usually well liked by an authoritarian teacher, who would much prefer the docile, obedient, neat, orderly, subservient student who always does exactly what he is told.

Thus, the tolerance, flexibility, and empathy of the faculty member is a major factor in promoting changes in students. (It must be said parenthetically that this does not mean that the teacher should not have goals and commitments of his own, in order to produce changes in his students. Far from it. He simply must be aware that the commitments of his students may differ from his own. Some college teachers do not plan class sessions on the grounds that they are encouraging "creativity" in their students—this dodge for laziness is usually detected very quickly by students.)

The heavy commitment which the young teacher, fresh from graduate school, gives to his *discipline* may be a major factor in the low impact of many high-status colleges. The freshman's ability to assimilate the concepts that the new Ph.D. has just learned may be so low that the new teacher may think of the teaching of freshmen as a derogation, an insult to his craft. (Also, increasing specialization in graduate programs may encourage the overloyal behaviorist teacher of psychology to fail the bright but Gestaltist-inclined undergraduate.)

What then *does* happen to a student in a college in which there are evidences of impact? There are many articles written by college counselors concerning patterns of development, but these are usually inferential, and usually based on the somewhat limited segment of the student population that uses the college or university counseling services. There is one well-conducted study of an entire student group as it moves through the four years—again, the Vassar student group was used. The material is presented in excellent detail in the original study for each of the four

---

[13] D. Brown, "Non-Intellective Factors and Faculty Nominations of Ideal Students," Mellon Foundation, Vassar College (dittoed).

years, and will only be summarized here, in terms of freshman-senior differences.[14]

The first three years are characterized by increasing solidarity within the college structure, reaching its apex in the junior year. The senior must suddenly begin responding to factors external to the college community, without diminishing her response to the continuing academic pressures and other demands of the college. The senior knows more than she did when a freshman, and some components of what she has learned are incompatible with other components. The senior often seems worried, anxious, and cynical, for she has more to be worried, anxious, and cynical about than she did as a freshman. She entered with a fairly stable and integrated notion of what she was and where she belonged, with identity and security based on her place in family and home town. Certain religious, social, and political convictions were accepted as given in the nature of things. College brought about changes in this identity, but the college community could substitute as a security-providing mechanism to reduce the stress inherent in changing major commitments and values.

The senior, however, becomes aware of the imminent cutting of the umbilical. The disparity between what she has learned and what she refers to as the "after-life" becomes readily apparent as graduation comes closer. For the first time, the student may realize that her total involvement in the college, usually in the junior year, was an experience almost totally unrelated to her future. As Freedman has said, "Many seniors are in a situation of having thrown off traditional values without having fully established others of their own, of having loosened long-standing inner controls at a time when new experiences have to be integrated, of having rejected old identities at the very time when important decisions have to be made." [15]

There are, however, several reasons for not overgeneralizing the results of this study. The Vassar senior feels a potential loss of community identity, because her college is small enough to allow the community feeling to develop. For the large institution, with thousands of commuters who go to school from 9:00 to 3:00 and then commute home, this sense of community may never have developed. Little is known about the student culture (if any) in the mass, urban, commuter institution. It may be that the student's passage through this sort of institution is much dif-

---

[14] M. Freedman, "The Passage Through College," *Journal of Social Issues,* 12 (1956), 13–28. The scales developed in the Vassar Research were the Developmental Status Scale, the Impulse Expression Scale, and the Social Maturity Scale. See also T. M. Newcomb's earlier studies at Bennington in *Personality and Social Change* (New York: Dryden Press, 1943).

[15] *Ibid.*

ferent because of this lack of community, particularly in terms of impact on student values and personality development.

Another way of looking at the problem of college impact has been developed by Pace and Stern at Syracuse. Through the use of factor analysis, they have developed two instruments, the CCI (College Characteristics Index) and the AI (Attitude Inventory). The CCI represents the college as an institution, while the AI represents the psychological parameters of the typical student profile at the institution. By comparing the "goodness of fit" of the two instruments, they have developed some interesting conclusions concerning which colleges have unusual impact on their students.[16]

A recent paper by Stern [17] describes a new analysis, this time breaking down the sample colleges into three categories: liberal arts, denominational, and universities. The profiles are extremely interesting, in that they support many of the stereotypes expressed about types of colleges. The liberal arts student is very interested in intellectual areas, very low on orderliness and applied interests, low on friendliness, high on expressiveness. The college program supports this—very high on intellectual climate and aspiration, very low on group life, social formality, and vocational interests. The university student profile (CCI) indicates a relatively low score on intellectual climate. The strongly denominational colleges, on the other hand, have on the student profile a very low intellectual orientation, low applied interests, and a surprisingly high sensuality score. On the college profile, they show a low intellectual climate, low self-expression, and very low on play or recreational interests.

There is also available some evidence on the American college population as a whole. The major ground-breaking effort was done by Philip Jacob, reported in *Changing Values in College*.[18] Based on a study of his own, as well as a review of the entire literature, Jacob sets forth a value profile which he claims holds for a majority of all American college students. They are, says Jacob, gloriously self-centered. Material gains are of the greatest importance. Their complaint is not "stop the world, I want to get off," but "keep things as they are until I can get a nice big slice of the good things of life." (Does this not explain the popularity of Goldwater among college students in 1964?) There are, of course, the

16 G. Stern, "Environments for Learning," in N. Sanford, ed., *The American College* (New York: John Wiley & Sons, Inc., 1962).

17 Syracuse: Syracuse University, 1963 (dittoed). See also Stern's "Student Values and Their Relationship to the College Environment," in H. Sprague, ed., *Research on College Students* (Boulder, Colo.: Western Commission for Higher Education, 1960), pp. 67–104.

18 (New York: Harper & Row, Publishers, 1957.)

Peace Corps and the student volunteers working on voter registration in the South through CORE and SNCC. But in terms of numbers, those *actively involved* in these activities constitute a very small fraction of the college population.

In an earlier chapter, the following statement was presented as typical:

> I'm not money-mad, by any means, but I'd like enough to buy a house, and have transportation, and of course good clothes for the family. Plus entertainments: I'd like to be able to see the good plays and movies. And I suppose I'd want a trip every year: visit in the big urban areas, you know, Berlin, Paris, Rome. I can't set any exact amount I'd like to make, so long as it's enough for the *necessities* of life.[19]

This statement points up the essentially self-centered, privatistic view of the world mentioned by Jacob. A study by Gillespie and Allport supports this notion. In studying American students compared with those from ten other countries, the authors found the Americans much more self-centered. There was no interest in national or international causes that the Americans *really* would devote themselves to. This was in marked contrast to the students from countries such as Mexico, whose greatest aspiration was to reduce disease, increase the standard of living, or help to promote world peace.[20]

American students are also, says Jacob, superficially tolerant, but this tolerance is usually due to a lack of commitment on their part to *any* core of values, rather than a belief in the liberal position of tolerance. The pull of college values is toward the values of college-educated men and women in the America outside the college walls, including the "fun culture" we have discussed.

Riesman has added an important qualification to this description. Although students are materialistic, it is not the materialism of the robber barons of an earlier era. They do not wish to destroy people or build huge fortunes. It is not the Protestant Ethic, with its Calvinist emphasis of self-denial in the present in return for future rewards. Instead, wealth is seen as something to be spent, for the pleasure of the individual and

---

[19] H. Hodgkinson, *Education in Social and Cultural Perspectives* (Englewood Cliffs, N.J.: Prentice-Hall, Inc., 1962), p. 231.

[20] J. Gillespie and G. Allport, *Youth's Outlook on the Future: A Cross-National Study* (New York: Doubleday & Company, Inc., 1955); Max Wise, *They Come for the Best of Reasons* (Washington, D.C.: American Council on Education, 1958); Edward Eddy, *The Impact of College on Student Character* (Washington, D.C.: American Council on Education, 1959). See also the fascinating study by Richard Peterson, *The Scope of Organized Student Protest* (Princeton, N.J.: Educational Testing Service, 1966).

his family. Loyalty to the nuclear family is extremely high, because the family is seen as a source of stability and security in a time of rapid social change.[21] Although the view of our student mentioned earlier may seem repulsive to those involved in college work, does it not, however, reflect with great accuracy the views of the good life professed by the American adult middle classes? And if this is true, is not the student's view of the good life (at least in American society) more realistic and perhaps more satisfying than the views many of us would wish he would present?

Before concluding, several comments must be added about this research. First, little account is taken of the almost infinite variety in types of students and types of institutions, and the "mix" or encounter is, therefore, more complex and sophisticated than one would surmise from many of the research studies. Much more needs to be known before we can make generalizations about the entirety of American higher education in terms of impact on student values—for example, we know little about impact in two-year or community colleges, although in a few years half of all American college students will be attending these institutions. (In fact, we do not even know whether or not these institutions see value change in students as one of their goals.) We know little about the commuting student in terms of what he seeks out of the college experience in addition to the desire for a larger paycheck, if anything.

Second, little of the research is designed to point out trends—to compare (some) students of today with (some) students of ten years ago, in order to make some judgments on trends in student personality development. Newcomb's study of Bennington seems to be the only data of this type available, although others are now in progress. It would seem consistent with our earlier analysis to conclude that today's students are influenced by common factors: relative affluence, the driving of social experiences down to earlier age levels in high school and before, generally more permissive home environments, and via the automobile, greater freedom from parental control with correspondingly greater influence on other young people on what behavior is acceptable. But we have little comparative data on how the entering student of today (our "raw material") differs from the entering student of ten or twenty years ago.

There is also a need to know what significance the college experience has throughout the life of the student: how relevant are college-inculcated values to the experiences and decisions which American society demands

[21] D. Riesman, "Review of the Jacob Report," *American Sociological Review*, **23** (1958), 732–38.

of its adults? For example, does the liberal arts graduate find retirement a less frustrating time of life because of artistic and intellectual experiences introduced in college? Are marriages of college graduates different in any important way from marriages of those who did not attend college? Does the college group raise its children differently? Will the college student who got A's do better on the job than the student who got C's? What is the impact, throughout life, of the nonclassroom educational experiences: the dormitory "bull sessions" which alumni can often remember with such astonishing accuracy many years later? Above all, how (if at all) does the college experience develop leadership in the relatively few people who will have a genuine impact on the directions our society will travel in the future? (At present, it would seem that a great many genuinely influential people were not very "successful" as college students.) To what extent is the high-school experience of today equivalent to the undergraduate college experience of a decade ago?

Returning now to the quotations that set the scene for this chapter, we can set individual colleges and individual students in a cultural context of fun, comfort, and consumership, of inconsistent values in a state of flux, of rampant materialism which many of the students will join and some will try to refute. The intellectual world has exciting new ideas, but none which contain a vision of how the world can be transformed into Utopia, none which seem to hold the key to individual, personal fulfillment. As Bell suggests, ideology seems to be on the way out, although student activism seems to be doing rather well without it.

Many of our previously untested assumptions clearly need rethinking. Do the liberal arts build "character"? Is the curriculum of today's undergraduate college relevant to the problems and lives of students in the latter half of the twentieth century? How do we ascertain its relevance?

The questions cannot be answered, but they point the way toward the need for a drastic reappraisal and testing of the goals of higher education. As Nevitt Sanford has said, if we were interested in stability alone, we would do well to plan a college program to keep freshmen just as they are, rather than trying to increase their education, their maturity, and their flexibilty. The senior who has been "educated" may be more unstable, simply because there is more to be stabilized; more uncertain about identity, because more possibilities are open. The essential dilemma of tradition and experimentation is detailed in a remark made to the late president of Bennington, William Fels, by a loyal graduate who gave him two bits of advice: keep it experimental but don't change a thing.

ADDENDUM: NEEDED RESEARCH

Some of the areas of needed research that are suggested in this chapter are listed here in outline form. These could well be accomplished by virtually any college that is interested in gauging its real impact on the values and personalities of its students (and faculty).

1. A longitudinal study, using a large number of college-age students, compared to a nearly identical group of the same age who did *not* go on to college. Comparisons of one college group with another will be of little use until the college and *non*college populations have been compared.

2. A cross-cultural study, comparing the student culture at an American college with, say, that of a British, French, Japanese, and Mexican institution of higher education. Obvious difficulties would be the development of research devices that would be fair to all the cultures and nationalities involved. Any school with an exchange program, or a "junior year abroad," could easily train students to do the actual gathering of data, so that cost would not be a major problem. Participant observer studies are often extremely effective.

3. A study of the *specific* impact of various "value-loaded" college experiences, such as compulsory chapel, required religion courses, courses in ethics, etc. The development of certain "before-and-after" measures would be difficult but by no means impossible. The situation would call for more than the usual questionnaire response; probably some depth interviewing over a period of time would be the best approach.

4. An analysis of teacher competence, focusing specifically on those aspects of the teacher's behavior that influence (or do not influence) the student in his own value choices. (Some teachers are considered brilliant by only a few students in their classes, while others may be considered brilliant by virtually *every* student they teach. It may well be that some teachers who are considered as poor by a majority of their students are nevertheless very influential in changing the values of a small minority.) Also, many teachers become known as perceptive influencers of student values, so that students come to their classes *expecting* to have things happen to them. The impact of the students' advance ideas of the teacher on what he learns would be interesting to study.

5. A study of "conversion," or the genuine acceptance of a particular religious outlook by a particular student or group of students. To what sort of student does this generally occur? What causes it? Is it true that the student who becomes the zealous Christian is often the student who has been rejected by certain other social groups on campus, such as fraternities, and turns to religion to establish his superiority

over others? How long do such conversions last? What other aspects of his thinking (political, vocational, economic, aesthetic) are modified in the process?

6. A study of the student's precollege expectations of the college experience, compared to his actual perceptions while a student, would be very interesting. The materials of Pace and Stern are useful in this connection. This approach would be of particular benefit to those colleges which are concerned with the problem of attrition on their campuses, because one of the major factors in attrition is that college is not quite what the students expected.

7. A study comparing student cultures on denominational and non-denominational campuses would be extremely interesting. Of particular interest here might be the process wherein the new recruit (freshman) is inducted into the *real* folkways and mores of student life (often very different from what the Dean of Students tells him college is all about). Many aspects of campus student life are, for better or worse, totally outside the control of the faculty and administration. These could be clarified, and the relative risks involved spelled out. Some colleges might be interested in investigating whether or not this campus culture can be moved in certain directions by the college— e.g., if the college wishes to increase students' interest in the intellectual or academic dimensions of experience, how should it go about it? (It is possible, of course, that if a girl *really* comes to college to get a husband, there is nothing much that can be done to change a whole college of husband-hunters.)

SELECTED BIBLIOGRAPHY

It is suggested that if the following are read somewhat in the order of their listing, it will allow the reader to develop sophistication as he goes along.

BOROFF, DAVID, *Campus U.S.A.* New York: Harper & Row, Publishers, 1961. An interesting series of descriptive accounts of Mr. Boroff's views of Harvard, Wisconsin, Claremont, Swarthmore, Brooklyn College, Parsons College, Birmingham-Southern, Smith, Sarah Lawrence, and the University of Michigan. Although this volume could only loosely be called social science, the interpretations of campus life and mores are stimulating and might be of assistance to individuals in setting up categories to examine their own campuses more closely. Easy, pleasant reading.

JACOB, PHILIP E., *Changing Values in College.* New York: Harper & Row, Publishers, 1957. This book is one of the first to make the case that American students are not much influenced by the college experience.

It is readable and contains a good summary of work done up to that time.

SANFORD, NEVITT, ed., *College and Character*. New York: John Wiley & Sons, Inc., 1964. This is a smaller and more useful version of the *American College*.

BARTON, ALLEN H., *Studying the Effects of College Education*. New Haven, Conn.: Hazen Foundation, 1959. A methodological examination of *Changing Values in College*.

SMITH, JOHN E., *Value Convictions and Higher Education*. New Haven, Conn.: Hazen Foundation, 1958.

RIESMAN, DAVID, "Review of the Jacob Report," *American Sociological Review*, 23 (1958), 732–38. This is an excellent short article which adds many new dimensions to the Jacob study.

FREEDMAN, MARVIN, "The Passage Through College," *Journal of Social Issues*, 12 (1956), 13–28. This is an excellent account of the Vassar Study, commenting both on the research methodology and the findings, which are of major significance. The material is also available in Sanford's book, but in a less interesting format. One gets a feeling for the individual student here.

RIESMAN, DAVID, "The Influence of Student Culture and Faculty Values in the American College," *Year Book of Education* (New York: Harcourt, Brace & World, Inc., 1959), pp. 386–404.

EDDY, EDWARD D., *The College Influence on Student Character* (Washington, D.C.: American Council on Education, 1958) and W. Max Wise, *They Come for the Best of Reasons* (Washington, D.C.: American Council on Education, 1959). These are books which try to get at the "big picture" of the entire United States. Both contain excellent information for any college interested in doing a self-study.

FREEDMAN, MARVIN, *Impact of College*, New Dimensions in Higher Education, No. 4. Washington, D.C.: U.S. Department of Health, Education and Welfare, 1960.

HABEIN, MARGARET, ed., *Spotlight on the College Student*. Washington, D.C.: American Council on Education, 1959. Addresses by Riesman, Jacob, Sanford, and others.

"Values of American College Students: A Symposium," *Religious Education*, 55 (1960), 15–48, 99–105. Good review of research at a variety of institutions.

WERNER, FRED. W., ed., *The World of the American Student*. Philadelphia: U.S. National Student Association, n.d. Good essays by Wise, Jacob, Riesman, Taylor, and others.

PRENTICE, W. C. F., P. JACOB, and R. J. HAVIGHURST, "Social Changes and the College Student," *The Educational Record*, 41, 4 (Oct. 1960), 329–58. A symposium.

SOUTHERLAND, R. L., W. H. HOLTZMAN, E. A. KOILE, and B. K. SMITH, *Personality Factors on the College Campus*. Austin, Tex.: Hogg Foundation for Mental Health, University of Texas, 1962. Review of a symposium.

SANFORD, NEVIT, *The American College*. New York: John Wiley & Sons, Inc., 1962. This book is probably the most important book on the list but is placed here because of its overwhelming format. It is virtually impossible to read it from cover to cover. However, if the reader has read some of the first five sources, he should be able to ask some specific questions with which this compendium can assist. As in all books of its type, the range of styles of the various contributors is unbelievable and disconcerting. As information, it is invaluable.

A few titles which deal more normatively than descriptively with values and the college student:

AUBREY, EDWIN E., *Humanistic Teaching and the Place of Ethical and Religious Values in Higher Education*. Philadelphia: University of Pennsylvania Press, 1959.

AVERILL, LLOYD, "The Climate of Valuing," *Current Issues in Higher Education*, 67–73. Washington, D.C.: Association for Higher Education, 1963.

CARPENTER, MARJORIE, *The Larger Learning*. Dubuque, Iowa: William Brown Co., 1960.

MOORE, JOHN M., *The Place of Moral and Religious Values in Programs of General Education*. New Haven, Conn.: Hazen Foundation, n.d.

9: some "revolutions" of our time— drastic social changes

Before proceeding, a word should be said about the current stage of development in the theory and research on social change. Workers in the field seem to be moving both to the global level, as in the case of W. E. Moore, and toward the individual level, as in the case of Homans.[1] This divergence of perspective has been helpful in dispelling certain monolithic notions of social change—we now know that what is seen as change will differ with the size of the focus, and that several contradictory changes are occurring simultaneously at all times on all levels of analysis, from a single person to a nation.

[1] W. E. Moore, "Global Sociology," in *American Journal of Sociology*, **71** (Mar. 1966), 475–82. See also his excellent summary volume, *Social Change* (Englewood Cliffs, N.J.: Prentice-Hall, Inc., 1963), and *Man, Time and Society* (New York: John Wiley & Sons, Inc., 1963). On the individual level, see George Homans' address, "Bringing Men Back In," a plea for sociology related to human beings, in *American Sociological Review*, **29** (1964), 809–18. Possibilities for the analysis of individuals interacting are expanded by Glazer and Strauss, "Awareness Contexts and Social Interaction," *American Sociological Review*, **29** (1964), 669–79.

theoretical perspectives

Certainly, we are being led to think that we are in an era of incredibly rapid social change. In many areas of endeavor, the change is said to be *exponential;* that is, the change increase is a multiple of the *rate* of change. From this has come the pattern of "log-log" acceleration, as used by Hart: [2]

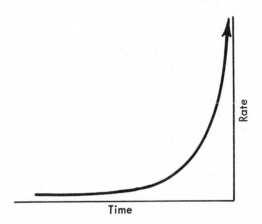

Many types of cultural change (particularly those dependent on technology) can be graphed on this curve; for example, speed records, cutting tool efficiency, speed of communication, number of new inventions. The exponential curve can make us a little paranoid about our environment at times—we think of the world as dashing away from us at the speed of light. Fortunately, all aspects of our lives are not subject to exponential change (number of children per family, for example). In fact, we tend to forget that in previous times, *other* factors were perceived by the populace as "getting out of hand"; for example, during the Middle Ages, the number of new scriptural interpretations per year, as well as the number of people dying of bubonic plague, may well have been described on an exponential curve. The point to be made, however, is that instead of screaming off the top of the graph, the exponentially increasing phenomenon tends simply to disappear, as society turns its interests and energies in other directions. *Social* change, like social stratification and so-

2 Hart's well-written article, "Social Theory and Social Change," in L. Gross, ed., *Symposium on Sociological Theory* (Evanston, Ill.: Row, Peterson & Company, 1959), pp. 196–240, is a classic on the topic.

cial mobility, must be perceived by individual members of the culture. A few years ago, there was an exponential increase in the number of hula hoops sold, but at "the top of the curve," when the change line was heading straight up, sales simply stopped as the fad wore off. (Whether or not this pattern is true for all changes, including present ones, is certainly debatable.)

The exponential model has increased recent interest in one of the major theories of social change, that of cultural lag. Originally put forth by Ogburn [3] (but with roots deep in the past), the theory suggests that technology is changing at a much faster rate than social institutions; therefore, we are not able to integrate new technology into the structure of values and perceptions that comprise culture. As the "gap" between values and technology increases, more and more "strain" is felt in individual lives, as people try to implement new technology with obsolete institutions and values.

There are many difficulties with the theory, as I have pointed out previously.[4] First, technology is certainly not valueless. Not only are there values inherent in the production processes of technology, but the things produced themselves have a definite set of symbolic value assumptions. A car or a toaster is a medium of *expression of symbols* as well as a thing, or as Marshall McLuhan puts it, "The medium is the message." Thus the dichotomy of technology and values is indeed fallacious. Secondly, change is both qualitative and quantitative, and rate of change may not be as disruptive as the quality of the change: "Devices and processes can change with great rapidity and cause no new problems, as long as the values and norms inherent in their form and function are compatible with the existing traditional values."[5] Finally, the lag model, suggesting as it does that values are "lagging behind" technology, also implies that the solution to our problem is to help values "catch up" with technology. But what does "catching up" mean? How would we know when we have "caught up"? It would seem, therefore, the major conclusion of the cultural lag position—that we should change "values" as fast as possible, in order to "catch up" with technology—should be subject to serious doubt.

There are several other ways in which social change can be viewed. In terms of the direction of change, we can say that there are three general positions: the Epiphany view, that we will someday be transformed

[3] W. F. Ogburn, Social Change (New York: The Viking Press, Inc., 1950) (revised edition, with excellent new summary chapter).

[4] Education in Social and Cultural Perspectives (Englewood Cliffs, N.J.: Prentice-Hall, Inc., 1962), Chap. 4.

[5] Ibid., p. 112.

into a Golden Age; the evolutionary view, that we are progressing toward more complex and efficient uses of energy; and the cyclical view, that social change is occurring in trendless fluctuations.[6] The major exponents of the first view of social change were probably Marx and Christianity, the second view was probably best presented by John Dewey and Herbert Spencer, and the third by Sorokin and perhaps Spengler. Each perspective has merit in terms of certain specific types of change; for example, change in political parties seems to be best described in cyclical terms, while U.S. economic growth seems to be a progressive, evolutionary, as well as cyclical, phenomenon. Although the earthly Epiphany has not yet occurred, it is reasonable to say that it has always been representative of the belief systems of many, particularly the poor and underprivileged (for example, in the words of "The Big Rock Candy Mountain").

The major difficulty with these three major propositions is that their supporters have tried to make them all-inclusive. It is clear that this cannot be, that there are different kinds of social change simultaneously moving us in different directions. For example, the number of marriages ending in divorce is increasing, as the age at time of marriage is decreasing. It also would appear that the number of teen-age marriages in which the wife is pregnant at the time of marriage is increasing (one out of six, in a recent Connecticut survey), while the use of birth control devices has increased. Alcoholism and venereal disease rates (especially among teen-agers) have shown large increases, as have the incidence of crimes of various types. On the other hand, comparative intelligence tests indicate that our draft age population knows more than did the draft age population in World War I, the number of years of formal education has increased, incomes have evened out, sales of books and records have increased drastically (more people go to symphony concerts than go to baseball games), more people are getting more hospital and medical care, church attendance is increasing, etc. Anyone who would generalize from this that we are "getting better" or "getting worse" is on rather shaky ground.

We also should not generalize from these and other data that social change occurs without any control by man, that, as Sumner and others have stated, the world is not subject to human efforts to change human conditions. For example, the number of air fatalities per 100,000 miles traveled has shown a marked decrease, as has child labor, and number of lynchings per year, as well as deaths from tuberculosis—all of these were accomplished by conscious intent. There are, then, many areas of endeavor in which man can direct his future, while there are others

---

[6] Adapted from Hart, *op. cit.*

which, at the present time, do not seem to be controllable. (To be able to see these latter as *potentially* controllable is a major task for all educational institutions.)

We should also point out here that, as with social stratification and social mobility, *social* change must be perceived by at least some members of any given society before we can say that change is taking place. It is interesting to note that certain societies perceive certain changes at certain times, but not at other times. For example, there seems to be a great deal of concern now over what we are doing to our natural environment (strip mining in Pennsylvania, regulation of the lumber industry, cleaning up rivers and ending air pollution), while in the 1920's (when exploitation of natural resources could have been stopped without major damage) there was little if any public *consciousness* of the changes that were taking place. We act on the basis of what we perceive, and what we perceive seems to be subject to rather wide variation, both for populations and within individuals. Why is it that at certain times people driving through a slum or a farm or forest decimated by strip mining "see" a social problem, while at other times they "see" nothing at all? The question cannot now be answered, but at least it is being asked. (In fact, the importance of the perceptions of individuals and groups may represent one of the major contributions of modern scholarship. It is one of the few centralizing concepts which pull the social sciences closer together, rather than tearing them apart.) [7]

Finally, it should be pointed out that in most discussions of social change, each change is considered as an independent entity. Because of our interactionist viewpoint, we must conclude that these areas of change are not isolated phenomena but are affecting each other. Some speculative suggestions along this line will be made.

i. cybernation

In the minds of many people, cybernation and automation are the same thing. There is, however, a very significant difference. The industrial revolution was accomplished with several theories; the first, that of identical or interchangeable parts, and the second, that the assembling or processing of these parts could be done by a machine regulated by a man, or perhaps several men. Thus, while output was

[7] For example, in history see H. Stuart Hughes, *Consciousness and Society* (New York: Random House, Inc., 1961), and Kenneth Boulding, *The Image* (Ann Arbor: University of Michigan Press, 1961). McLuhan's three major works, *The Mechanical Bride, The Gutenberg Galaxy,* and *Understanding Media,* also fit this theme. See also Leo Marx, *The Machine in the Garden* (New York: Oxford University Press, 1964), and Floyd Matson, *The Broken Image* (New York: George Braziller, Inc., 1964).

drastically increased, there was still plenty of work for people to do. Cybernation, however, has established that the machine can be regulated by *another machine:* for example,

> ... an automatic lathe ... which gauges each part as it is produced and automatically resets the cutting tools to compensate for tool wear. In addition, when the cutting tools have been worn down to a certain predetermined limit, the machine automatically replaces them with sharp tools. The parts are automatically loaded onto the machine and are automatically unloaded as they are finished. These lathes can be operated from 5 to 8 hours without attention, except for an occasional check to make sure that parts are being delivered to the loading mechanism.
>
> The R. H. Macy Co. is trying out its first electronics salesgirl. This machine is smart enough to dispense 36 different items in 10 separate styles and sizes. It accepts one to five dollar bills in addition to coins and returns the correct change plus rejecting counterfeit currency.[8]

Basic to these developments is the concept of *self*-regulation or feedback, which, according to its founder, "... is a method of controlling a system by reinserting into it the results of its past performance."[9] The thermostat is a relatively simple example of the concept in action.

Before proceeding to a discussion of the impact of cybernation on society, we might detour a moment to point out that the idea of self-regulation of systems has been a major factor in new thinking in a variety of areas, from communication theory to biology and anthropology. The diagram on page 206 could be used to explain the behavior of cells, people, ants, or perspiration.[10]

The model is extremely useful, not only in explaining feedback processes as they are, but also in explaining how new systems of feedback can be developed ("new circles" in the diagram), allowing the cell, organism, or organ to modify itself to meet new conditions. Also important in the model is the concept of information: the organism must have feedback information which is "coded" in a language that it can use. Be it perforated paper tape in a computer, or DNA in a cell, the communication of information in and out must be compatible, because what is being fed back is *information.*

[8] Both from an excellent summary pamphlet, *Cybernation: The Silent Conquest,* by Donald Michael (Santa Barbara, Calif.: Center for the Study of Democratic Institutions, 1962).

[9] Norbert Wiener, *The Human Use of Human Beings* (Garden City, N.Y.: Doubleday & Company, Inc., 1954), p. 61. Also his *Cybernetics* (Cambridge, Mass.: The M.I.T. Press, 1965).

[10] From Robert McClintock, "Machines and Vitalists," in *American Scholar,* **35** (1966), 249–57, p. 252. This whole issue, devoted to communication theory and cybernetics, is highly recommended.

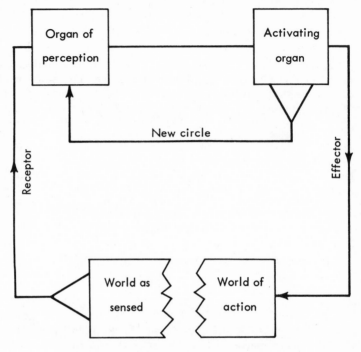

(From Uexküll, modified by McClintock)

The impact of cybernation is immense, both ideologically and economically, and will probably increase in the future. Many of our cherished ideas about man (and work) will no longer stand. For example, wealth, which has always been produced by human hands and human effort, can now be produced *automatically*. An individual's economic wealth has been for centuries a valid index of his personal worth (even Warner used it in Yankee City), but if those are correct who say that by the year 2,000 all the work there is can be done by 2 per cent of the people, then clearly human work has lost its wealth- (and status-) producing power for virtually everybody.

Between now and then, we must make some drastic changes in how we train people for work. Increasingly, we will run the risk of training people for jobs which, by the time training is completed, will no longer exist. Men will no longer have a one-job career; the prevalent pattern will be a succession of jobs, with intensive retraining after each. Vocational education will become a lifelong thing; people will no longer say that they have finished school. The consequences of cybernation will affect all areas of the occupational world: the farmhand replaced by the automatic milking machine lines up with the miner displaced by the electric shovel, the machinist by the automated lathe, the white-collar worker by the electric salesgirl and (in a couple of years) by the electric secretary, who can type directly from dictation with no mistakes and file everything perfectly; the linotype operator by the automatic type-setter; and even in the professions, the lawyer and doctor are finding some of their functions limited by computers (searching the medical or legal literature for precedents, for example).

As of now, these problems do not appear to be too great, since there are other jobs for these displaced workers. The time may soon come, however, when relatively large segments of our work force may be out of work at the same time, with no other work for them to do. At present, overproduction has led often to overconsumption, which has kept things relatively even. But the question remains, is there an upper limit to the amount of goods and services that a human being can consume?

The aspirations of youth (and particularly of parents for their children) in relation to vocation may have to be reviewed seriously, along with the desire for increased education on grounds of occupational mobility:

> Parents send their young to schools, at all levels of education, to acquire a skill with which to earn money. They are resentful of spending money for any purpose other than for education, and they measure the success of the process by the average beginning salary of the senior class. If it is high, they are pleased, for the future of their offspring is secure. They believe this delusion even though grandfather was a blacksmith and father is an unemployed coal miner.[11]

The schools, as well as the American family, must begin to develop some other standards of "success" (worth as a person) besides occupational status. Basic to this difficulty is the deeply rooted notion that the individual is competing for survival against a basically hostile world, and it is through work that one survives. Contrast this attitude with the new proposals being made in Washington that every citizen should be guaranteed a minimum number of dollars per year, whether he works or not. If the individual loses the responsibility for his material well-being, then enormous changes can be expected in family structure, and particularly in sex roles. Through the ages, man has been the protector of and provider for his family—it is through his energy and effort that they survive. If machines can provide the energy and effort (and money), what is

[11] From William Matheo, "When Men and Machines Work Together," in Brickman and Lehrer, eds., *Automation, Education, and Human Values* (New York: School & Society Books, 1966), p. 48.

there left for man to do, as a father, husband, and "supporter"? For example, in articles dealing with automated machines for teachers, doctors, and others, the conclusion is usually reached that the new technology releases the professional to perform those tasks which can only be performed by human beings—but these tasks are seldom stated specifically. We may have to find out what they are.

ii. leisure

The problem here is clearly a consequence of the preceding discussion, because leisure is only possible when large amounts of nonhuman energy are made available to do what was man's work. The difficulty is simply stated: we still feel guilty for not working, not only because the Devil finds work for idle hands to do, but because work (vocation) provides us with one of our principal sources of self-identity, and one of our major devices for classifying and evaluating other people. (All people may be of equal worth in some abstract sense, but we seldom act as if we believed it.) In that we have learned that time is money, *free* time is therefore immediately translated into worthless time. As we have seen in our studies of suburbia, people budget every minute of "free" time just as rigorously as they do on the job, even though there is no conceivable reason for their doing so. The American is often an activist because he is afraid to be anything else.

In other nations with greater respect for the speculative, philosophical life, the problem will not be as severe. But as Hofstadter has brilliantly pointed out, our entire history has been anti-intellectual; it has been the "can-do" person who has been praised and emulated. The reflective person has seldom if ever been praised (Thoreau was, of course, snickered at as the Village Idiot, and Einstein was thought by many to be a trivial figure playing with numbers, until the results developed into something frighteningly material.) Thus the adaptation to leisure will be extremely difficult for Americans, particularly at the present time when a large proportion (perhaps one fourth, if Harrington is correct) of people are living in poverty, while two thirds of us have both higher incomes and more leisure.

American education at all levels seems singularly unqualified to help young people make effective use of future leisure. In the first place, the "fun culture" we have spoken about as typical of high schools and colleges supports *activities*, not private cogitation or speculation. In an other-directed society, to be alone is to be without direction, which is terrifying to a person who has no core of interests of his own. Even in the area of independent study, there are some students who simply cannot manage to "call their own shots"; they must be told what to do. Even within the formal curriculum, elementary schools, high schools, and colleges seem still to place major emphasis on the rapid regurgitation of the "right" answer. This emphasis on "output" in schools leads to the view that ". . . the life of leisure is anti-democratic, antisocial, against organization, opposed to work and to most of the things men work for, and indifferent to home, mother, and perhaps even country." [12] (To make the point, it could be said that Socrates, were he alive today, would be arrested in almost every state in the Union for violation of vagrancy and loitering statutes.) Even that venerable institution, the study hall, is used for getting assignments done, period. This author has seen students whose homework had been completed, censured for looking thoughtfully out the window—the ground being that they "were not working." Schools and colleges command students not to think but to produce. The very notion of "goofing off" suggests that not to be fully occupied with *doing* things is cheating on the rest of us; yet, when we leave our friends, what do we say? "Take it easy"! The expression is generally meant to be mutual assurance that we have worked hard enough.

Leisure in the American mind has always been associated with an aristocracy of wealth—we think of Mozart performing for a privileged class of libertines, while peasants starved. In the American ethos, every man must "do his share" or the whole system is threatened. The discomfiting fact is, however, that we may have to begin restricting people's working hours through force, if necessary. (In many instances, an electrician who *wants* to work a 60-hour week will be restrained from doing so, even by legal means.) The problem is a real one: in 1850, the average workweek for all industries was 69.7 hours; in 1960, it was 38.5 hours.[13] Vacations (paid) are getting longer at the same time, and monthly vacations are by no means a rarity. In fact, some companies are establishing orientation programs to help workers adapt to the longer vacation periods. A major fear during the turn of the century, when major reductions in the workweek were being accomplished, was that more hours off would mean more drinking and brawling (work was good in that it gave the workingman little time and energy to manifest his baser—or his better—impulses). It is at least clear that this danger was ill-founded. We may not like the way workers *spend* their time (and note the economic metaphor in this phrase), but at least they are not killing each other in large numbers.

It seems unlikely that schools and colleges can contribute to a revolu-

[12] S. DeGrazia, *Of Time, Work, and Leisure* (Garden City, N.Y.: Doubleday & Company, Inc., 1964), p. 411.
[13] *Ibid.*, p. 419.

tionary change in the use of more and more "free" time by the American people. Those things which can only be accomplished with leisure—philosophy, art and music, the writing of literature—have never been the keystone to our educational system, at any level. Above all else, our educational system has perpetuated the occupational structure, and it has functioned primarily in this way. Although we claim to be "making good citizens" who "understand their cultural heritage," educational status has always been closely linked with occupational status. Another unanswered question is significant here: What proportion of the populace is *capable* of acquiring sophisticated taste and contemplative skills? History tells us little on this point, because no culture has ever had the economic ability to produce, not Veblen's leisure *class*, but a leisured *society*.

At the present moment, the whole system of values that goes with the work ethic seems to be in a state of flux. Reducing the workweek does not reduce the worker's hunger for more money and goods, so that one major consequence of the six-hour day is the acquisition of a second job—"moonlighting"—on a major scale.[14] In fact, at least one study of the introduction of a four-day workweek indicated that most workers didn't like it, even though they were paid the same amount as in their previous five-day week. A day off during the week meant that the children were at school, the wife had her regular tasks to do, and the male had nothing to do but sleep or watch television. There apparently was nothing else that he wanted to do. The central dilemma this raises for educational institutions has been nicely put by Riesman:

> It is discomfiting to reflect on the complexity and scope of the programs that would be required to overcome this legacy of passivity and aimlessness. What sort of adult-education program could meet these workers halfway in helping them plan their leisure in terms of lifelong opportunities? What sort of change of perspective on the world and the self is required before muted and barely realized dissatisfactions can become a lever for individual development?[15]

Although no revolutions can be accomplished through education, certainly a beginning can be made. The central problem may be that, while we must motivate some young people to *want* a job, we may have to motivate some other students to want something else as well. How are we to explain to students that their fathers were wrong in wholehearted, slavish devotion to their jobs and not to their inner resources? Certainly, the next twenty years will show enormous dislocations in the occupational

[14] S. Swados, "Less Work—Less Leisure," in Larrabee and Myerson, eds., *Mass Leisure* (New York: Free Press of Glencoe, Inc., 1958), pp. 353–63.

[15] David Riesman, "Some Issues in the Future of Leisure," pp. 174–84, p. 179, in *Abundance for What* (Garden City, N.Y.: Doubleday & Company, Inc., 1965).

structure—how can we prepare youth for the possibility that the job for which they've trained may not exist when they are ready to take it? How can we help them to develop self-respect in an era in which the state makes sure that no one will starve or be short on medical care?

Certainly, one solution for these major problems is *not* the institution of a required course in art or music. But how do we justify the fact that philosophy is ignored in virtually every American high school? At the same time we are pushing social experiences into earlier and earlier grades, we seem to avoid doing so with the arts and humanities. Perhaps the time has come to at least begin experimenting along these lines.

iii. the family

Clearly, the problems emergent here are related to the first two categories. In an economy of scarcity, every worker was needed; ideally, 24 hours a day. In an economy of abundance, the young and the old are kept from vocational responsibility (often against their will). By expanding number of years of schooling, a glut on the labor market is avoided.

But at the same time we prevent youth from assuming occupational responsibility until a later and later time in life, other kinds of social maturity are occurring at even earlier levels (girls mature earlier physically today due to the better diet, etc.). The contradictions here are going to be incredibly difficult to resolve, particularly if the age at marriage continues to decline. Can a couple marrying at age sixteen be happy with each other at forty-five? How can a father, working a twenty-hour week, show his leadership and masculinity within the family? Where will discipline come from? When children work longer and harder hours in school than their father does on the job, what will be the results? The mother is in a much better position on this score, as DeGrazia has commented that the more laborsaving devices she possesses, the *more* time she spends on housework.[16] She at least has things in the home to make her feel essential.

The "trauma" of adolescence may be caused, more than any other single factor, by the delaying of vocational and economic responsibility conflicting with a social code that encourages earlier and earlier social maturity. If children are encouraged to date at puberty and before, is it any wonder that they want to "play house" at fifteen? The contradiction here is direct and traumatizing for the adolescent. The mass media suggest (or insist) that they live in a sex-filled world, yet there is no socially

16 *Op. cit.*, p. 72.

approved way of releasing this drive which has been prematurely developed and heightened. The kind of titillating published material that only a generation ago had to be smuggled under a drugstore counter can be found today in entirely legitimate form, not only in magazines devoted exclusively to that purpose, but even in the movie advertisements in the venerable *New York Times*, which still claims to publish only the *news* (but not the ads) "that's fit to print." Most of us who have reached something like adult status and have resolved some of these conflicts have little idea about how (and how constantly) the adolescent is forced to look at sex, particularly of the pre- and extramarital variety. It is hard to believe that the combination of very early marriages based on virtually irrational romanticism, plus the Hugh Hefner "Playboy Philosophy," which suggests that the good life is a string of superficial sexual conquests, will act in the future to *reduce* the divorce rate.

Partially as a consequence of these disjunctures in the world of work and leisure, we can expect that family structure will alter significantly. Although all the dimensions cannot be postulated, several can be. First, one chief source of male identity in the family will be as *head consumer*. Already the problems of how and what to buy, the styles of consumership to be adopted, seem to occupy an increasing amount of the family's time and energy. Even more than today, the family unit will be perceived and evaluated in terms of what it owns. Particularly is this true in terms of leisure gear. (Someone could write an interesting paper on the status systems involved in camping—both the equipment and the "one-upmanship" rules of displaying it at the campsite.) Anyone who has been in an airplane recently can testify to the astonishing increase in the number of *large* suburban backyard swimming pools. In fact, as a source of personal identity for the individual and the family unit, these products may be better symbolically than the older ones of car and house. At least leisure products tell the observer something about what these people are like and what they think is important.

Control of parents over children's behavior will certainly not be strengthened in the future. As more and more of the child's activities become the property of "specialist" outside agencies, and as the guns of the consumer marketeers are trained more directly on children and the enormous amount of wealth they can influence, as geographical mobility of the family increases, and with it the increase of mobility of youth through the acquisition of two cars per family, the harder it will be for parents to take a firm stand. Another source of difficulty is that the "fun culture" appears to make the teen-ager the model for *everybody's* behavior, and if everyone wants to be like youth (which means do what the young people are doing), how can we adults at the same time chastise them?

It has been widely proclaimed that the existence of cheap, oral contraceptives will be the end of the American family, since youth will therefore drop all its scruples and engage in orgiastic behavior. Thus far, there is little reason to believe that this will happen. Sophisticated observers of the college scene indicate that the "sexual revolution" is probably not a revolution at all in terms of *behavior*, but that students are much more open about their problems, and wish moral decisions to be made personally, not brought about by the imposition of outside authority. It would appear (and there is some evidence for this) that a greater danger to family solidarity may come from the freedom which the new contraceptives make possible not for the children but for the parents, especially among those who wish to emulate, or who are envious of, the adolescent's position in the "fun culture." [17] In certain high-status suburbs, for example, the Search for Kicks seems to occupy more of the parents' time and energy than the children's, indicating that this pattern may filter down to other economic levels in the future. Some of the reasons for this were pointed out in the chapter on communities.

One of the basic difficulties in all this is a pervasive inability to separate love and sex. The qualities of warmth, tenderness, affection, sympathy, and understanding are seldom, if ever, purveyed through the mass media as qualities (of adults) which youth should emulate. As an astute observer of the contemporary scene has put it, the Victorians, afraid of sex, took refuge in love, while the contemporary American, afraid of love, takes refuge in sex.[18] We are conditioned to look at all contacts with the opposite sex as potential conquests, and to look at all relationships with the same sex as extremely suspect. To this degree, our pervasive concern with sex limits drastically the extent of human relationships we permit ourselves, and threatens not only family solidarity but also our ability to have interesting and meaningful nonsexual relationships with a wide range of people. It suggests once again that Puritanism (the tendency to see oneself as an isolated individual, keeping the rest of the world outside) is still with us, because sex can be accomplished in a mechanistic, isolated, impersonal way, while love cannot, by definition. This preoccupation with sex *may* be what has been called "The New Puritanism," [19] but it certainly is the consequence of a materialistic, individualistic culture, in which the person is pitted against a hostile environment.

One of the most insidious aspects of contemporary family culture is

[17] See Donald Michaels, *The Next Generation* (New York: Random House, Inc., 1965), pp. 76–77. This volume is an excellent summary of trends in the next twenty years. Highly recommended for general background.
[18] See Rollo May, "Antidotes for the New Puritanism," *Saturday Review*, March 26, 1966.
[19] *Ibid.*

the way in which many parents manipulate their children through the denial of love. To say to a child that "Mommy won't love you if you do that" is to suggest that the child is loved only for his actions, not for himself. More than any other, this action is bound to make the child suspicious later of love "with no strings attached." The permissive environment of the contemporary family is not necessarily full of love because it is permissive; in fact, earlier families, more restrictive of the children's behavior, may have actually been more supportive, because the parents' love for the child was never called into question and never used as a bribe. Since there are few other ways for today's parents to manipulate their children, this use of the denial of love as a threat will probably increase.

On the other hand, the future will hold more time and more opportunity for the family to share experiences together. For those who take advantage of it, the opportunities to learn and explore as a family are certainly present. The high divorce rate does *not* mean that marriage as an institution is declining; it may mean that the qualifications for a successful marriage and family are becoming more difficult, complex, and sophisticated; therefore, harder for many to achieve. It is clear that many of the institutions that have in the past been sources of identity for youth no longer serve this function. It is largely the family and the school at present which have relatively constant access to youth, and which will, therefore, teach the child who he is and what he may (and may not) become. It is extremely unlikely that the age of entering school can be moved much lower, although universal ("free" and "compulsory") education of four-year-olds is certainly possible. During these first four or five formative years, the parents (and the "second parent"—the television set) have relatively complete influence, and the school must necessarily inherit, for better or worse, the product of this interaction.

If father is to be home more hours of the week, at least one problem *may* be solved, in that there will be a real adult male around for the boys in the family to identify with. But if father-at-home is a lazy, indolent watcher of TV and consumer of beer (as seems to be the case very often), then the problem of identification models for male children may be intensified.

In conclusion, there is little reason to expect that the family as a social institution is about to shrivel up and die. It will, however, become a family organized around leisure and consumership, rather than work and frugality. In one way, the opportunities for meaningful family relationships have never been greater, because the father now has time and energy to take a productive role in the developing family *as a person,* not as a disembodied breadwinner who collapses immediately on his arrival home, exhausted from the toils of work. If he is humble enough to admit what he does not know, he and his family may even engage in really significant learning experiences together. This possibility—the family as an *educational* unit for all members—could be productive indeed. There are indications that many alert publishing companies have seen the opportunities here, and the array of materials for *family* study—from classical Greece, to animal life, from higher mathematics to opera—is heartening to see. If this movement were to take hold, the family could become a unit for *self*-education which would have a pervasive effect on American education and American culture. Involving Father will be a crucial step.

iv. the evolution of a world perspective

Certainly, one of the factors that has continually arisen in this volume is the coordination of larger and larger entities—in bureaucracies, in government, in business, and in communities. Clearly, in twenty years the United States will be controlled and coordinated largely through a series of eight to ten megalopolitan areas. Existing state and local governments (the parameters of which were established, in part, due to notions of communication and transportation which are now outmoded) may still have an important place, but quite likely some form of formal governmental system will evolve for megalopolitan-level problems.

Moving out from the megalopolis, it is also clear that our national government is increasingly involved in coordination with other nations. Particularly because of rapid increases in travel and communication speeds, the businessman in Chicago today can have better contact with business prospects in Rome than his predecessor did with contacts in Peoria. This has produced the standardized system of secondary group associations we have spoken about. (To have breakfast in India and have nothing but fried eggs and "Rice Krispies" available is strange but often true.) There is little doubt that we are giving up much that is good in local, indigenous cultures in order to achieve this higher level of coordination.

The individual citizen probably still feels little sense of responsibility or allegiance to the world as a political, social, or economic entity. The time is coming, however, when this will be a necessity, and Willkie's vision of One World may become *perceptual* reality. As travel and communication with the rest of the world increase for a wide range of citizens, better information on nations we used to think of as light-years away should make us see how close we really are. Eventually, the fact that American dogs are better fed, according to standards of human nutrition, than 30 per cent of the world's *people*, will enter into the perceptual fields of many of the American citizenry.

Similarly, many Americans are now cognizant of the problems of pollution and waste of natural resources at the *national* level. It may soon be obvious that this is a world problem as well. The telling analogy is that of a space ship. Everything which is used in the ship for life-support systems must be made reusable somehow—nothing can be wasted, nothing can be thrown away. In the future, people may begin to perceive the *earth* as a space ship (which it is), with a "life support" system based on reuse of materials. Were this to occur, it would add new impetus to the problem of waste. (We currently have to get rid of five pounds of waste for every American every day.) When we bury a wrecked car, we are not "throwing it away," any more than an astronaut is throwing away packaging materials by stuffing them behind his seat. The air, water, minerals, and organic living material are all that we have on this space ship in which all men are riding. When people begin to perceive this larger level of organization, they may also begin to see local *problems* extended to this larger context. Examples of coordination like NATO and the Common Market indicate that megalopolis applies to supranational levels as well as within one nation. It would be logical to expect that more and more formerly "local" problems will come to be perceived on national and supranational levels, where more effective action on the entire problem is possible.

These problems of perceiving new and larger levels of human activity will probably be more difficult for most persons than the problems of dealing directly with new technological innovations. In many ways, we are becoming increasingly sophisticated and blasé about technological innovation, and many changes, such as learning to use a push-button telephone instead of a revolving dial one, or flying in a 2,000-miles-per-hour jet instead of a 600-miles-an-hour one, seem to be problems we can all deal with. But to perceive human problems on terms larger than those of the nation will be difficult indeed for certain types of people. Genuinely to realize that what happens in India affects our economy directly will be extremely difficult, especially for those whose current perceptions of the world are limited to the local community and perhaps the state. One of the most optimistic aspects of this problem is the relatively large number of college students who seem to have acquired at least some understanding of the international level of human organization. Businessmen also seem to have realized, for the most part, that international commerce implies international travel schedules, shipping arrangements, monetary exchanges, and even international law. Even high-school students are involved in exchange programs with students from other countries, helping to push the international perspective into new areas, both in this country and abroad. Since the first step in dealing with a problem is that of perceiving the problem in its entire dimensions, this tendency toward international perceptions can be a force for good.

conclusions

Many other examples of "drastic" social changes could have been presented here. However, it is the view of the author that most of these areas are interdependent—as we have seen here, social changes in different aspects of life often stem from the same source, and interact with each other to a significant degree. It is through the interrelationships of these changes that we can see them with greatest clarity. Many pundits have shown exponential curves of technological advances in many fields, which makes us think that the world is about to come to an end. However, when these data are put together with others, and the *cultural* implications are sketched out, it becomes clear that we can survive the next few years and retain our humanity. There are new forms of coercion present, and new forms of freedom as well. There will be new sources of tension, along with relief from previous tensions. The young and the old will not understand each other perfectly, but they never have, and probably never will.

During the sixties, some major changes have occurred in our perceptions of the role of educational institutions. First and foremost, it is now widely recognized that what they do is not only local but has regional, national, and ultimately, international implications. The boy in Middletown, Ohio, will probably not live out his life in Middletown, and we cannot educate him on any other assumption than that he will live in the nation and the world as well as in Middletown.

Also, the formal function of educating is being more widely dispersed, both in terms of the length of time a person is subjected to it, and in terms of the variety of media and institutions which are responsible for it. Vocational training and retraining are unquestionably carried on more expeditiously in the immediate context of the job, and more and more industries are establishing their own training and retraining facilities. The two-year colleges seem to be the major recent educational development in terms of numbers, and soon will be in the majority in terms of higher-education enrollments. They currently are serving vocational needs for large groups, and are a "bridge" to four-year colleges for others, just as the junior high schools evolved to "bridge" the gap between elementary and high schools, as universal high-school education became a reality. They seem the natural institution to begin providing large groups of people with experiences in the arts and humanities which would make enlightened mass leisure a reality, but they currently do not seem to see this as a major task. Adult education programs, sponsored by community school districts and private agencies, seem to be springing up at a great rate, and it may be through these programs that extravocational emphases can be at least begun. With younger parents completing the childbearing phase earlier and earlier, it may be that more educational programs geared for entire families will be available, both through the mass media and in institutions of learning.

There is one expected consequence of social precocity that should be pointed out. As we drive social skills further down the age continuum, we can expect the same kind of "rebellion" in high schools that now seems to be prevalent at many colleges. Already, high-school students who have been expelled from school for the way they wear their hair or clothes are taking their cases to court—and winning. For a high-school student to spend the summer as a civil rights worker is no longer impossible. More and more colleges are reporting that experimentation with glue sniffing, marijuana, and even LSD is something which the entering college freshman brings with him from secondary school. It seems that we cannot push forward just the "desirable" social experiences to earlier age levels; we get not only earlier dating but earlier necking and drinking as well. For example, it is hard to believe that if public school teachers continue to use the strike in the future, high-school students will be sitting quietly on the sidelines. More political acuteness will bring for the high-school student, as it has for the college student, a desire to try out his knowledge. The high-school equivalent to the Berkeley revolt may be just around the corner.

One major problem for education in the future involves organization and communication *within* the educational profession. Although there are presently some promising developments in this area, it remains to be said that, compared with the business and political enterprises, education is very poorly organized. People at different levels seldom have a chance to discuss common problems (and, as we have seen, their institutions and problems are really very much alike). Status systems in education, whereby the primary school teacher is looked down on as being "inferior" to the high-school or college teacher, are largely responsible for this insularity within the profession. It is particularly strange because of the fact that the central questions of education—motivating students, evaluating their learning, selecting criteria for teaching excellence, administrative organization for effective and flexible teaching, financing of education, teacher preparation, etc.—remain so constant at all educational levels. We have spoken often in this book of the importance of perceptions, and it may be a just conclusion to say that maturity in the educational profession will be attained when all teachers perceive all other teachers as colleagues, allied in a common enterprise.

author and title
index

The index is offered in this form both to assist the reader who is searching for a particular reference and also to provide a working bibliography for the reader who wishes to engage in further study.

a

Adorno, T. W., *et al.*, *The Authoritarian Personality*, 166

Aldrich, Thomas Bailey, *Story of a Bad Boy*, 145

Amis, Kingsley, *Lucky Jim*, 8

Aubrey, Edwin E., *Humanistic Teaching and the Place of Ethical and Religious Values in Higher Education*, 199

Averill, Lloyd, "The Climate of Valuing," 199

b

Barber, Bernard, "Structural-Functional Analysis: Some Problems and Misunderstandings," 60
Social Stratification, 93
Barton, Allen H., Studying The Effects of College Education, 198
Beck, James, Our Wonderland of Bureaucracy, 26
Becker, H. & B. Geer, "Student Culture in Medical School," 132
"The Fate of Idealism in Medical School," 188
Behavioral Science & Educational Administration, 35
Bell, Daniel, The End of Ideology, 98, 182, 183
Bendix, R., Max Weber: An Intellectual Portrait, 116
Bendix, R. & S. Lipset, eds., Class, Status, and Power, 78, 81, 84, 97, 116
Social Mobility in Industrial Society, 118, 123
Benjamin, Harold, The Saber-Tooth Curriculum, 69
Bensman, J. & B. Rosenberg, Mass, Class, and Bureaucracy, 26
Bickel, Alexander, "Much More than Law Is Needed," 58
Black, Max, ed., The Social Theories of Talcott Parsons, 79
Blau, Peter, Bureaucracy in Modern Society, 26, 32, 44
"Occupational Bias and Mobility," 119
Blum, A., "Social Structure, Social Class, and Participation in Primary Relationships," 122
Bock, K., "Evolution, Function and Change," 84
Boroff, David, "The Air Force Academy: A Slight Gain in Altitude," 131
Campus U.S.A., 197
Boulding, Kenneth, The Image, 114, 204
Bowers, William J., Student Dishonesty and Its Control in College, 131, 132
Breed, W., "Occupational Mobility and Suicide Among White Males," 96
Brickman & Lehrer, eds., Automation, Education and Human Values, 207
Bromfield, Egghead, 16

Bronfenbrenner, Urie, "Socialization and Social Class Through Time and Space," 177
Brown, D., "Non-Intellective Factors and Faculty Nominations of Ideal Students," 174, 190
Bruin, Frederick S., "Bureaucracy and National Socialism: A Reconsideration of Weberian Theory," 31
Buckley, Walter, "Social Stratification and the Functional Theory of Social Differentiation," 55, 84
Burgess, Anthony, A Clockwork Orange, 147
Burnham, James, The Managerial Revolution, 26
Butcher, Margaret, The Negro in American Culture, 102

c

Callahan, Raymond, Education and the Cult of Efficiency, 44
Calvin, J., Institutes of the Christian Religion, 116
Campbell, Roald, "Implications for the Practice of Administration," 41
Cannon, The Wisdom of the Body, 53
Carpenter, Marjorie, The Larger Learning, 199
Cartter, Allan, "A New Look at the Supply of College Teachers," 133
Centers, Richard, The Psychology of Social Classes, 94, 97
Chinoy, Automobile Workers and The American Dream, 125
Clark, Burton, Educating the Expert Society, 69
Cloward, R. & L. Ohlin, Delinquency and Opportunity, 145
Cohen, A., Delinquent Boys, 145
Cohen, John, Chance, Skill and Luck: The Psychology of Guessing and Gambling, 6
Coleman, James, The Adolescent Society, 69
"The Adolescent Subculture and Academic Achievement," 188
Corson, John J., Governance of Colleges and Universities, 44
Coser, Lewis, The Functions of Social conflict, 53, 54
Cox, Harvey, The Secular City, 144
Cox, O., "Race and Caste: A Distinction," 99

Crutchfield, "Conformity and Creative Thinking," 170, 171
Cuber, J. & W. Kenkel, *Social Stratification*, 92
Current Issues in Higher Education, 199

d

Dain, Norman, *Concepts of Insanity in the United States, 1789-1865,* 166
Davis, A. & B. Gardner, *Deep South,* 99
Davis, A., *Social-Class Influences Upon Learning,* 108
Davis, Kingsley, "The Myth of Functionalism as a Special Method in Sociology and Anthropology," 78
"A Conceptual Analysis of Stratification," 82
Human Society, 82
Reply to Tumin, 84
Davis, K. & W. E. Moore, "Some Principles of Stratification," 82
DeGrazia, S., *Of Time, Work, and Leisure,* 124, 209, 211
Dennis & Kauffman, eds., *The College and the Student,* 187
Dichter, Ernest, *The Strategy of Desire,* 51
Dobriner, W., ed., *The Suburban Community,* 122, 149, 156
Dore, Ronald, "Function and Cause," 51, 79
Dressel, P. & L. Mayhew, eds., *General Education—Explorations in Evaluation,* 188
Driesch, Hans Adolph, *The History and Theory of Vitalism,* 55
The Science and Philosophy of The Organism, 55
Durkheim, Emile, 139

e

Eddy, David D., *The College Influence on Student Character,* 198
Eddy, Edward, *The Impact of College on Student Character,* 193
Elias, C., *Metropolis: Values in Conflict,* 142
Eliot, T. S., "Love Song of J. Alfred Prufrock," 8
Notes Towards the Definition of Culture, 83
Emmet, Dorothy, *Function, Purpose and Powers,* 52

"The Notion of Biological Functionalism," 55

f

Fallding, Harold, "Functional Analysis in Sociology," 56, 84
Festinger, L., *When Prophecy Fails,* 166
A Theory of Cognitive Dissonance, 166, 185
Form, W. & J. Geschwender, "Social Reference Basis for Job Satisfaction," 119
Form, W. H., "Status Stratification in a Planned Community," 122, 156
Fortes, Meyer, *The Institutions of Primitive Society,* 140
Foss, Daniel, "The World View of Talcott Parsons," 78
Freedman, M., *Impact of College,* 183, 198
"The Passage Through College," 191
Fromm, Erich, *Escape from Freedom,* 41, 77, 166
Fuguitt, Glenn, "The Growth and Decline of Small Towns," 89
Functionalism in the Social Sciences, 62

g

Gerth & Mills, eds., *From Max Weber: Essays in Sociology,* 26, 116
Getzels, Jacob & Phillip Jackson, *Creativity and Intelligence,* 173, 180
Ghiselin, B., *The Creative Process,* 162
Gillespie, J. & G. Allport, *Youth's Outlook on the Future: A Cross-National Study,* 193
Glass, V., ed., *Social Mobility in Britain,* 118
Glazer, B. & A. Strauss, "Awareness Contexts and Social Interaction," 17, 200
"Temporal Aspects of Dying as Unscheduled Status Passage," 17
Goffman, Erving, *The Presentation of Self in Everyday Life,* 6, 19
Stigma: Notes on the Management of Spoiled Identity, 6, 19
Goldsen, Rose, *What College Students Think,* 131
Gomberg, A., "The Working-Class Child of Four and Television," 111
Goodman, Percival & Paul Goodman, *Communitas,* 158

Gordon, E. Wayne, *The Adolescent Society*, 17
The Social System of the High School, 69
Gordon, A., *Jews in Suburbia*, 152
Gottman, J., *Megalopolis*, 153
Gouldner, Alvin, "Red Tape as a Social Problem," 32
"Reciprocity and Autonomy in Functional Theory," 54
Granick, David, *Management of the Industrial Firm in the USSR*, 26
Green, Arnold W., *Sociology*, 55
Gross, E., *Work and Society*, 118
Gross, L., ed., *Symposium on Sociological Theory*, 49, 54, 201
Grossack, M., *Mental Health and Segregation*, 103
Gruber, Howard, *et al.*, eds., *Contemporary Approaches to Creative Thinking*, 163, 164, 170, 172
Guest, Edgar, *The Favorite Verse of Edgar Guest*, 115
Gunzberg, R., *One Hundred Years of Lynching*, 103

h

Habein, Margaret, ed., *Spotlight on the College Student*, 198
Haer, J., "A Comparative Study of the Classification Techniques of Warner and Centers," 94
Harmin, M. & S. Simon, "The Year the Schools Began Teaching the Telephone Directory," 68
Harrington, M., *The Other America*, 100, 146
Harris, C. & E. Ullman, "The Nature of Cities," 142
Hart, "Social Theory and Social Change," 201, 203
Hatt, P., "Occupational and Social Stratification," 97
Hatt, P. & A. Reiss, *Reader in Urban Sociology*, 141
Haydn, Hiram, "Humanism in 1984," 24
Heist, P., *et al.*, "Personality and Scholarship," 189
Hempel, Carl, "The Logic of Functional Analysis," 49
Hemphill, John K., "Personal Variables and Administrative Styles," 42
Henry, Jules, "Working Paper on Creativity," 63, 75

Hodge, R., "Status Consistency of Occupational Groups," 96
Hodgkinson, H. L., *Education in Social and Cultural Perspectives*, 71, 104, 126, 165, 193, 202
Hoffer, Eric, *The True Believer*, 166
Hofstadter, Richard, *Anti-Intellectualism in American Life*, 7, 16
Social Darwinism in American Thought, 103
Hollingshead, A. & F. Redlich, *Social Class and Mental Illness*, 97, 146
Homans, George C. & David Schneider, *Marriage, Authority, and Final Cause*, 49, 56
Homans, George, "Bringing Men Back In," 200
Horrocks, John, *The Assessment of Behavior*, 167
Hsu, F. L., *Caste, Clan and Club*, 99
Hughes, E., "Dilemmas and Contradictions of Status," 101
Hughes, H. Stuart, *Consciousness and Society*, 204
Huxley, Aldous, *Brave New World*, 154
Hyman, H., "The Psychology of Status," 94, 269
Hyneman, Charles, *Bureaucracy in a Democracy*, 26

j

Jackson, E. F., "Status Consistency and Symptoms of Stress," 96
Jackson & Crockett, "Occupational Mobility in the United States," 119
Jacob, Philip, *Changing Values in College*, 192, 197
James, William, Philosophy of, 2
Jones, Maxwell, *The Therapeutic Community*, 140

k

Kafka, Franz, *The Trial* and *The Castle*, 26
Kahl, J., *The American Class Structure*, 93
Kaplovitz, D., "The Problem of Blue-Collar Consumers," 111
Karacki, L. & J. Toby, "The Uncommitted Adolescent: Candidate for Gang Socialization," 145
Katz, Fred, "The School as a Complex Social Organization," 69

Keniston, Kenneth, *The Uncommitted: Alienated Youth in American Society,* 145

Kenkel, W., "Social Stratification in Columbus, Ohio," 92, 93

Kerr, Clark, *The Uses of the University,* 36

Kluckholm, Clyde, "Shifts in Values during the Past Generation," 126
Mirror For Man, 52

Koestler, Arthur, *The Art of Creation,* 162, 163, 169, 172

Kogan, Nathan & Michael Wallach, *Risk-Taking: A Study of Cognition and Personality,* 170

Kornhauser, R., "The Warner Approach to Social Stratification," 91

l

Landecker, W., "Class Crystallization and Class Consciousness," 96

Lauman, E., "Subjective Social Distance and Urban Occupational Strata," 96

Larrabee & Myerson, eds., *Mass Leisure,* 210

Lavin, David E., *The Prediction of Academic Performance,* 187

Lazarsfeld, P. & R. Merton, eds., *Continuities in Social Research,* 94

Lee, Dorothy, *Freedom and Culture,* 61
"Personal Significance and Group Structure," 75

Lee, Robert, *The Church and the Exploding Metropolis,* 144

Lenski, G., "America's Social Class: Statistical Strata or Social Groups?" 92, 95

Lerner, D., "Comfort and Fun: Morality in a Nice Society," 69

Linton, Ralph, *The Study of Man,* 81

Lipset & Bendix, "Social Mobility and Occupational Career Patterns," 119

Lynch, K., "The Pattern of the Metropolis," 142

m

Maccoby, Newcomb & Hartley, eds., *Readings in Social Psychology,* 177

Machiavelli, N., *The Prince,* 8

Mack, M., *et al., Social Mobility: Thirty Years of Research and Theory,* 118

Marquand, John, 26

Marx, Leo, *The Machine in the Garden,* 204

Matheo, William, "When Men and Machines Work Together," 207

Matson, Floyd, *The Broken Image,* 204

May, Rollo, "Antidotes for the New Puritanism," 213

Mayo, Elton, *The Human Problems of an Industrial Civilization,* 29

McClelland, David, *The Achieving Society,* 127
"Some Social Consequences of Achievement Motivation," 127
"On the Psychodynamics of Creative Physical Scientists," 172

McClelland *et al., Talent and Society,* 129

McClintock, Robert, "Machines and Vitalists," 205

McConnell & Heist, "Do Students Make the College," 186

McKinley, Donald, *Social Class and Family Life,* 128

McKinsey, J. C. C., *Introduction to the Theory of Games,* 6

McLuhan, Marshall, *The Mechanical Bride, The Gutenberg Galaxy, Understanding Media,* 204

Mendelson, W., *Discrimination,* 103

Merton, R. K., *et al., Reader in Bureaucracy,* 26

Merton, R. K., "Bureaucratic Structure and Personality," 34, 39
"Manifest and Latent Functions," 49, 145
Estimates (for 1950), 57, 58
Social Theory and Social Structure, 62

Merton, R. & A. Kitt, "Contributions to the Theory of Reference Group Behavior," 94

Michael, Donald, *Cybernation: The Silent Conquest,* 205
The Next Generation, 213

Miller, Arthur, *Death of a Salesman,* 26

Miller, Daniel R. & Guy E. Swanson, *The Changing American Parent,* 25

Miller, S. M., "The 'New' Working Class," 100
"The Outlook of Working-Class Youth," 133, 134

Miller, S. & I. Harrison, "Types of Dropouts: The Unemployables," 133

Millett, John D., *The Academic Community: An Essay on Organization,* 44

Mills, C. Wright, "The Grand Theorists," 78
White Collar, 26
Mizruchi, *Success and Opportunity*, 125
Mooney, Ross L., "The Problem of Leadership in the University," 44
Moore, John M., *The Place of Moral and Religious Values in Programs of General Education*, 199
Moore, W. E., "Global Sociology," *Social Change, Man, Time and Society*, 200
Morison, E., ed., *The American Style*, 126
Morse, Chandler, "The Functional Imperatives," 60
Murray, H. A., *Explorations in Personality*, 185
Myrdal, Gunnar, *An American Dilemma*, 100
"The Swedish Way to Happiness," 138

n

Nagel, Ernest, "A Formalization of Functionalism," 53, 55
Nebraska Symposium on Motivation, 127
"The Negro Protest," 103
Newcomb, T. M., *Personality and Social Change*, 191
North & Hatt, "Jobs and Occupations: A Popular Evaluation," 97

o

Ogburn, W. F., *Social Change*, 202
Orwell, George, *Animal Farm*, 135
1984, 154
Osofsky, Gilbert, *Harlem: The Making of A Ghetto*, 148

p

Packard, Vance, *The Hidden Persuaders*, 51
Park, R. E., *Race and Culture*, 2
"The City; Investigations of Human Behavior in the Urban Environment," 141
Parsons, Talcott, *The Social System, Essays in Sociological Theory, Structure and Process in Modern Societies*, 78
"A Revised Analytical Approach to the Theory of Social Stratification," 84

Peterson, Richard, *The Scope of Organized Student Protest*, 193
Pfautz, H., *et al.*, "The Current Literature of Social Stratification," 91
Plato, *The Republic*, 86
Pope, Alexander, "The Rape of the Lock," 8
Prentice, W. C. F., P. Jacob & R. J. Havighurst, "Social Changes and the College Student," 199
Presthus, R., *The Organizational Society*, 26, 41

r

Riesman, David, "Some Dilemmas of Women's Education," 17
The Lonely Crowd, 26, 69
"Review of the Jacob Report," 194
Year Book of Education, 198
"Some Issues in the Future of Leisure," *Abundance for What?* 210
Roethlisberger, F. L. & W. L. Dickson, *Management and the Worker*, 29
Roethlisberger, F. L., *Training for Human Relations*, 29
Management and Morale, 29, 30
Rogoff, N., *Recent Trends in Occupational Mobility*, 118, 119
Rokeach, M., *The Open and Closed Mind*, 93, 166, 167, 168
Rose, A., "The Negro Problem in the Context of Social Change," 102
Rosen, Bernard, "Socialization and Achievement Motivation in Brazil," 129

s

Salisbury, Harrison, *The Shook-Up Generation*, 147
Sanford, Nevitt, *The American College*, 182, 193, 199
College and Character, 198
Sanson, Eric, *A Contest of Ladies*, 8
Sartre, *Being and Nothingness*, 1
Sayres, W., "The Singular Society of Loscho," 69
Schwartz, R., "Functional Alternatives to Inequality," 84
Seeley, J. R., *et al.*, *Crestwood Heights*, 71, 129, 151
Segal, B. & R. Thomsen, "Status Orientation and Ethnic Sentiment Among Undergraduates," 96
Sexton, P., *Education and Income*, 108

Shackle, G. L. S., *Decision, Order, and Time in Human Affairs*, 6, 164

Shostak & Gomberg, *Blue Collar World*, 99, 103, 107, 111, 122, 133, 145

Shubik, Martin, *Strategy and Market Structure*, 6

Simon, Herbert, *et al.*, "The Processes of Creative Thinking," 164

Simpson, R., "A Modification of the Functional Theory of Social Stratification," 84

Sinclair, Upton, *The Jungle*, 33

Skinner, B. F., *Walden Two*, 84

Smiley, M. & J. Diekhoff, *Prologue to Teaching*, 20

Smith, John E., *Value Convictions and Higher Education*, 198

Snygg, Donald & A. W. Combs, *Individual Behavior: A Perceptual Approach to Behavior*, 163, 166

Sorokin, P., *Social Mobility*, 117

Southerland, R. L., M. H. Holtzman, E. A. Koile & B. K. Smith, *Personality Factors on the College Campus*, 199

Spectorsky, A. C., *The Exurbanites*, 149

Spenrad, W., "Blue Collar Workers as City and Suburban Residents," 122

Sprague, H., ed., *Research on College Students*, 193

Srole, L., *et al.*, *Mental Health in the Metropolis*, 146

Stanislavski, C., *Stanislavski's Legacy*, 3, 10

Acting—A Handbook of the Stanislavski Method, 10

Stein, Maurice, *The Eclipse of Community*, 92, 140

"Toward a Theory of American Communities," 142, 158

Stein & A. Vidich, eds., *Sociology on Trial*, 78

Stern, George, "Characteristics of the Intellectual Climate in College Environments," 17, 69

"Environments for Learning," 192

"Student Values and Their Relationships to the College Environment," 192

Strasser, Stephen, *Phenomenology and Human Sciences*, 50, 59

Strodtbeck, F., "Family Interaction, Values, and Achievement," 129

Swados, S., "Less Work—Less Leisure," 210

Swanson & Miller, *The Changing American Parent*, 128

t

Taylor, Frederick, "Behavioral Science and Educational Administration," 41

Thernstrom, S., "Yankee City Revisited: The Perils of Historical Naivete," 90

Toffler, Alvin, *The Culture Consumers*, 69

Tumin, M., "Some Principles of Stratification: A Critical Analysis," 82, 84

v

Van Den Haag, Ernest, *Education as an Industry*, 35

Vidich & Bensman, *Small Town in Mass Society*, 92, 156

von Eckhardt, W., *The Challenge of Megalopolis*, 153, 155, 157

Von Neumann, John & Oskar Morgenstern, *Theory of Games and Economic Behavior*, 6

w

Walker, Edward & Heyns, Roger, *An Anatomy for Conformity*, 6

Walker, Willard, *The Sociology of Teaching*, 69, 188

Warner, W. L., *American Life: Dream and Reality*, 89, 120

The Status System of a Modern Community, 89

Yankee City, The Living and The Dead, A Study of the Symbolic Life of Americans, 89, 90

Warner & Lunt, *The Social Life of a Modern Community*, 89

The Social Systems of American Ethnic Groups, 89

The Social System of the Modern Factory, 89

Warner, W. L., M. Meeker, K. Eells, *Social Class in America*, 91

Wattell, Harold, "Levittown: The Suburban Community," 149

Weber, Max, *From Max Weber: Essays in Sociology*, 26

The Protestant Ethic and the Spirit of Capitalism, 116

Weinstein, E., "Children's Concept of Occupational Stratification," 96
Werner, Gred. W., ed., *The World of the American Student,* 198
Wertheimer, Max, *Productive Thinking,* 163, 168
White, R. H., *Lives in Progress,* 185
White, Winston, *Beyond Conformity,* 137
Whyte, W. E., *The Organization Man,* 26, 44, 122, 129, 135, 139, 150, 155, 156
Whyte, William F., *Street Corner Society,* 144
Wiener, Norbert, *The Human Use of Human Beings, Cybernetics,* 205
Wilson, Edmund Beecher, *The Cell in Development and Heredity,* 55
Wise, W. Max, *They Come for the Best of Reasons,* 193, 198

Wohl, "The 'Rags to Riches' Story: An Episode in Secular Idealism," 116
Woodward, C. Vann, "After Watts, Where is the Negro Revolution Heading?" 101

y

Yasada, S., "A Methodological Inquiry into Social Mobility," 118
Year Book of Education, 198
Young, Michael, *The Rise of the Meritocracy,* 66

z

Zola, Émile, *Germinal,* 33